Voices of African-American Teen Fathers
"I'm Doing What I Got to Do"

HAWORTH Health and Social Policy
Marvin D. Feit, PhD

Maltreatment and the School-Age Child: Developmental Outcomes and Systems Issues by Phyllis T. Howing, John S. Wodarski, P. David Kurtz, and James Martin Gaudin Jr.

Health and Social Policy by Marvin D. Feit and Stanley F. Battle

Adolescent Substance Abuse: An Empirical-Based Group Preventive Health Paradigm by John S. Wodarski and Marvin D. Feit

Long-Term Care: Federal, State, and Private Options for the Future by Raymond O'Brien and Michael Flannery

Health and Poverty by Michael J. Holosko and Marvin D. Feit

Financial Management in Human Services by Marvin Feit and Peter Li

Policy, Program Evaluation, and Research in Disability: Community Support for All by Julie Ann Racino

The Politics of Youth, Sex, and Health Care in American Schools by James W. Button and Barbara A. Rienzo

Race, Politics, and Community Development Funding: The Discolor of Money by Michael Bonds

Changing Welfare Services: Case Studies of Local Welfare Reform Programs edited by Michael J. Austin

Accountability in Social Services: The Culture of the Paper Program by Jill Florence Lackey

Voices of African-American Teen Fathers: "I'm Doing What I Got to Do" by Angelia Paschal

Making Business Districts Work: Leadership and Management of Downtown, Main Street, Business District, and Community Development Organizations edited by David Feehan and Marvin D. Feit

Voices of African-American Teen Fathers
"I'm Doing What I Got to Do"

Angelia M. Paschal, PhD, MEd

Routledge
Taylor & Francis Group
NEW YORK AND LONDON

First Published by
The Haworth Press, Inc., 10 Alice Street, Binghamton, NY 13904-1580.

Transferred to Digital Printing 2009 by Routledge
711 Third Ave, New York NY 10017
2 Park Square, Milton Park, Abingdon, Oxon, OX14 4RN

© 2006 by The Haworth Press, Inc. All rights reserved. No part of this work may be reproduced or utilized in any form or by any means, electronic or mechanical, including photocopying, microfilm, and recording, or by any information storage and retrieval system, without permission in writing from the publisher.

PUBLISHER'S NOTE
The development, preparation, and publication of this work has been undertaken with great care. However, the Publisher, employees, editors, and agents of The Haworth Press are not responsible for any errors contained herein or for consequences that may ensue from use of materials or information contained in this work. The Haworth Press is committed to the dissemination of ideas and information according to the highest standards of intellectual freedom and the free exchange of ideas. Statements made and opinions expressed in this publication do not necessarily reflect the views of the Publisher, Directors, management, or staff of The Haworth Press, Inc., or an endorsement by them.

Names of individuals discussed in this book have been changed to protect confidentiality.

Cover design by Lora Wiggins.

Library of Congress Cataloging-in-Publication Data

Paschal, Angelia M.
    Voices of African-American teen fathers : I'm doing what I got to do / Angelia M. Paschal.
       p. cm.
    Includes bibliographical references and index.
    ISBN-13: 978-0-7890-2737-5 (hard : alk. paper)
    ISBN-10: 0-7890-2737-2 (hard : alk. paper)
    ISBN-13: 978-0-7890-2738-2 (soft : alk. paper)
    ISBN-10: 0-7890-2738-0 (soft : alk. paper)
    1. African American teenage fathers. 2. Child rearing. 3. Parenting. I. Title.

HQ756.7.P37 2006
306.874'2—dc22

2005029267

To the young fathers who committed their time
to this study and shared their stories so that
we might better understand their experiences.

ABOUT THE AUTHOR

Angelia Paschal, PhD, MEd, is an assistant professor of preventive medicine and public health at the University of Kansas School of Medicine in Wichita (KUSM-W). Her expertise is in the areas of health disparities, cultural competency, and program evaluation, and her research interests include health literacy and the prevention and intervention of chronic diseases. Dr. Paschal also serves as the Director of Grants Development in the Office of Research at KUSM-W, advisory council member for the Kansas Public Health Leadership Institute, and holds membership on an African-American Foster Care and Adoption Fair committee.

CONTENTS

Preface	**xi**
Acknowledgments	**xiii**
Introduction	**1**

Chapter 1. Literature Review	**5**
Teen Pregnancy Statistics	5
Teen Childbearing Statistics	6
Consequences of Teen Motherhood	7
Sociopolitical Issues of Teen Parenthood	10
Explaining Teen Motherhood	12
Adolescent Fathers	16
Explaining African-American Teen Fatherhood	18
Perceptions of Fatherhood by African-American Youths	20
African-American Adolescents and Fatherhood Involvement	22
African-American Teen Fathers and Their Relationships with Others	25
Theoretical Perspective: Social Ecology and Gender Theory	28
Research Questions	41

Chapter 2. Research Methods	**43**
The Teen Fathers	43
Environmental Factors	46
Recruitment Strategies	47
The Interviewing Process	47
Reliability, Validity, and Generalizability	57
Transcription	57
Data Analysis	58

Chapter 3. How and Why African-American Teens Become Fathers	**61**
Carelessness: "If It Happened, It Happened"	61
Lack of Communication: "We Just Didn't Talk About It"	64

Getting "Trapped": "I Think She Got Pregnant on Purpose" 66
Intentional Pregnancies: "We Wanted to Have a Baby" 68
Limited Alternatives: "Abortion and Adoption Were
Not Options" 69

Chapter 4. How Teen Fathers Think About and Do Fatherhood 75

Father As Provider: "I'm Not Running from
My Responsibilities" 76
The Involved Nurturer: "I'm Being There for my Child" 85
The Independent Father: "It's Not My Responsibility!" 92

Chapter 5. Teen Fathers and Their Families of Origin 97

Relationships with Their Fathers 97
Relationships with Their Mothers 108

Chapter 6. Teen Fathers and the Mothers of Their Children 117

Amicable Associations 118
Loving, Intimate Affairs 126
Antagonistic Relationships 130

Chapter 7. Teen Fathers and Peer Influence 137

Fatherhood Affecting Friendships 137
Warning from Friends 138
Fatherhood As Status Symbol 139
Peer Influence Before Fatherhood 142

Chapter 8. The Challenges and Concerns of Teen Fathers 145

Youth-Related Issues 146
Fear of Losing Independence 148
Relationship Problems 153
Concerns About Child Support 154
Socioeconomic Challenges 156
Transportation Issues 159
Cultural Influences 161
Drug Issues 162

Daily Survival	165
Racism and Discrimination	167

Chapter 9. Discussion and Conclusion — 171

Research Questions and Major Findings	171
Theoretical Relevance of Findings	180

Chapter 10. Where Do We Go from Here?
Designing a Plan of Action — 189
Rhonda Lewis

Theoretical Frameworks	190
Recommendation #1: Develop an Assessment Tool	190
Recommendation #2: Use the Stages of Change Model to Address Condom Use	191
Recommendation #3: Identify the Risk, Protective, and Cultural Factors Associated with Early Adolescence	192
Recommendation #4: Use the Three Identified Categories of Fathers to Develop an Effective Intervention	193
Limitations	196

Appendix A. Interview Guide — 199

Personal Demographic Information	199
Identity Questions	199
Socioeconomic Circumstances and Perceived Future Outlook	200
Transition to Fatherhood	200
Definition of Fatherhood	201
Sexual Experience and Background	201
Fatherhood Involvement and Parental Support	201
Relationship with Mother of Child	202
Peer Relationships	202
Relationship with Family of Origin	203
Other Questions	203

Appendix B. Brief Biographies of Participants (Listed by Age) — 205

References — 213

Index — 223

Preface

Despite the proliferation of literature on adolescent pregnancy and parenthood, most research has focused on teen mothers. Information gathered on teen mothers is not necessarily applicable to adolescent fathers because of the different factors that influence their parental behavior and experiences. The purpose of this study is to provide insight into and understanding of the experiences of African-American teen fathers. Because the voices of young African-American male parents are not adequately represented in the discourse of social science literature and social policy, this book provides an account of their experiences and examines the social context in which their experiences occurred. First, the factors that influenced their fatherhood status were examined. Second, how fatherhood was conceptualized and practiced by the adolescent fathers was explored. Third, how the fathers' relationships with significant others, including parents, the mothers of their children, and their friends, impacted their fathering beliefs, attitudes, and behaviors were studied. Finally, the concerns and challenges the fathers faced were determined. Although the study confirmed some of the literature on this subpopulation, many interesting and surprising results occurred. Using social ecology and gender theory, understanding and insight into the young mens' fatherhood experiences is provided. The final chapter provides policy implications and practical steps in dealing with these findings.

Voices of African-American Teen Fathers
© 2006 by The Haworth Press, Inc. All rights reserved.
doi:10.1300/5477_a

Acknowledgments

This book would not have been possible without the participation of the teen fathers. Allowing me to share their lives with others was selfless and generous. I extend my deepest, sincerest thanks to them for their contributions, and I wish them the best.

Acknowledgment is also granted to my former dissertation co-chairs, Drs. Kathryn M. Feltey and Ellen K. Scott, who provided invaluable assistance and support in conducting and writing this study. I could not have made it without their expertise and endless hours of support, compassion, and patience. Their continued commitment led to the culmination of this work.

Gratitude is also given to my husband, Samuel A. Paschal Jr., for his love, patience, and understanding during my undertaking of this project. He is the epitome of a supportive and caring partner. I cannot thank him enough for calming me through the storms and for his timely advice for this study. I likewise thank my parents, Walter and Barbara Sanders, and my siblings, Walter Jr., Lorinda, and Rosaline, who have always encouraged me and whose faith in my abilities has led me to this path. During moments of doubt they never stop believing in me.

My colleague Dr. Rhonda K. Lewis deserves recognition for this book as well. Her support and advice has been most appreciated, and I am honored to have her contribute to this book.

Last, and most important, I give thanks to God for this opportunity and for making this study a reality.

Voices of African-American Teen Fathers
© 2006 by The Haworth Press, Inc. All rights reserved.
doi:10.1300/5477_b

Introduction

Over the past few decades, both teen pregnancy and adolescent parenthood have received increased attention in social policy debates and social scientific research as well as in the medical, nursing, and public health literature and popular forums. Approximately 870,000 teenagers between ages fifteen and nineteen become pregnant each year, with some by adolescent boys (Centers for Disease Control 2004). Documentaries, newspaper and magazine articles, and speeches graphically illustrate the dilemmas faced by adolescents becoming pregnant and bearing and raising children. Myriad research studies have associated adolescent parenthood with school dropout rates, poverty, welfare receipt, criminal activity, lowered social productivity, as well as a host of other social problems (e.g., Lerman 1993a; Ventura 1994; Pirog-Good 1995; Centers for Disease Control 2004). The "causes" of teen parenthood are complex and multifaceted, and teen pregnancy has been associated with a number of factors ranging from ignorance about reproduction to a lack of educational and economic opportunities (Sidel 1996; Xie et al. 2001).

Nonetheless, teen pregnancy and birth rates in the United States have declined for more than a decade (Ventura et al. 2001; Martin et al. 2002). In fact, most teenagers who become pregnant are eighteen to nineteen years old (Martin et al. 2002). Although they represent about a third of all unmarried mothers, teenagers give birth to just 12 to 13 percent of all children (Alan Guttmacher Institute 1999a), and most of these are to youths eighteen to twenty years old (Ventura et al. 2001). Although pregnancy rates are decreasing, the proportion of teens who have sex at an early age has increased (Ventura et al. 2001; Kalmuss et al. 2003). Moreover, 2003 results from surveys administered across the United States to youths in grades nine through twelve show that among male and female youths reporting to be sexually active, approximately 37 percent did not use condoms during sexual intercourse, and about 83 percent did not use birth control pills to prevent pregnancy while being sexually active (Grunbaum et al. 2004).

Voices of African-American Teen Fathers
© 2006 by The Haworth Press, Inc. All rights reserved.
doi:10.1300/5477_01

2 VOICES OF AFRICAN-AMERICAN TEEN FATHERS

Unfortunately, teen birth rates in the United States remain the highest among developed countries (Ventura et al. 2001).

Birth rates for African Americans declined more than any other population group during the 1990s in the United States (Ventura et al. 2001). In 2000, this rate was 79.2 per 1,000, compared to non-Hispanic white teenagers at 32.8 per 1,000. Thus, while the birth rates for African-American teenagers have significantly decreased since the 1990s (when it was 115.5 per 1,000 in 1991), with the exception of teenagers with Hispanic origin, rates for African-American teenagers continue to be substantially higher than for other groups (Ventura et al. 2001). Several studies have been conducted to examine those factors associated with African-American teen parenthood and/or to make recommendations for pregnancy prevention measures (e.g., Dallas et al. 2000; Gasden et al. 2003).

Teen fatherhood is not as widespread as adolescent motherhood. Nearly one-half (47 percent) of babies born to female adolescents have fathers who are twenty years of age or older. The incidence of adolescent fatherhood may be higher among African Americans than for whites because African-American adolescent mothers are disproportionately represented in teen pregnancy and birth statistics (Centers for Disease Control 2004).

Unlike single motherhood, however, the roles and experiences of fathers have largely been ignored in politics and research (Sidel 1996; Fagot et al. 1998). Thus, most of the available research on adolescent parenthood focuses on the mother. However, these data are not necessarily applicable to adolescent fathers because different factors influence the parental behaviors and experiences of the fathers. As with single motherhood, most of the literature on teen fathers has focused on the risk factors associated with teen fatherhood (Thornberry et al. 1997; Fagot et al. 1998; Xie et al. 2001) and/or the consequences of young fatherhood (Pirog-Good 1995; Dallas and Chen 1998; Harris 1998).

Although structural explanations (Anderson 1989, 1990; Wilson 1987) and cultural accounts (Anderson 1989, 1990; Sullivan 1989) have been used by researchers to explain the overrepresentation of African-American adolescent fathers, very few of them provide accounts of their fatherhood experiences. Therefore, questions remain about how these young fathers experience, define, and perceive their experiences. Not much is known about their perspectives, for example,

Introduction 3

on their cultural and socioeconomic conditions and how these are perceived to influence their fatherhood experiences. Little data exist regarding how they view their relationships with others, and how others, in turn, affect their fatherhood perceptions, experiences, and paternal behaviors. Although some progress has been made in research on African-American adolescent fathers, still too little is known about them and their circumstances.

Because African-American young males are especially hard to recruit for research (Hendricks and Solomon 1987), it is essential that greater efforts be made to study this population. Using in-depth interviews, the current study contributes to the social science literature on adolescent parenthood by examining the lived experience of fatherhood from the perspectives of unmarried, low-income, African-American adolescent fathers in a Midwestern urban area. Young African-American fathers must be understood on their own terms in order to address their needs or to accurately provide information about them. As Luker (1996) explained in *Dubious Conceptions,* teens of today live in a very different world than did those in former generations. Thus, the current world of these young parents needs to be understood from their own viewpoints if their needs are to be adequately addressed and participation in public discourse about their lives is to occur appropriately and accurately. The following chapters will provide insight into and understanding of African-American adolescent fatherhood. In addition, information about teen motherhood will be presented first in order to enhance our understanding of teen fatherhood.

Chapter 1

Literature Review

When childbearing occurs outside the norms of a socially constructed ideal path to parenthood, as in the case of teenage parenthood, it is characterized as "deviant" (Furstenberg 1985). Teenage parents have been characterized as too young, too poor, uneducated, single, and unemployed (Pirog-Good 1995). Becoming a public concern around the 1970s (Furstenberg et al. 1987), teen parenthood was and is defined from a deficit perspective according to its distance from the "normal" and ideal state of parenthood, which involves individuals who are of the right age, the right class, and who are parenting under the right circumstances, which usually include marriage (Furstenberg 1985; Sidel 1996). Concerns about this phenomenon have focused on the public costs and personal tragedy of teen childbearing, including such factors as truncated schooling and long-term poverty (Furstenberg et al. 1987; Xie et al. 2001). Since teenage childbearing has become a social issue, a plethora of strategies and solutions to preventing teenage parenthood have been proposed (Gasden and Smith 1995; Jaccard et al. 2000; Kalmuss et al. 2003; Philliber et al. 2003).

TEEN PREGNANCY STATISTICS

Approximately 870,000 teenagers become pregnant each year (Centers for Disease Control and Prevention 2004), and nearly 80 percent of these pregnancies are unintended (Henshaw 1996; Alan Guttmacher Institute 1999a). Moreover, about 79 percent of pregnant adolescents are unmarried (Martin et al. 2002).

Voices of African-American Teen Fathers
© 2006 by The Haworth Press, Inc. All rights reserved.
doi:10.1300/5477_02

6   *VOICES OF AFRICAN-AMERICAN TEEN FATHERS*

Racial and ethnic group differences also exist. The prevalence of having been pregnant or having gotten pregnant was higher among black (9.1 percent) and Hispanic (6.4 percent) than among white (2.3 percent) students in 2003 (Centers for Disease Control and Prevention 2004). These data were based on a student sample size of 15,214 using thirty-two state surveys (using the Youth Risk Behavior Surveillance System [YRBSS] survey) and eighteen local surveys administered to students in grades nine through twelve from February to December 2003.

Within Sedgwick County, Kansas (including Wichita, the city in which this study was conducted), the overall teen pregnancy rates were higher than the rest of the state of Kansas and of the United States. Per 1,000 youth ages fifteen to nineteen, Sedgwick County reported 96.9 pregnancies collectively, among all races (Kansas Department of Health and Environment 1998). For the state of Kansas in 2002, the overall pregnancy rate for female youths aged ten to nineteen decreased 18.7 percent from 34.8 pregnancies per 1,000 in 1992 to 28.3 per 1,000 in 2002 (Kansas Department of Health and Environment 1998). In that same year, births to white teenage mothers represented 84 percent, and African Americans represented 12.9 percent. The teen pregnancy rates for African Americans declined more than in other population groups from 1992 to 2002, decreasing 39 percent, from 79.5 pregnancies per 1,000 in 1992 to 48.5 in 2002 (Kansas Department of Health and Environment 1998).

TEEN CHILDBEARING STATISTICS

Approximately 13 percent of all births in the United Stated are to teens (Ventura et al. 2001). Most of these births are to young women between eighteen and nineteen years of age (Martin et al. 2002). The United States adolescent birth rate for year 2000 was 48.7 births per 1,000 women aged fifteen to nineteen years compared to 62.1 per 1,000 in 1991(Ventura et al. 2001; Martin et al. 2002). This is the lowest level ever reported in the country's history. Despite this trend, the teen birth rate in the United States remains notably higher than the rates in other industrialized democracies (Martin et al. 2002).

The largest decline in birth rate has been for African-American adolescents. The birth rate for African Americans aged fifteen to

Literature Review 7

nineteen fell 31 percent between 1991 and 2000. Overall, the rate for African-American adolescents giving birth is 79.2 per 1,000 in the year 2000 (Ventura et al. 2001). Nonetheless, the rates for African Americans, as well as Hispanics, who have a birth rate of 94.4 per 1,000, remain significantly higher than that of other groups. Teenagers of Asian and Pacific Islander descent aged fifteen to nineteen have a birth rate of just 21.8 per 1,000 and non-Hispanic white teenagers have a birth rate of 32.8 per 1,000 (Ventura et al. 2001).

In the state of Kansas, whites have 38 births per 1,000 for girls aged fifteen to nineteen (the national rate in the United States is 32.8 for whites), while the rate for African-American girls of the same age range is 97 per 1,000 (which is also higher than the national rate of 79.2 per 1,000 for African-American youths aged fifteen to nineteen) (Kansas Department of Health and Environment 1998).

Births to African-American adolescents in the United States are likely to be nonmarital (Alan Guttmacher Institute 1999a). In Kansas, births to unmarried white teenagers ages fifteen to nineteen compose 72 percent of all births to white teens (which is similar to the national rate of 71 percent), whereas births to unmarried African-American adolescents comprise 95 percent of all births to African-American teens (the national rate is 96 percent) (Ventura et al. 2000a).

A great racial disparity exists in teen parenthood for adolescents. African Americans have a higher likelihood than whites of becoming adolescent mothers (Alan Guttmacher Institute 1999a). In order to fully comprehend patterns of early childbearing in the African-American population, studies must focus on adolescents and explore their perceptions, attitudes, beliefs, and behaviors in regard to pregnancy and parenthood.

CONSEQUENCES OF TEEN MOTHERHOOD

A number of studies have focused on teen parents and on teens' adjustment to parenthood and the adaptive strategies they have employed for this life-altering experience. Many studies discuss the consequences of adolescent parenthood, such as high rates of school dropouts, increased poverty, a cycle of teen and/or single parenthood, and low-income jobs (e.g., Harris 1998; Pirog-Good 1995). A number of negative consequences are associated with teen pregnancy and

8   VOICES OF AFRICAN-AMERICAN TEEN FATHERS

early childbearing. Compared to older mothers, teen mothers are less likely to receive adequate prenatal care, more likely to have only marginal gestational weight gain, and more likely to smoke during pregnancy (Ventura 1994). Nationally, 25 percent of teen mothers have a second child within two years of their first child (Alan Guttmacher Institute 1999a). In addition, teen mothers experience restricted educational attainment, increased risk of lifetime poverty, and curtailed childhood (Ventura 1994; Pirog-Good 1995; Harris 1998). These findings indicate that teens do not effectively adapt to the changes adolescent parenthood brings. It is simply difficult to simultaneously parent, go to school, and work to support a family.

Negative consequences of adolescent childbearing for the infant include increased risk of low birth weight, childhood health problems, and hospitalization (Alan Guttmacher Institute 1999a). Furthermore, the sons of teen mothers are 13 percent more likely to end up in prison, whereas daughters are more likely to become adolescent mothers themselves (Haveman et al. 1997).

Some studies suggest that these negative outcomes and consequences are not inevitable (Furstenberg 1976; Furstenberg et al. 1987). Bearing and raising a child as an adolescent do not predictably lead to truncated schooling and economic hardship, either for the parent or for the child (Luker 1996). For instance, in the first of two books of a longitudinal study mentioned previously, Furstenberg (1976) examined the consequences of teen parenthood by studying a sample of 300 low-income African-American adolescent mothers and their families. He conceptualized out-of-marriage birth in adolescence as a deviation from the traditionally acceptable sequence of life events. In other words, out-of-marriage childbirths to teens represented a disturbance in the normative schedule (or an ill-timed or off-schedule timing) of life events. Furstenberg (1976) studied the coping strategies, strategic planning, rearrangement of schedules, and educational aspirations of the adolescent mothers as they attempted to "repair the damage" of their early births to their life chances. He concluded that the negative consequences of an unplanned pregnancy could potentially be rectified by certain actions and events.

The adaptation to teen parenthood may include adjustments such as postponement of marriage, the rescheduling of schooling; and/or the control of fertility (Furstenberg 1976). With these adjustments, adolescent parents may overcome their early setbacks with childbearing

Literature Review 9

and parenting and later still become as "successful" as their peers (success defined as equivalent educational attainment, comparable socioeconomic status, and economic independence). Still, most researchers generally conclude that adolescent mothers and their children will be much worse off in almost all respects than if the teenagers had given birth later in life. Generally, adolescent parenthood is not without negative consequences in the teen parents' lives or in their children's lives.

Nevertheless, a fifteen-year follow-up (Furstenberg et al. 1987) of the same young women in Furstenberg's (1976) earlier five-year study revealed that a substantial minority of the young women was doing just as well in life as their former classmates who did not become premaritally pregnant. For instance, some of the young women had married the fathers of their children, others postponed marriage and focused on their education, some delayed further childbearing, and many achieved economic independence. Their later life circumstances closely resembled their counterparts who did not become adolescent parents.

However, as found in other studies, successful coping strategies were not found with the majority of the women in the sample (Furstenberg et al. 1987). Despite previous problems, the young women had, other problems emerged with adolescent parenthood—thus, pregnancy was a confounding factor. Many of the young mothers were not able to cope with the problems precipitated by their early pregnancies, for example their prospects of achieving a stable marriage were hindered by the early pregnancy and they had great difficulty supporting families on their own. They were often poorly educated, unskilled, burdened by additional small children, and living with economic deprivation. So, although adolescent parenthood does not always lead to poverty and deprivation for the parent or child, it is a very likely outcome.

Since poverty has been associated with teen parenthood, and African Americans in general are overrepresented in the lower end of the socioeconomic scale (Wilson 1987; Hajnal 1995; Sampson and Wilson 1995), it becomes vitally important to understand the influences of poverty and other forms of social structure on the African-American adolescent parenthood experience.

SOCIOPOLITICAL ISSUES
OF TEEN PARENTHOOD

Although teen parenthood might lead to increased poverty, most teen mothers are already from poor or low-income families (Sidel 1996; Alan Guttmacher Institute 1999a; Xie et al. 2001). For instance, regardless of race, teen parents are already far more likely to come from economically disadvantaged families (Sidel 1996; Xie et al. 2001). In general, 38 percent of all female teenagers are from poor or low-income families, but 83 percent of teenage mothers are from such families (Alan Guttmacher Institute 1999b). This suggests that teen mothers tend to be poor prior to becoming pregnant, and, therefore, teen pregnancy or childbearing does not necessarily cause young women to become poor, since poverty usually precedes adolescent parenthood. This situation becomes problematic in the sociopolitical sphere. Similar to the poor, teen parents are blamed for creating the conditions and circumstances in which they live and are also blamed for the social problems associated with their parental status.

Although teens are often blamed for their pregnancies or young parenthood, one important factor is not usually the center of attention: teen pregnancies often involve adult fathers. For example, in an earlier study conducted in 1991, the National Center for Health Statistics (quoted in Sidel 1996:131) reported that out of approximately 300,000 teen mothers, more than 60 percent revealed that they were impregnated by men over the age of twenty. According to the Annual Summary of Vital Statistics for 2001 for the state of Kansas (where this book's study was conducted), among the cases in which the age of the father was known, nearly two-thirds (67.1 percent) of the fathers were aged twenty and over and were responsible for births to mothers aged ten to nineteen years (Kansas Department of Health and Environment 2002). Furthermore, Lindberg and colleagues (1997) reported that the fathers of children born to teenage mothers are likely to be older than the women, estimating that one in five babies born to unmarried minors are fathered by men five or more years older than the mother. Yet, as Sidel (1996) points out, injunctions against these men who are responsible for adolescent pregnancies are usually not enforced (for example, through enforcement of statutory rape laws). Despite adult men's involvement in teen pregnancy, teen pregnancy is not viewed politically or socially as an adult problem (Sidel 1996).

More than half of all babies born to teen mothers are fathered by legally adult men (and it is statutory rape in most cases). This should be a bigger public concern.

Teen parenthood is perceived to be a financial problem in our society. Single teen mothers are generally considered to be a burden on the welfare system. Some of these young mothers must seek public assistance if they and/or their families of origin are unable to sufficiently provide for the children themselves, yet the reliance of teen mothers on Temporary Assistance for Needy Families (TANF) has typically been viewed as a problem by policymakers. Hence, the welfare reform of the late 1990s required that teen parent recipients live with their parents (Edin and Lein 1997). This was designed to discourage teens from "using" welfare to set up an individual home. These regulations also established caps or restrictions on the level of funding and the number of children covered. Moreover, these benefits are not always fully available, and when they are they are not usually enough to sustain financial independence (Edin and Lein 1997).

Sidel (1996) wrote that the widespread campaign against single mothers is a form of scapegoating in which attention is deflected from other problems, such as the growing gap between the rich and poor, widespread unemployment, increasing political apathy and alienation, and extraordinary levels of violence. Prevalent stereotypes of the "welfare queen" and of mothers "living off the system" persist in our society (Zucchino 1997), even though studies such as Edin and Lein's (1997) *Making Ends Meet* clearly demonstrate that single mothers cannot provide for themselves and their families solely from their receipt of government assistance. As Sidel (1996) mentioned, the message has become that single-parent families breed trouble, and that poor single mothers breed catastrophe. When it comes to teen motherhood, especially when the parents are minority and poor, these same assumptions are made.

In *Keeping Women and Children Last,* Sidel (1996) argued that single motherhood is demonized because those in powerful, affluent positions seek to blame the problems of society on the poor and powerless. For example, many policymakers do not appear to be concerned when children are reared by single adult fathers, by single middle- to upper-class mothers, or by white parents in general (Luker 1996; Sidel 1996). In fact, Luker (1996) pointed out that unlike the teen mother, the affluent unwed older mother is rarely seen as a social

12 VOICES OF AFRICAN-AMERICAN TEEN FATHERS

problem, yet few studies have been conducted to examine these women's "motives" for having children (as opposed to the many studies conducted on the topic for adolescent mothers). Whether receiving state or federal assistance or not, single motherhood is problematic. The absence of fathers (including teen fathers) from their children's lives is thought by some to be a contributing factor in the "moral decline" of our nation's values. Nearly forty years after Daniel Patrick Moynihan stated in his 1965 report to President Lyndon Johnson that posited that black matriarchal families constitute a problem, or crisis, in society, the sentiment still resonates in current politics and social policies. The Moynihan Report described African-American, female-headed families as being demoralized and disorganized, and this view has carried over to female-headed families in general (Sidel 1996). For instance, unmarried mothers are often blamed for the breakdown of the family, high crime rates, drug and alcohol addiction, poverty, poor school performance, and so on (Sidel 1996). Terms persist that describe female-headed families as "broken families," whereas terms such as "stable" and "intact" are used to describe two-parent families. The perception remains that female-headed families (especially those in which the mother is an adolescent) are negative and undesirable. Single parenthood and raising children outside of heterosexual, legally recognized marriages are thought to invite the destruction of the family as a social institution (Blankenhorn 1995; Popenoe 1996).

EXPLAINING TEEN MOTHERHOOD

Various reasons why teenagers become pregnant and why they choose to become parents exist (Luker 1996). Female teenagers might become pregnant because they are not rational actors who put themselves first in their own lives, according to Luker (1996). She explained that adolescents do not believe in adult conventional wisdom—not because they are defiant or because they are too developmentally immature to process the information (although many are one or the other and some are both), but because the conventional wisdom does not accord with the world they see around them. Adults tend to draw upon a "lived reality" that may be decades in the making. However, today's adolescents live in a world with very different demographic, social, economic, and sexual circumstances than the

Literature Review   13

older generations (Luker 1996). Therefore, studies similar to this book's study are very important in helping us understand the teen parent's world and his or her experiences. In particular, it is critical that studies focus on African-American and Hispanic teens, who are more likely to become parents.

Luker's (1996) assertion that female adolescents are not rational actors who put themselves first is conceivable given their youth, immaturity, and gender. For example, young women often have sex in order to please their male partners, and they may not use contraception if the male partner objects to it (Wingwood and DiClemente 1998). They believe that if they try to enforce condom usage they might offend their male partners and/or jeopardize their relationships with them. Wingwood and DiClemente (1998) interviewed 128 African-American women between eighteen and twenty-nine and found that the women were unlikely to be assertive with condom usage if the partner resisted. They also found that some women thought that asking their partners to use condoms implied that their partners were unfaithful. According to Franklin (1987), contraceptive use is also influenced by sexual exclusivity and frequency of intercourse. If a woman is deeply involved with her male partner, his influence regarding contraception is predominant (Franklin 1987; Wingwood and DiClemente 1998). Male partners in general tend to possess more influence and control of contraceptive use. However, Battle and Battle (1987) wrote that contraception is still perceived by African-American young men as being the woman's responsibility.

In *Not Our Kind of Girl,* Elaine Bell Kaplan (1997) wrote that it is the absence of support, mainly from the teens' parents, that best explains why teenagers get pregnant and decide to keep their children. For instance, when some young women feel unloved, ignored in school, and rejected by their fathers and/or boyfriends, they tend to be more open to having a child in order to feel loved and to give love. Kaplan (1997) explained that a child represents a way of making a relationship—by having a baby these teens hoped to become relationship rich under circumstances in which they felt alienated, even from their close family members. Kaplan interviewed a sample of thirty-two unmarried African-American teen mothers. Her research provided an in-depth look at the lives and parenthood experiences from the perspectives and accounts of African-American teen mothers.

14 VOICES OF AFRICAN-AMERICAN TEEN FATHERS

Kaplan called for the same type of study on African-American teen fathers.

Furstenberg (1976) did not conclude that adolescent mothers have an increased commitment to having children, in or out of marriage, thus the position that adolescent mothers were specially motivated to bear children did not have enough support. Among the reasons for pregnancy identified by Furstenberg (1976) were peer pressure to engage in sexual relations, the neutralization of restrictive norms of premarital sex by their peers, encouragement by parents to conceal their sexual status from them (therefore, removing "controls" that might have otherwise been exercised by the parents), the adult parents' disregard of sexual activity signs in their teen children, and parents' general preparation or expectation of teen pregnancy.

As Wilson (1987) wrote, many teen pregnancies are not planned and are not wanted. With African-American teens the situation is, however, somewhat different. He found that although African-American adolescents reported fewer unwanted pregnancies than other race or ethnic groups, pregnancy was not sufficiently unwanted to prevent it. Adolescents without a strong deterrence to childbearing do not effectively use contraceptives, he stated. Because children born out of marriage do not present a strong stigma in the African-American community, a lack of social pressure exists for adolescents not to bear children. Similarly, Furstenberg and colleagues (1987) found that although 75 percent of the young women in their study did not want nor plan the pregnancy, the other 25 percent either desired pregnancy or were not regretful that it occurred.

As Furstenberg and colleagues (1987) and Kaplan (1997) supported, African-American teens often become pregnant because of cultural expectations. They are *expected* to become teen parents—more so than their white counterparts (Wilson 1987). Although the environments of African-American communities may not directly encourage teen pregnancies, they do not strongly discourage them either. This situation is a result of the poor economic conditions in which many African Americans live, according to Wilson (1987).

In a similar vein, Lewis's (1966) Culture of poverty theory stated that because of long-term poverty conditions, some groups create a culture that perpetuates poverty from one generation to the next, and in response to these conditions, a distinct culture is created. Responses to pregnancy for those who live in poor economic conditions are markedly different from those who do not, and distinct patterns of behavior or values may develop. On the other hand, women with educational and/or career plans manage to avoid pregnancy or, if they become pregnant, they often decide to have abortions. For instance, teenagers from more affluent families are more likely to terminate their pregnancies than those from poorer families (Sidel 1996).

Researchers also contend that some adolescents become parents in order to gain a measure of status and respect among their peers (Dash 1989; Anderson 1989, 1990). They suggest that adolescents are more likely to bear children because childbearing represents a symbol of achievement or adulthood in an environment in which they perceive that little opportunity to achieve or accomplish exists. As a result, teens do not perceive that they have much to lose if they have a child (Dash 1989; Anderson 1989, 1990; Wilson 1987). In Carol Stack's (1974) study, *All Our Kin,* she discussed how she spent time living in a poor, urban, African-American community studying their collective adaptation to poverty. She concluded that African-American young women who became parents were in some ways reinforced because they gained respect and were regarded as adults by their families and others around them. Thus, parenthood was a passage into adulthood for these individuals.

In summary, teen pregnancy is complex and is associated with a number of factors (Furstenberg 1976; Furstenberg et al. 1987; Sidel 1996). Although teen motherhood is not without disadvantages and tends to exacerbate negative socioeconomic circumstances, it does not always lead to such conditions (Furstenberg 1976; Furstenberg et al. 1987; Sidel 1996). Most teen mothers are already from economically disadvantaged families prior to their pregnancies. These poor economic living conditions frequently result in a culture that perpetuates teen pregnancy and subsequent poverty (e.g., having babies to obtain adult status).

Finally, although teen pregnancy and parenthood are largely defined as social problems, it is important to explore this topic from different perspectives. With so much focus on teen mothers, little attention has been given to teen fathers, who are clearly involved in a significant number of teen pregnancies. More effort should be made to investigate the boys' perspectives on fatherhood and paternal involvement, and to explore policy alternatives that might be suggested by these studies.

ADOLESCENT FATHERS

The current study developed out of concern that the voices of young African-American fathers, speaking about their own experiences, are not heard or are not well represented in the mainstream discourse of social science research and social policy on teen parenting. Little is known about adolescent fatherhood. Although some (e.g., Anderson 1989, 1990; Sullivan 1989; Allen and Doherty 1998; Gasden et al. 2003) have acknowledged the importance of relating the sociocultural meanings of fatherhood to the adolescent fathers' own experiences, this field remains largely under-explored. Much of what we know about African-American adolescent fathers is based on adult male African-American fathers (e.g., Hamer 2001) and from retrospective studies using adult participants who were once teen fathers (e.g., Gasden et al. 2003).

Focusing on African-American teen fathers and other minority groups is important. Allen and Doherty (1998) and Gasden et al. (2003) explained that race and ethnicity are important to concentrate on in studies about adolescent parenthood because race and ethnicity can have an impact on preferences regarding pregnancy resolution, for example. This was exemplified in Sullivan's (1989) study in which he found that African-American, white, and Hispanic young men had different responses to pregnancy. Because few studies have focused exclusively on the African-American teen father, the present study will fill a gap in the literature by addressing in greater depth the unique subjective aspect of African-American adolescent fatherhood.

Adolescent Father Statistics

Statistics indicate that birth rates for teen fathers (ages fifteen to nineteen) have declined over the past decade, with the greatest decline being among African Americans (Martin et al. 2003; Kimball 2004). The incidence of African-American teen fathers in the United States declined from 54 per 1,000 in 1994 to 32.5 per 1,000 in 2003. This was a 29 percent decrease. These rates are relatively high considering that in comparison the overall teen father population was 16.9 in 1,000 for 2002 (Martin et al. 2003, Kimball 2004). Furthermore, the incidence of fatherhood might be higher than statistics indicate for African-American teens because African-American adolescent mothers are overly represented in teen pregnancy and birth rates. In addition, the 2003 YRBSS survey conducted across the country indicated that the prevalence of having gotten someone pregnant was 7.6 percent for African-American male students compared to 1.7 percent for white male students (Centers for Disease Control and Prevention 2004). As previously stated, Kansas statistics indicate that out of the adolescent females aged ten through nineteen who gave birth in Kansas in 2002, more than two-thirds (67.1 percent) of the fathers were twenty years old and over (Kansas Department of Health and Environment 2002). These figures probably underestimate the incidence of teen male involvement in adolescent pregnancies, especially for African Americans.

Obtaining a good approximation of the number of teen fathers is difficult. Robinson (1988) and Dallas and Chen (1998) explained that it is difficult to ascertain precise estimates of the number of adolescent fathers for several reasons. First, adolescent males have a relatively low rate of paternity affirmation (Allen and Doherty 1998). In a study by Weinman and colleagues (2002), less than half of the fathers studied had declared paternity for their children. Second, a social stigma is attached to early childbearing, discouraging fathers from admitting paternity (Allen and Doherty 1998); thus, many are unlikely to admit to parenthood. Third, in some cases adolescent mothers refuse to name the fathers (Christmon 1990), and the age of the father may be omitted from the birth certificate (Christmon 1990). These missing data on birth certificates make adolescent fatherhood statistics unreliable (Kimball 2004).

Regardless of underreporting, clearly racial and ethnic variations in adolescent fatherhood exist, with the proportion of African-American teen fathers being higher than adolescent white and Hispanic males (Centers for Disease Control 2004). The previous statistics point to a need to examine factors that influence beliefs, attitudes, and behaviors that might lead to African-American adolescent fatherhood status. Although structural explanations (Anderson 1989, 1990; Wilson 1987) and cultural accounts (Anderson 1989, 1990; Sullivan 1989) have been used by researchers to explain the overrepresentation of African-American adolescent fathers, very few provide information from the teen fathers' perspectives about their fatherhood experiences, beliefs, attitudes, and practices. Even though some progress has been made

18 VOICES OF AFRICAN-AMERICAN TEEN FATHERS

researching African-American adolescent fathers, still too little is known.

EXPLAINING AFRICAN-AMERICAN TEEN FATHERHOOD

The factors associated with adolescent fatherhood are similar to those associated with teen motherhood. They include low socioeconomic status (Xie et al. 2001; Gasden et al. 2003), reduced income potential (Marsiglio 1987; Castiglia 1990), poor academic performance, and higher school dropout rates (Marsiglio 1987; Castiglia 1990; Fagot et al. 1998; Xie et al. 2001), desire to achieve symbolic adult status (Anderson 1989, 1990) and/or peer admiration and approval (Anderson 1989, 1990), and careless sexual practices or infrequent use of contraceptives (Sullivan 1989; DiClemente et al. 1992; Dawsey 1996). African-American young men are less likely to use contraceptives than are white teens (Centers for Disease Control and Prevention 2004), and they are more likely to reject abortion as an option to unplanned pregnancies (Sullivan 1989; Joshi and Battle 1990).

Most studies on adolescent fathers do not focus upon cultural differences in parenting or on the experiences of becoming fathers. However, in "Absent Fathers in the City," Mercer Sullivan (1989) studied cultural influences on fatherhood. He used ethnographic methods in his study on young father involvement among three racial/ethnic and culturally diverse populations, including men from a white Catholic neighborhood ($n = 15$), a predominantly African-American neighborhood ($n = 16$), and a largely Hispanic neighborhood ($n = 17$). Sullivan spent much time in the three neighborhoods, took field notes, conducted extensive interviews with the participants, and collected life-history reports. Some of the young men in the study were legal adults at the time of the study, and each had fathered at least one child by a teen mother. Sullivan used a general interactionist view of culture, society, and economy in his study of young fatherhood, as well as social ecology theory to guide his research. He wrote that it was essential to consider the effects of culture in order to understand how people deal collectively with economic disadvantage, prejudice, and procreation issues, for example. However, it is equally as important to situate the behaviors of those studied in their proper context, including the consideration of social and socioeconomic settings and educational influences. According to Sullivan (1989), neighborhoods and communities were distinctive in his study because of the variations in cultural values, as well as their "ecological niche in relation to the regional economy, the educational system, and other institutions of the larger society" (p. 60).

Sullivan's (1989) study demonstrated comparative differences in adaptive strategies of the young men in dealing with parenting. For instance, although he did not find any differences between the groups in regard to early sexual activities and contraceptive use (nearly all in each group experienced intercourse by age fifteen, and few had used contraceptives), differences existed in the *responses* to pregnancy (whether abortion was sought, whether marriage or coresidence was entered into, and/or whether the children were economically supported to some extent by the fathers). He found that most of the African-American fathers were opposed to abortion, and they were not generally encouraged by their community to marry or reside with the mothers of their children. Furthermore, most of the young African-American fathers reported provision of care and support for their children to the extent that they were able. The responses to pregnancy in the white neighborhood indicated that the majority of the young men were not strongly opposed to abortion and that marriage was a more common choice. The Hispanics in his study were even more opposed to abortion than were the African-American young fathers. They were more likely to pursue marriage and coresidence than the other two groups because of their cultural influences regarding tradition and religion.

In another ethnographic study examining the sexual conduct, pregnancy, and parenthood of socioeconomically poor urban African-American adolescents, Elijah Anderson (1989) interviewed approximately forty persons, including adolescent mothers, pregnant teenagers, teen fathers, prospective adolescent fathers, and several close relatives of the adolescents. The interviews took place in natural settings throughout the neighborhood. Anderson's intent was to create conversations about the general subject of sex and pregnancy among poor, inner-city, African-American young people in the fifteen- to twenty-three-year-old age range. Similar to Stack (1974) and Wilson (1987), Anderson (1989, 1990) found that adolescent parenthood in poor urban communities was a symbol of status and a rite of passage into adulthood. Adolescent parenthood as a status symbol, he explained, is a

20 VOICES OF AFRICAN-AMERICAN TEEN FATHERS

cultural manifestation of various social and structural conditions, including the lack of jobs that pay a living wage, the stigma of race, rampant drug use, and the alienation and lack of hope in the community. Because of such conditions, explains Anderson (1989, 1990), young men must assert their manhood in other ways (e.g., parenthood) since they cannot do so in the traditional American way (namely through gainful employment opportunities). Robert K. Merton's strain theory indicates that such behavior is not pathogenic but rather outcomes of a society that emphasizes material success and nice job, for example, but also deprives access (via racism, classism, and sexism) to such goals (Huang and Anderson 1991).

PERCEPTIONS OF FATHERHOOD
BY AFRICAN-AMERICAN YOUTHS

Understanding how African-American teens perceive and experience their fatherhood is important in understanding how we must address it. In one study, Allen and Doherty (1998) explored the perceptions of fatherhood among African-American teen fathers. They were primarily interested in how their subjects conceptualized fatherhood and, to some extent, whether these perceptions were reflected in their paternal behavior. In-depth interviews were used with a sample of ten fathers aged fifteen to nineteen in the Minneapolis-Saint Paul, Minnesota, area. One of the major themes found in Allen and Doherty's (1998) data was the young men's perception of fatherhood as being physically and emotionally present in the lives of their children. They conceptualized fatherhood as "being there," which referred to having been present at the birth of their children and/or being physically and emotionally present in the children's lives. The majority of the fathers were dedicated to being involved with their children and to performing roles as fathers, according to their assessments. Furthermore, they found that the fathers' families of origin played an important role in the way the adolescent fathers thought about their paternal role. The absence of fathers was a primary influence on the young mens' perceptions of fatherhood. For example, the young fathers reported that not having fathers involved in their lives motivated them to be involved with their own children, in large part because of their conviction that they would have benefited from the involvement of a father.

On the other hand, these young men also had mothers and other significant women in their lives who played an important role in how they perceived fatherhood.

Although the present study addressed similar issues explored by Allen and Doherty (1998) (e.g., definition of fatherhood and parenting behavior), this book takes a broader approach to exploring the experiences of adolescent fatherhood. Perhaps the biggest distinction emphasized in the current study was the subjective accounts of how and why the male teens became fathers. Moreover, the present study extensively explored actual parenting behavior and how it was associated with the conceptualization of fatherhood, relationships with significant others, and with the challenges and concerns the males had. In addition, the theoretical orientations between the former and the current study differed somewhat, with Allen and Doherty (1998) using symbolic interactionism as a general framework, with specific concepts from identity, role, and human ecology theory. The current study used gender theory and social ecology theory as theoretical paradigms (discussed in the following sections).

Kenneth Christmon (1990) investigated the willingness of African-American teen fathers to take responsibility for their children and studied the factors that influenced this willingness. He carried out the study with forty-three African-American adolescent fathers, fifteen to twenty-one years old, from the Washington, DC, area, and used questionnaires as assessment tools. Even though Christmon (1990) did not explore actual parenting behavior, he found that African-American adolescent fathers' sense of parental responsibility was more influenced by their own role expectations and self-images than by those of others. The teens' parental responsibilities were not influenced by the role expectations they perceived their partners and parents had for them. Furthermore, adolescents with good self-images were more prepared to handle their roles as fathers. The relationship with the young fathers' peers was not examined.

Various researchers (Dash 1989; Anderson 1989, 1990) have found peer influence to be a major factor related to African-American teens' perceived fatherhood role and behavior. They submit that the inner-city young man is heavily influenced by members of his peer group who often set the standards for his conduct. African-American teens and their peers who are socioeconomically poor may have different views from other groups regarding sexuality, pregnancy, and teen parenthood (Andersen 1993; Allen and Doherty 1998). To most poor, urban, African-American youths, according to Anderson (1989, 1990), personal independence and freedom are highly valued. Because of the young men's limited financial abilities and their desire for personal independence, their perception of fatherhood is often negative. Subsequently, they come to view women and children as a financial burden and begin to devalue marital relationships. This perception is further intensified by young fathers' male peers who generally share the same views (Anderson 1989, 1990). Their negative perceptions of such relationships and responsibilities are further affirmed as adults when they find it difficult to provide economically for their children and families (Wilson 1987; Anderson 1989, 1990).

Hendricks and Montgomery (1983) provided a preliminary account of African-American teen fathers' subjective experiences on parenting, fatherhood readiness, and their basic views about the relationships with the children's mothers. A comparison was made between two samples of unwed African-American first-time fathers under the age of twenty-one in Tulsa, Oklahoma ($n = 20$), and Chicago, Illinois ($n = 27$). Using open-ended and closed-ended questions, they found that the young men in both samples were more likely than not to be accepting of their fatherhood, which contrasts with Anderson's later findings (1989, 1990). Furthermore, most of the fathers also believed that their experiences as unwed fathers would change their lives in a positive way. Although the researchers explored just a few dimensions of adolescent fatherhood, their findings provided an additional explanation or factor that may be associated with why young fathers may not be strongly opposed to adolescent fatherhood—mainly because they do not perceive early parenthood to be detrimental or a negative factor in their lives.

AFRICAN-AMERICAN ADOLESCENTS
AND FATHERHOOD INVOLVEMENT

As previously stated, the presumed absence of fathers (which includes adolescent fathers) from their children's lives has been considered a major factor in the "moral decline" of our nation's values by politicians and social scientists (Blankenhorn 1995; Popenoe 1996). Blankenhorn (1995), for instance, contended that our "culture of fatherlessness" has perpetuated various social problems such as

Literature Review 23

unwed motherhood and poverty-stricken, female-headed households. In turn, these conditions have promoted a cycle of familial poverty, youth and neighborhood violence, and vulnerable family situations in which a steady weakening of parental authority in the home occurs. Thus, increased efforts have been made to hold nonresidential fathers accountable in terms of their financial responsibilities (Johnson et al. 1999; Rhodes 2000). Attempts have been made to collect child support payments from "deadbeat dads" who are considered able but unwilling to provide financial assistance (Johnson et al. 1999; Rhodes 2000). However, less attention has been given to programs and policies that focus on the social aspects of fatherhood, the individual situations of fathers, and father-child involvement in general.

Although studies differ in how parental involvement is defined, many, including Sullivan (1989), Danziger and Radin (1990), and Gasden et al. (2003) have found that in general African-American adolescent fathers tend to be involved in their children's lives. Danziger and Radin (1990) conducted a study on a sample of 289 teen mothers receiving Aid to Families with Dependent Children (AFDC, currently Temporary Assistance for Need Families, TANF) by administering thirty to forty minute telephone interviews. Their findings indicated that adolescent mothers of color reported higher levels of paternal involvement than did their white counterparts. Involvement was measured by four factors: perceived father-child relationship quality, diversity of paternal help with the baby, father's discussions about the baby with the teen mother, and the mother's perception of the father's overall or total fathering.

Some researchers have found that African-American adolescent fathers are not very involved or economically supportive of their children (Dawsey 1996; Kaplan 1997). The African-American adolescent mothers in Kaplan's (1997) study, for example, reported that the fathers of their children did not participate very much in their children's lives. Kaplan was unable to explore the fathers' points of view about parenting because the fathers (although not the target participants of her study) of the children of her female subjects chose not to participate, were hard to contact, or because the mothers of their children were unable to contact them.

In another example, Dawsey (1996) interviewed several young African-American men between fifteen to twenty-four years of age from various socioeconomic groups in nine major cities over a six-month time period. He did not indicate how many men he interviewed but stated that in their interviews they discussed a variety of topics including fatherhood, sex, work, and employment. The results of his study are somewhat inconclusive as far as involvement because he reported that many young fathers participated considerably in their childrens' lives whereas many others did not. He defined being involved as providing economic support, spending time with the children, and participating in the childrens' socialization processes.

The majority of other social science work on father-child involvement points to socioeconomic status as the most important determinant of father-child interaction and economic support among African-American fathers (Wilson 1987; Anderson 1989, 1990; Danziger and Radin 1990; McCall 1994; Xie et al. 2001). For instance, Danziger and Radin (1990) found that the more economic resources young men provided (which was sometimes determined by their socioeconomic status and ability to provide these resources) to the mothers of their children, the more likely they were to want and to be allowed to participate in child care tasks and to be viewed as nurturing by the mothers of their children. Similarly, Stack (1974) found the mothers in her ethnographic study of low-income, urban African Americans were more likely to consider a father (or the father's family) to be supportive and involved if the father and/or his family contributed economically or materially to the welfare of the child.

Joblessness or lack of gainful employment diminishes the family role of the father in economically disadvantaged communities (Wilson 1987; Anderson 1989, 1990; Danziger and Radin 1990). Wilson's (1987) study found that men were more likely to marry the mothers of their children and/or to become more involved in the lives of their children if they could provide financial support. He also explained that rapid postindustrialization and displacement of unskilled jobs accompanied by gender-specific academic problems in the public schools placed African-American fathers at an alarming risk for chronic joblessness, provider-role failure, familial estrangement, and high levels of personal distress. In "Understanding African-American Teen Fathers" John McAdoo (1990) concurred. McAdoo presented a structural and cultural perspective and overview of the teen father literature from various disciplines using a modified social exchange theoretical perspective. He determined that the findings on teen fathers were consistent with choice and exchange theory, which suggests that the greater the economic resources, the more likely adolescent fathers of all ethnic backgrounds are to provide economic and emotional support for their children. He maintained that when African-American adolescent fathers are able to overcome economic and educational barriers they are able to provide the social, emotional, and material support for the mothers of their children.

In addition to socioeconomic status, other factors associated with paternal involvement are the age of the father and of the child. For example, besides finding that mothers of color reported higher amounts of father participation than did white mothers in their sample, Danziger and Radin (1990) also found that younger fathers (regardless of race or ethnicity) participated more in their children's lives than did older fathers. Rein et al. (1997) also found that the fathers' increasing age was as an important barrier for fatherhood involvement among non-African-American fathers. Danziger and Radin (1990) explained that the fathers' greater involvement with younger children was possibly due to an "excitement period" in which more interest and involvement with children existed in the beginning of the child-rearing stages. This excitement period is thought to eventually dwindle as the complexities of being a father become a reality. Furthermore, Danziger and Radin (1990) found that the younger the child, the more involved the father, regardless of the father's age. Thus, the age of the father (Danziger and Radin 1990), age of child (Danziger and Radin 1990), low socioeconomic status (Wilson 1987; Anderson 1989, 1990), and general economic provision by the father to his child (Stack 1997; Wilson 1987; Danziger and Radin 1990) are all factors associated with father involvement.

AFRICAN-AMERICAN TEEN FATHERS AND THEIR RELATIONSHIPS WITH OTHERS

The primary socialization of adolescent fathers occurs in the family (Seward 1991). According to Seward (1991), the family provides the primary means of social control over teen fathers, and it influences teen fathers' behaviors more than other social groups or institutions. Franklin (1984) wrote that the family facilitates the socialization of young men in two ways: it provides a setting in which the youth can observe and learn how men are expected to behave, and it provides direct and indirect guidance about the male role. Because many African-American youths are raised in single-parent, female-headed households (Taylor 1997; Chadwick and Heaton 1998), much of their socialization begins with their mothers (Billingsley 1992). However, many African-American single mothers have relied on extended family support systems (Stack 1974; Billingsley 1992; Collins 1994) to help them raise their children. Therefore, due to the collective effort of families and community, many African-American youths have been raised by, or have been greatly influenced by, individuals other than their mothers and fathers (Billingsley 1992; Collins 1994).

Hendricks and colleagues (1981) conducted a cross-sectional study with ninty-five unwed, African-American adolescent fathers in Tulsa, Oklahoma; Chicago, Illinois; and Columbus, Ohio, and found that they were more likely to go to their families than to anyone else for help with a problem. The person most likely to provide assistance was the young father's mother.

Virtually no studies have been done that explore the relationship between the African-American teen father and his own father. However, Allen and Doherty's (1998) study was able to capture some of the dynamics that occur with this relationship. The relationship had a positive influence on some teen fathers, which helped shaped positive views about fatherhood. However, some of the teens did not feel "fathered" and struggled with abandonment issues. Eight of the ten participants in their study indicated that their fathers had been teen parents similar to themselves.

The relationship of the teen father with the mother of his child is very important and influences the emotional welfare of the young fathers. In an earlier study, Hendricks and colleagues (1981) found that the problems young African-American fathers experienced with the mothers of their children were related to the fathers not being able to see the children as often as they would have liked. The investigators used open-ended and closed-ended questions to examine the kinds of problems the teen fathers were likely to seek help from others to resolve. The males' relationships with the mothers of their children were often a source of stress for them.

Contrasting results were found in a study by Hendricks and Montgomery (1983), in which they analyzed the teens' perceptions of fatherhood and their relationships with the mothers of their children. The young African-American fathers reported their relationships with their partners to be meaningful for the most part. For instance, most of the young men felt some love existed between them and the mothers of their children—or at least friendship. The relationship with the female partner was also perceived to be a close one after the birth of the child. However, Hendricks and Montgomery (1983) mentioned that these findings did not indicate how committed these young men were in these relationships, nor did they demonstrate whether the fathers viewed their relationships or involvement as long term.

Even though Hendricks and Montgomery (1983) found that adolescent African-American fathers perceived their relationships with the mothers of their children to be meaningful, several researchers (Wilson 1987; Anderson 1989, 1990; Dawsey 1996; Allen and Doherty 1998) found that the fathers tended to experience relationship difficulties. Allen and Doherty (1998) found that in addition to relationship problems with the mothers of their children, African-American adolescent fathers experienced relationship problems with the adolescent mothers' families as well. Often the relationship with the family of the adolescent mother was perceived positively until the young mother became pregnant (Allen and Doherty 1998). These relationships were very strained, and the problems sometimes extended to the young mothers' friends and acquaintances, who often adopted similar negative attitudes and beliefs toward the adolescent fathers.

Some research findings suggest that urban African-American male youths are greatly influenced by their peers (Dash 1989; Anderson 1989, 1990; Meyers 1998; White and Cones 1999). Anderson's (1989, 1990) study showed that the peer group is very important to the inner-city male youth. He stated that for inner-city male youths, the most important people in their lives are members of their peer groups. "They set the standards for conduct, and it is important to live up to those standards, to look good in their eyes," he wrote (1999: 150). Myers (1998) contended that the peer group is second only to parents in socializing adolescents, and that it is an important factor in the adolescent socialization process. White and Cones (1999) supported this position and stated that the peer group replaces the parents during adolescence and becomes the source of support, understanding, and guidance. The peer group gives African-American males the opportunity to enact the masculine behaviors that can be practiced, including competitiveness and aggression, which are even more important

28 *VOICES OF AFRICAN-AMERICAN TEEN FATHERS*

in the overall socialization process of lower-class adolescents (Myers 1998; White and Cones 1999). Virtually no studies have been done on how the peer group influences African-American fathers in regard to their behaviors and involvement as fathers.

Many problems and challenges that teen fathers experience are not directly tied to their relationships with others. For example, Hendricks and colleagues (1981) further indicated that the young African-American fathers also experienced restriction of freedom, not seeing the children as often as they would like, financial difficulties and lack of employment, and academic problems, such as not being able to finish school. Furthermore, Allen and Doherty (1998) discovered that African-American teen fathers believed that various social service institutions, such as public assistance and child protection organizations, were intimidating and created barriers to them becoming the fathers they believed they could be. Finally, young fathers were not likely to seek community resources (e.g., social service agencies, clergypersons, teachers, etc.) for assistance or help with their problems (Hendricks et al. 1981).

In summary, not a lot of sociological research on teen fathers is available. Among the existing studies that specifically focus on African-American adolescent fathers, a limited set of issues is examined. The lack of literature on male teen parents is an indication that this area of study is still in its exploratory stages. The existing studies indicate that teen fathers tend to be relatively involved with their children. The extent to which they are involved is affected by both cultural and structural factors. Furthermore, the adolescent father's perceptions of fatherhood tend to influence fatherhood readiness and his level of paternal involvement and parent-child interaction. Nonetheless, some research points to inconsistencies in regard to the teens' perceptions of fatherhood and paternal behavior. Finally, African-American teen fathers experience many challenges, including problems with female partners and their families as well as financial and educational barriers or difficulties.

THEORETICAL PERSPECTIVE:
SOCIAL ECOLOGY AND GENDER THEORY

As previously stated, the goal of this study is to understand how African-American teens understand and experience fatherhood. The subjective meanings that they create are best understood through the lens of both social ecology and gender theory. These paradigms provide some of the structural and social psychological explanations for the particular meanings of fatherhood constructed by these boys and young men. In addition to their individual interpretations and experiences of fatherhood, these paradigms direct us to examine the structural conditions and social contexts in which the teens became fathers.

The social ecological paradigm is rooted in concepts or core themes regarding interrelations among environmental conditions and human behavior and well-being (Bubolz and Sontag 1993; Stokols 1996). It suggests that it is important to view social phenomena in the context of social structure and the particular cultural milieu, which produce specific meanings (Brofenbrenner 1979; Bubolz and Sontag 1993).

The ecological framework depicts environmental settings as having several physical, social, and cultural dimensions that influence a variety of outcomes, including developmental maturation, emotional well-being, and social cohesion (Stokols 1996). Urie Bronfenbrenner (1979), a major influence in human ecology theory, promoted the practice of providing a contextual emphasis on ecological research. Specifically he stated that four levels of environmental systems exist: micro-, meso-, exo-, and macrosystems.

The family is the primary microsystem context in which development takes place (Bronfenbrenner 1979). For example, the dyadic relationship between the teen father and his child is an example of a microsystem. Bronfenbrenner discussed the mesosystem in terms of the relationships or interactions between microsystems or between microsystems and other settings for developments, such as the school. The exosystem is referred to as broader institutions, for example the economic and political institutions that affect the microsystems. Finally, the macrosystems are explained as the broad ideological values, norms, and culture in which the micro-, meso-, and exosystems occur. For instance, macrosystems may involve current and historical images of fatherhood.

Bronfenbrenner (1979) provided a useful framework to explore ways in which teen fatherhood is influenced by familial conditions and by extrafamilial circumstances and environments. Thus, adolescent fathers' subjective accounts of their experiences for the present project should be studied in their proper social context because their

30   VOICES OF AFRICAN-AMERICAN TEEN FATHERS

perspectives are affected by both social structure and the cultural context for meanings.

Mercer Sullivan (1989) used social ecology as a basis for writing his study about fatherhood in the inner city. In doing so, he illustrated the importance of family location within the broader social structure and how this location influences the events that family members experience. As earlier explained, the study observed young fathers from three different neighborhoods, and it was found that each neighborhood was distinctive not only because of their cultural values (e.g., neighborhood differences in responses to pregnancy), but also because of their relation to the economy, educational system, and other institutions (e.g., the neighborhoods were socioeconomically different). Thus, the social meanings attached to events (including teen parenthood) are a product of one's local social environment (Bengtson and Allen 1993). This position is taken by several scholars, as will be described in the following sections.

Social constructionist theory emphasizes how interaction processes both produce and reproduce gender in everyday life (Chafetz 1999). What distinguishes this perspective from other gender theories is the emphasis placed on the individual interpretations of situations and how meanings are ascribed to behaviors. Furthermore, this theory emphasizes individual agency and the ongoing social construction of gender in face-to-face interaction. Drawing on West and Zimmerman's (1987) concept of "doing gender," this book's study examines the production of masculinity in a small sample of African-American men, as evidenced by their accounts of their fatherhood. Borrowing further from Franklin's (1989) approach to gender, specifically African-American masculinity, the goal was to explore how structure, interaction, and masculinity intersect in the lives and experiences of African-American adolescent fathers.

Social Ecology Theory and African-American Teen Fatherhood

Many of the social problems and issues that confront African-American youths (drugs, teen pregnancy, violence, HIV/AIDS infection, etc.) are in large part due to poor socioeconomic conditions, the hopelessness they feel, and the bleak futures they perceive (Staples 1985; Wilson 1987; Myers 1998). For example, in the United States,

African Americans disproportionately reside in severely impoverished areas of the Northeast and Midwest that are characterized by high levels of unemployment, dependency on public assistance, violent crime, educational deficiencies, and teenage pregnancy (Wilson 1987; Anderson 1990). These conditions of poverty are important to understanding the experiences and culture of African-American youth. Among persons residing in concentrated poverty in the nation's metropolitan areas, 67 percent are African-American, 20 percent are Hispanic, and 12 percent are white (Hajnal 1995).

Because of racism, deindustrialization, and the exodus of major corporations from inner, urban areas during the 1970s and 1980s, many African Americans suffered from unemployment and low-paying jobs that did not provide sufficient living wages (Wilson 1987; Anderson 1990; Hill 1990). Many had difficulty finding work in the regular economy and resorted to criminal activities. As meaningful employment became increasingly scarce for African Americans, crime and drugs became a way of life for many. Illegal activities, such as the sale of drugs, became particularly alluring for youth when prospects for legitimate employment disappeared (Wilson 1987).

Moreover, research by Sampson and Wilson (1995) found that conditions of concentrated poverty, African-American male joblessness, and residential instability led to high rates of family disruptions and accounted for high levels of violent crime. In their study, they examined poverty, joblessness, residential instability, and crime and found the association almost identical in size and magnitude among whites and African Americans. They wrote, "The sources of violent crime appear to be remarkably invariant across race and rooted instead in the structural differences among communities, cities, and states in economic and family disorganization" (Sampson and Wilson 1995:41). Even so, they write that it is not possible to control fully for ecological characteristics in African American–white comparisons, because even among the poor, African Americans and whites do not live in the same neighborhoods characterized by concentrated poverty or family disruption. For instance, among the 171 largest cities in the nation, Sampson and Wilson (1995) contend that not even one city exists in which whites live in ecological equality to African Americans in terms of poverty rates or rates of single-parent households. They summarized that even when compared to the average urban context of

32   *VOICES OF AFRICAN-AMERICAN TEEN FATHERS*

African-American communities, the worst urban context in which whites reside is considerably better.

Douglas Massey and Nancy Denton (1993) argued that the critical factor in the development of an underclass in American society was not African-American poverty but rather the geographical segregation of that poverty. This residential segregation and the social conditions associated with it are important to understand because they affect educational and employment opportunities—which have meant curtailed economic mobility for African Americans (Williams 1998; Massey and Denton 1993). Because of residential segregation and other aspects of institutional discrimination, racial differences still exist today in the quality of education and income returns for a given level of education (Williams 1998; Massey and Denton 1993). Because of institutional discrimination and segregation, racial differences exist in the stability of employment and in the wealth or assets associated with a given level of income (Williams and Collins 1995; Massey and Denton 1993).

Even when jobs are available, African Americans must still contend with racism (Wilson 1996). In *When Work Disappears,* William Julius Wilson (1996) wrote that inner-city residents are often denied employment simply because of their inner-city addresses or neighborhoods. Although this type of discrimination may appear to be more of a class than race issue, this type of selective job recruitment screens out far more African Americans than inner-city Hispanics or white workers from the same types of backgrounds. African Americans report being denied employment because of their race. Their perception that employers or potential employers have negative attitudes about them were supported by survey and interview data from white employers who indicated judgment and attitudes that were more critical toward inner-city African-American male workers than others (Wilson, 1996). Furthermore, Kinder and Mendelberg (1995) using the 1990 General Social Survey (GSS) reported that half of all whites believe that African Americans are prone to violence, prefer to live off of public assistance, and lack the motivation and willpower to pull themselves out of poverty. However, a 2000 GSS study by Dixon and Rosenbaum (2004) indicated that regular contact with blacks at school and at work helps to disconfirm antiblack stereotypes among whites.

Literature Review 33

Since the civil rights movement and social policy changes such as affirmative action, African Americans have experienced some socioeconomic improvement (Franklin 1989). However, despite socioeconomic gains among African Americans in recent years, the vast majority of African Americans did not reap these gains and very little structural change actually occurred (Franklin 1989). For instance, even though the African-American middle class of educated professionals has expanded since the civil rights movement, socioeconomic conditions deteriorated for the majority of African Americans (Messner 1997). Because very little change occurred at the structural level, African-American youth live in a society today in which they are confronted with higher infant mortality rates and high mortality rates due to homicide, accidents, suicide, and drug overdose (Staples 1985; Franklin 1989). Furthermore, it does not escape these youth, especially male youth, that a high rate of incarceration (Franklin 1989), underemployment, and unemployment exists among African-American men (Staples 1985; Franklin 1989). Thus, African-American male youth observe and/or perceive limited educational and career options for themselves (Staples 1985; Franklin 1989).

In *The Truly Disadvantaged,* William Julius Wilson (1987) discussed how underemployment and unemployment had a severe, long-term impact on the ability of African-American men to marry and/or support families. Marriages do not happen just because of family values, he stated, but are also greatly shaped by the larger social environment. Unemployment, insufficient incomes, and high job-turnover rates are all associated with increased rates of marital dissolution (Williams 1998). The number of female-headed households declines when male earnings rise, and the number rises when male unemployment increases. Thus, an inverse association exists between employment opportunities for African-American men and the rates of African-American female-headed households (Wilson 1987). In the following sections is a discussion of how socioeconomic and structural conditions interact with and create/re-create gender in the African-American community and how it might shape young males' perceptions of fatherhood.

Socioeconomic status and other factors not only shape a family's resources but also influence family structures. Variations in the traditional nuclear family (in which the parents are married, heterosexual, and living in the same household) are adaptations to limited

34   *VOICES OF AFRICAN-AMERICAN TEEN FATHERS*

resources and opportunities (Myers 1998). Out of a sample of 8,186,828 African-American households with children under eighteen years of age, 46 percent were married couples and 45 percent were female headed, compared to 14 percent and 8 percent for whites, respectively, in a sample of 56,204,069 (U.S. Census Bureau 2000). African-American children are three times more likely to live in single-parent homes than are white children (Taylor 1997). In many inner-city African-American communities, more than half of the children are born to unwed mothers, and approximately 70 percent of children grow up without a biological father in the household (White and Cones 1999). Female-headed households are more strongly associated with poverty than are households containing two parents. In a sample of 70,505,715 households, female-headed households represented 55 percent of all households living in poverty (U.S. Census Bureau 2000).

For various reasons, a limited number of marriageable African-American men exist (Wilson 1987). Few become family leaders and providers, thus, not being able to enact the most important, traditional forms of masculinity. According to Robert Staples (1985), the problem does not lie in the quantity of African-American men but rather in what he defines as the "quality" of these men in terms of socioeconomic status and position. The vast number of African-American women who are not married is a function of limited choice from a small pool of potential husbands "who can successfully fulfill the normatively prescribed familial roles" (Staples 1985:1005). The factors associated with this limited pool of marriageable or suitable African-American men are poverty, high incarceration rates, drug addiction or involvement, and unemployment or underemployment (Wilson 1987). Chronic poverty in itself is simply not conducive to forming stable marriages (Roberts 1998).

In addition, many African-American female-headed households are socioeconomically poor and a disproportionate number of them receive TANF, a system that in the past required men be absent from the home (Staples 1985). Thus, when men were needed most, and when many of them were in need themselves, the very system (public assistance) that was put in place to assist women and children in need also prevented the formation of a household in which African-American men were able to enact the family-leader role. Although this policy no longer requires that men be absent from the homes in order to receive public assistance, the ramifications of the prior policy are still seen today, as many poor African-American youth were raised without the benefit of two parents, thus, two incomes and parental assistance.

Furthermore, poverty creates conditions in which the men do not see marital formation or nuclear family formations as advantageous. As Elijah Anderson (1989) wrote, "In the social context of persistent poverty, young men have come to devalue the conventional marital relationship, easily viewing women as a burden and children as even more so" (p. 65). When men have neither employment nor sufficient incomes, Staples (1985) explains that they do not feel good about themselves or act very positively toward women and their children. As a result, they are less likely to marry. Serial mating and having children by multiple partners have served to exacerbate their economic inadequacies (Aronson et al. 2003). In analyzing life history data collected from twelve adult African-American men participating in a parenting program, Aronson and colleagues (2003) observed that multiple factors impacted family formation and family involvement at the intrapersonal, interpersonal, community, and broader societal levels. Socioeconomic disadvantages influenced issues on several levels.

As earlier stated, societal and structural barriers inhibit African-American men's upward mobility and "render millions of Black males socially impotent and/or socially dysfunctional" (Franklin 1989:370). As Messner (1997) stated, young African-American men are now living with the legacy of more than twenty years of deindustrialization, rising joblessness, and declining quality of inner-city schools. The socioeconomic conditions of these young fathers cannot be understated. In "The Absent Black Father," Dorothy Roberts (1998) asserted that "Making Black men symbols of fatherlessness serves two specific functions: This racial association automatically brands fatherlessness as a depraved condition and it offers a convenient explanation for Black people's problems" (p. 146). The African-American family has been blamed for its own plight and for many of society's problems, yet lesser attention is given to the socioeconomic and social context (including racism and poverty) that have shaped the family's structure as well as its socially defined problems.

Gender Theory and Masculinity

One of the more severe ways that poor socioeconomic conditions, various structural factors, and feelings of hopelessness and alienation have affected African-Americans is in the ways that African-American men and male youths have come to express masculinity (Kimmel 2000) and experience and perform fatherhood (Messner 1997). For example, the changes in how masculinity is expressed have negatively affected the interaction in male-female relationships (Staples 1985; Franklin 1989) as well as worked to reproduce the very circumstances (e.g., high poverty and high crime rates) that influenced these changes in the first place (Anderson 1989, 1990).

Traditional masculinity, or what Connell (1987) refers to as hegemonic masculinity, demands that men exhibit traits such as independence, pride, resiliency, self-control, and physical strength (Thompson 1989). Traditional masculinity also suggests attributes such as competitiveness, toughness, aggressiveness, and power. However, many scholars theorize that masculinity and femininity are learned (West and Zimmerman 1987; Kimmel and Messner 1989). For example, in *Men's Lives,* Matt Groening (1989) wrote that "Men are not born, they are made" (p. 127). The differences between masculinity and femininity are not natural, inherent, or necessary, but are activities or attributes that have been prescribed. Gender is performed always in interaction with race, class, sexuality, etc., and is a "product" that is accomplished in and sustained by social interaction, and is also learned and repeated.

For instance, West and Zimmerman (1987) wrote that "Doing gender involves an intricate system of socially guided perceptual, interactional, and micropolitical activities that cast particular pursuits as expressions of masculine and feminine 'natures'" (p. 126). This position was supported by Michael Kimmel in *The Gendered Society* (2000) when he argued that no great differences exist between men and women, and in fact, gender differences are really the product of gender inequality. The perceived and practiced differences between the sexes legitimate inequality. Thus, one of the basic assumptions of traditional masculinity that still persists today is the subordination of women (Connel et al. 1989).

Therefore, gender is "a powerful ideological device, which produces, reproduces, and legitimates the choices and limits that are predicated on sex category" (West and Zimmerman 1987:147), and it legitimates one of the most fundamental divisions of society—male and female. The interviews in the present study will reveal something about the opportunities these young men perceive to be available as well as their construction of their own masculinity and of the femininity of the mothers of their children. These stories are ways of doing gender or expressing gender roles.

The roles of American fathers have been traditionally confined to those of economic provider and family leader; however, the majority of African-American men are not able to implement these roles due to structural barriers (Robert Staples 1985; Hill 1990). As Franklin (1989:369-370) wrote:

> Our society today undoubtedly remains structured in such a manner that the vast majority of Black men encounter insurmountable barriers to the attainment of a "masculine" status as defined by most Americans (black and white Americans). Black men still largely are locked within the Black culture (which has relatively limited resources), unable to compete successfully for societal rewards—the attainment of which defines American males as "men."

An issue then is what happens when the enactment of socially approved expressions of masculinity (e.g., breadwinner or provider) cannot be enacted by a significant number of African-American men. Franklin (1989) wrote that the consequence has been that many African-American men have adopted only a part of the general culture's definition of masculinity. He explained that the significance of masculinity remains important even to those who are not able to express it in fundamentally perceived ways. Thus, masculinity does not become lost among African-American men simply because they are not able to fully enact it; instead, traditional forms are partially enacted and masculinity becomes overemphasized in other areas of their lives or expressed in other forms. Understanding this concept may help in understanding the behaviors of African-American male youths, especially in their relationships with others and as young fathers.

Clyde Franklin (1989), in *Black Male-Black Female Conflict: Individually Caused and Culturally Nurtured*, maintained that it is because African-American men encounter structural barriers and receive mixed, noncomplementary messages, that they have conflict in

38   VOICES OF AFRICAN-AMERICAN TEEN FATHERS

their relationships with African-American women. This situation, he suggested, explains why few African Americans are married and few have father figures in their homes. He argued that African-American men are taught and socialized to acknowledge and accept the importance of being masculine, which means being dominant, aggressive, decisive, responsible, and, in some instances, violent in social encounters. Yet the second message they receive is that they cannot exhibit these attributes in the workplace or in their careers because of racism and the injustices they will encounter. They are taught that white Americans will not let them progress very far in the work force, and that the masculine attributes they are socialized to express would not be accepted in the workplace.

Thus, although they are taught that as a man they must exhibit certain masculine qualities, it does not hold true for employment or in the pursuit of their careers, where essentially they cannot be a "man," according to Franklin (1989). Because they are socialized to believe that employment and income are a measure of their masculinity, they are negatively impacted by this gender-created notion that posits that being male means being a provider and family leader, when in reality the African-American males are structurally hindered as well as discouraged by the negative messages they have been taught and have internalized (Franklin 1989). These messages are reified when they see the high unemployment rates and low socioeconomic conditions of others around them.

According to Billson (1996), one of the factors that encourages the decision to accept a new identity (such as fatherhood) is having models to demonstrate appropriate behavior for that particular identity. Thus, when African-American male youth do not see "appropriate" fathering behaviors demonstrated they are less likely to enact such behavior. Many young African-American men do not believe they can become adequate family leaders and providers, or they believe that it will be a great challenge to achieve. Franklin (1989) further stated that the expectations and pressure they feel from themselves and their female partners to become providers can create dissonance and conflict in their relationships.

In *Black Man Emerging,* White and Cones (1999) posit that African-American youth face four challenges, which include "constructing an identity and defining themselves as persons; developing and maintaining close relationships with others; coping with racism; and

Literature Review 39

discovering adaptive possibilities . . ." (p. 131). The first two challenges, they state, are concerns that all American men must face. However, coping with racism and discovering adaptive possibilities are challenges unique to African Americans and other minority men. Messner (1997) wrote that men of color "have often faced a lifetime of influences that call their basic sense of manhood into question" (p. 64).

For African-American men who are not able to express masculinity in the workplace or in their homes as breadwinners (a notion that society tells them that a "responsible" man does) enact their masculinities by "proving themselves" (Thompson 1989). For instance, in *Streetwise,* Elijah Anderson (1990) observed that African-American youth gain respect, admiration from peers, and a sense of manhood by being street tough, becoming drug dealers, and amassing cash and weapons. In *Code of the Street* (1999), he wrote that African Americans in inner cities learn the rules or appropriate behaviors of the streets (which is the "code") that help them survive the dangers they face daily. This code of the streets and its emphasis on toughness and gaining respect is an oppositional culture in poor inner cities that is developed out of the circumstances of poverty, racism, joblessness, and prevalent exposure and use of drugs and other substances. Negotiating respect is the basis upon which violent behavior occurs, yet it is also a cultural adaptation to the lack of jobs that pay living wages, the poverty in which they live, the lack of hope they have for the future, the stigma of race, and the lack of faith they have in the legal system (Myers 1998; Anderson 1999).

Messner (1997) found the notion of respect to be important to African-American men as well. After interviewing former male athletes about their lives and discussing their motivations for becoming athletes, he observed that achieving respect from others, at least through sports, was very important to African-American and Latino men. However, among the white men interviewed, respect was never mentioned unless Messner raised the issue himself.

The "code" and the negotiation of respect that is at its core are adaptations of masculinity in response to being poor, oppressed, and minority (Anderson 1999). Anderson's contentions are supported in *Black Man Emerging,* in which White and Cones (1999) discussed how African-American youth are swayed by the excitement, adventure, and macho image of gang life and street behavior. This dangerous

VOICES OF AFRICAN-AMERICAN TEEN FATHERS

display of masculinity is exacerbated by the proliferation of drugs and easy access to guns. White and Cones (1999) indicated that middle-class African-American youths are affected by this culture as well, indicating that they tend to emulate gang fashions and behaviors as a way of proving their masculinity, achieving notoriety, and gaining respect. White and Cones (1999) provided two case examples of middle-class male youths who were enticed and influenced by this lifestyle. This violent, dangerous notion of masculinity is strengthened further by the media and pop culture, as seen in movies, music, and in rap videos (Myers 1998; White and Cones 1999).

Lena Myers (1998), in *Black Male Socialization,* contended that mass media has enormous effects on young men's attitudes and behaviors, making them central to their socialization. Consequently, pop culture has partially socialized African-American men to violence because these men are commonly depicted as violent or as threatening characters. These media portrayals are important because they project expected role behavior for and by the larger society while showing the lack of conformity to expected roles on the part of African-American men (Myers 1998). Their masculinity is portrayed differently from white men's masculinity, and is enacted differently—with African-American men often depicted as criminals, drug addicts, and gang members (Myers 1998). This problem is further compounded when African-American youth already perceive a justice system that treats them differently than whites. When not depicted as criminals, White and Cones stated (1999), they are projected as superathletes, entertainers, and clowns. They write, "A foreign visitor watching American TV could easily conclude that all Blacks are natural athletes, can sing and dance, and spend the day making up funny one-liners" (p. 69).

In summary, African-American men face many challenges in their efforts and abilities to enact the traditional forms of masculinity, which are to become adequate providers and family leaders. Their inability to do so is associated with high rates of unemployment and incarceration and holding jobs that do not pay living wages (Franklin 1989). These structural forces are associated with variations in family structure (e.g., high rate of African-American female-headed households), changes in community culture (e.g., masculinity that involves interaction with others that places emphasis on gaining "respect" and being tough and a street culture that glorifies violence), and negative

Literature Review 41

perceptions (e.g., internalized thoughts about inabilities to gain upward socioeconomic mobility). These conditions are viewed as cultural adaptations to these challenges; however, they have made it more difficult for the African-American man (especially the African-American teen father) to assume a breadwinner or provider role. Poor socioeconomic conditions, his definition of masculinity, and his culture and interaction with others intersect to create and re-create conditions that counter such development.

RESEARCH QUESTIONS

As previously stated, most of the available research on adolescent parenthood focuses on teen mothers. A limited number of studies about African-American teen fathers and their support networks, processes of accommodation, roles as parents, or overall subjective fatherhood experiences exist. Few sociological studies exist that strive to give voice to these young men; therefore, our knowledge about them is limited. The primary purpose of this study is to provide insight into the issue of adolescent pregnancy and parenthood as it is viewed through the eyes of African-American teen fathers. This study seeks to explain how limited resources and structural constraints, perceived career and educational opportunities, and social definitions influence and shape African-American male adolescent behaviors, perceptions, and experiences as young fathers. To this end, the research questions were the following:

1. How and why do African-American teens become fathers?
2. How do African-American adolescent fathers define or conceptualize fatherhood?
3. How do African-American teen fathers enact fatherhood, and does a relationship exist between their enactment and their conceptualizations of fatherhood?
4. How do the relationships that African-American teen fathers have with significant others impact their fatherhood experiences and vice versa?
5. What challenges to African-American teen fathers perceive, and how do these challenges influence their fatherhood experiences and conceptualizations?

6. How do African-American adolescent fathers construct masculinity, and how does it impact their fatherhood experiences and conceptualizations?

The next chapter will describe how the teen fathers were recruited for this study, discuss the interviewing processes, and explain how data were collected and analyzed.

Chapter 2

Research Methods

As discussed in the literature review, only a few studies on African-American teen fathers exist. Accordingly, the questions guiding this research were exploratory and designed to enter the experience of teen fatherhood as understood and enacted by African-American young men. The study used qualitative methodology. Qualitative research adds knowledge and understanding about a particular social phenomenon, and helps reveal social processes and events (Gilgun 1999).

THE TEEN FATHERS

Previous studies on adolescent fathers had disparate sample sizes, ranging from as few as five (Dallas and Chen 1998) to more than forty-two (Christmon 1990; Pirog-Good 1995). In this study, thirty African-American teen fathers, forteen to nineteen years of age, were interviewed. Because in-depth information was sought, lengthy interviews were conducted; hence, a smaller sample size was optimal for this study.

The population of African-American teen fathers varies in age, socioeconomic status, the ages at which they become fathers, and other factors (Lerman 1993b). The sample of thrity adolescent fathers in the present study reflects some of this diversity, although the primary criteria used to select participants were race/ethnicity, sex, and fatherhood status. The author interviewed nonresidential African-American fathers residing in Wichita, Kansas, during the years 2000 to 2002. With the exception of two participants, these young men were socially and/or financially dependent on their parents or other adults.

Voices of African-American Teen Fathers
© 2006 by The Haworth Press, Inc. All rights reserved.
doi:10.1300/5477_03

Although an attempt was made to target fathers between the ages of thirteen and nineteen, the fathers actually interviewed ranged in age from fourteen to nineteen years of age. Because of potential cohort differences in the social experiences of fathers, fathers over the age of nineteen who were once teen fathers were not included in the study. Most of the young men in this study were between seventeen and nineteen ($n = 17$), with age seventeen representing the modal category ($n = 8$) (see Table 2.1). The fathers' education levels ranged from eighth grade to college, with twelfth grade representing the modal category (see Table 2.2).

The majority ($n = 21$) were from families of low socioeconomic status, having a combined family income of less than $25,000. Six of the thirty fathers were employed part-time, with one employed full-time. Most of the fathers were residing with one parent or another family member (e.g., grandmother) at the time they were interviewed. Six of the boys, or one-fifth of the sample, were living in two-parent families.

Three of the young fathers had two children. The participants' children ($n = 33$) ranged in age from two months to three years old, with the majority of the children ($n = 22$) being less than one year of age. Eighteen of the children were boys, and all of the children resided with their mothers. The mean age of the mothers of the children was seventeen years old (see Table 2.3).

TABLE 2.1. Age of participants.

Age $\overline{X} = 16.67$	Total (N)	Percent
14	3	10
15	4	13
16	6	20
17	8	27
18	5	17
19	4	13
Total	30	100

Research Methods 45

TABLE 2.2. Education level.

Education	Total *(N)*	Percent
Eigth grade	2	7
Ninth grade	3	10
Tenth grade	7	23
Eleventh grade	5	17
Twelfth grade	8	27
College	1	3
Completed high school (not in school)	3	10
Did not complete high school (not in school)	1	3
Total	30	100

TABLE 2.3. Teen fathers, children, and the mothers of their children by age.

Age of fathers (*n* = 30)	Age of partners (*n* = 33)	Age of children (*n* = 33)
All fathers	$\overline{X}$ = 17.1 years	$\overline{X}$ = 11.1 months
Fourteen to fifteen years old	$\overline{X}$ = 16.3 years	$\overline{X}$ = 7.1 months
Sixteen to seventeen years old	$\overline{X}$ = 16.8 years	$\overline{X}$ = 14 months
Eighteen to ninteen years old	$\overline{X}$ = 18.09 years	$\overline{X}$ = 17.2 months

ENVIRONMENTAL FACTORS

The majority (n = 26) of the participants were recruited from neighborhoods located in an urban area that is approximately 6.2 square miles in size, identified as the inner northeast neighborhood of Wichita, Kansas, in Sedgwick County. This area has a population of approximately 50,000, with 94 percent of this population being African Americans and the other 6 percent including whites, Hispanics, and Asians (Wichita-Sedgwick County Dept. of Community Health et al. 1997). The average household income was $16,000 at that time. Furthermore, a 1997 Community Health Assessment Project (CHAP) revealed that the health indicators of the residents in the northeast community were worse than those of other Wichita areas (Wichita-Sedgwick County Dept. of Community Health et al. 1997). Children born to African-American teenagers between the ages ten and nineteen accounted for 17.9 percent of teen births in the county. This was more than twice as many as any other zip code in the county (Wichita/Sedgwick County Weed & Seed Steering Committee 2002). Moreover, more than one-third of pregnant women in this area did not obtain care in their first trimester (Wichita-Sedgwick County Dept. of Community Health et al. 1997), and the infant mortality rate was 28.6 per 1,000 live births, which is much higher than the rate of 17.2 for African Americans nationally (Centers for Disease Control and Prevention 2005).

CHAP also revealed that the health indicators of the residents of the northeast community were worse than those in other areas of the city (Wichita-Sedgwick County Dept. of Community Health et al. 1997). For instance, African Americans were three times more likely to have a stroke than were other races residing in the area. The incidence rate of diabetes was 60 percent higher among African Americans than the rest of the city. In addition, more than 45 percent of the northeast population had no health insurance, the unemployment rate was very high, and the high school dropout rate was 26.4 percent. This area also had an annual death rate of 701 to 1,410 per 100,000 in the twenty-five to sixty-four age group compared to 150 to 300 per 100,000 in other sections of the city (Wichita-Sedgwick County Dept. of Community Health et al. 1997).

RECRUITMENT STRATEGIES

Although aware of the need to include African-American teen fathers in adolescent parenthood studies, many researchers often exclude them because of the difficulty in recruiting them (Johnson et al. 1999). For example, in Mercer Sullivan's foreword to Johnson and colleagues' (1999) *Fathers' Fair Share*, he writes that it is possible that social scientists have avoided focusing attention on poor, noncustodial fathers because these men avoid persons related to authority and bureaucracy. As stated in the literature (Miller 1997; Dallas and Chen 1998), African-American men are an especially difficult group to access for research, and this was also found to be the case in the present study. Many of the teen fathers that were approached were reluctant to be interviewed, and some failed to keep the arranged appointments and were never interviewed. Two of the interviews were rescheduled several times before taking place.

According to Cannon and colleagues (1988), the recruitment of African-American respondents requires labor-intensive strategies that include personal contact—usually face-to-face contact. This tactic was more rewarding than allowing a third party (e.g., a social service agency employee) to make the contacts and arrangements. In those cases involving a third party, the potential subject was less likely to participate. Nine of these fathers had been involved in a school-based ($n = 4$) and a community-based ($n = 5$) program that offered services to adolescent fathers. Most effective in my recruitment efforts was the snowball technique in reaching potential participants. In these cases, the recruited participants had not used such services and were referred through personal acquaintances, church contacts, middle school and high school counselors, and other adolescent fathers.

THE INTERVIEWING PROCESS

Conducting in-depth interviews was advantageous to this study because it allowed the teen fathers to describe their experiences in their own words. Using an open-ended format provided the opportunity for the interviewer to clarify and probe issues mentioned during the course of the interviews. The interviews were conducted over the course of two years and lasted from forty-five to ninety minutes. Two

48 VOICES OF AFRICAN-AMERICAN TEEN FATHERS

of the interviews were interrupted before their completion because one young father's transportation arrived earlier than expected, and the other because the young man wanted to end the interview. Ten of the interviews took place in the homes of the fathers, seven in an office or classroom at a community-based facility, four in my home, six in churches, and three at the home of a third party.

Although initially I believed the fathers' responses in the church settings to be somewhat subdued, I did not find differences when the content of the data was analyzed. For example, although the fathers that were interviewed in churches did not use profanity (and one apologized for "slipping" up), many others did, although they may not have started out using such during the onset of the interviews. Furthermore, when the responses from fathers interviewed in the churches were compared to those interviewed in other settings, again, no differences were found in relation to their sexual experiences and their descriptions of their relationships. Therefore, it was concluded that the settings did not make a difference in the content of their responses.

According to my recollections and field notes, fathers who were interviewed in the churches or in my home appeared to be more uncomfortable in the beginning of the interviews (e.g., an unrelaxed posture, reticence to divulge information, fidgeting, etc.) than those fathers who were interviewed in settings more familiar to them, such as their own homes or at the community-based organization where they were recruited. Therefore, a degree of difference occurred in this regard. Still, it was concluded that the interview settings did not make a significant difference in the responses given during the interviews. As the interviews progressed, participants appeared comfortable with the interviews regardless of setting, and no differences in content of discussion were noted. It probably helped that I was open to interviewing the fathers wherever they suggested or felt comfortable interviewing. Although none of the fathers suggested interviewing in my home, this alternative was suggested only when other options did not seem agreeable to the participants.

The Interview Guide

The interviews were conducted face-to-face and included open-ended questions designed to explore how the fathers perceived or experienced the meaning of fatherhood, their roles and what they believed to be expected fatherhood behavior, how involved they were with their children, the relationships they had with their children's mothers and others, and the challenges they encountered as adolescent fathers. The interview guide is included in Appendix A.

I conducted two pilot interviews to test the interview guide, to explore what needed to be asked, and to determine what teen fathers thought was important for others to know. These interviews proved to be very useful in formulating the final interview guide. The final interview questions covered a wide range of issues, including the socioeconomic circumstances of the subjects, the perceived outlook for their socioeconomic future as adults, their parenthood transitional experiences, how they defined fatherhood, the fatherhood activities in which they participated, their fatherhood experiences in general, the participants' relationships with their children's mothers and with significant others (e.g., family members, friends and peers, other female partners), and their sexual experiences and backgrounds, especially as it related to the pregnancies. As previously stated, each interview varied in length and sometimes in issues discussed.

Holstein and Gubrium (1995) posit that interview schedules may be used as guides, not scripts, for the interview process. In other words, they could serve as advisories or conversational agendas rather than as procedural directives (Holstein and Gubrium 1995). This approach was used in composing the interview questions. A set of questions was developed to use in the interviews, but I tried to allow the father's responses to determine whether particular questions were necessary or appropriate as leading frames of references for the interviews (Holstein and Gubrium 1995). Although efforts were made to ensure that the central topics were covered in each interview, the manner in which these questions unfolded varied from participant to participant. Thus, each interview was different in length and content.

To assess as much information and data as possible, field notes were also used during the research process. For instance, observations including thoughts and impressions generated during the recruitment and interviewing processes were noted. The plan was to be able to recall the context within which the participants' stories were related to me. The end goal was to maintain perspective when the data were analyzed and interpreted.

Communication with Participants

Establishing rapport with some of the participants was difficult at times. However, it was my goal to establish trust and confidentiality, to make the participants feel as comfortable as possible with the interview process, and to communicate the importance of their contribution to the study. It was explained to the fathers that they did not have to answer questions they felt uncomfortable discussing, and that they could stop the interview at any time.

The majority of the interviews proceeded without interruption or problems, although some of the fathers appeared to be oppositional at times and/or noncommunicative in their responses to many of the questions. For example, a few consistently gave brief or curt answers to questions. The following dialogue illustrates one father's opposition when he playfully admitted to trying to give me a "hard time" when I asked him why he had decided to do the interview for the study:

INTERVIEWER: Well, it certainly wasn't for the money. But what made you decide to do it then?

PARTICIPANT: I don't know. I don't know. Hmmm. I guess I was just interested in seeing what you were going to ask. Then I was going to give you a hard time.

INTERVIEWER: Really?

PARTICIPANT: Yep.

INTERVIEWER: Why?

PARTICIPANT: Because I get off on giving people a hard time.

INTERVIEWER: Really. So, how do you think you're doing?

PARTICIPANT: I think I've made you a little nervous. But you're too nice for me to fool with too much.

This participant became more cooperative and was very amiable throughout the remainder of the interview.

Some of the difficulty in establishing rapport that would lead to fuller, richer conversation was due to my inexperience in conducting interviews. For instance, in some of the earlier interviews I sometimes asked leading questions and failed to ask follow-up, probing questions. However, the more interviews I conducted, the more experienced I be-

Research Methods 51

came, and the participants became more elaborate in their responses, with later interviews lasting longer than the earlier ones.

Participant Incentives and Informed Consent

The literature indicates that the provision of a small financial incentive, primarily to cover the respondent's time, is an appropriate procedure when it can be used (Coates 1987). The young fathers were provided a stipend of $25.00 for participating in the study. It was anticipated that this gesture would apprise the young fathers of the importance of their contribution to this research. It was also done to demonstrate appreciation for their willingness to participate in the study. The fathers were given the stipend at the beginning of the interview, and it was explained that their receipt of the money was not contingent on their answering every question in the interview or dependent on their completing the interview.

Approval for this study was granted by the Human Subjects Review Board at Kent State University, in Kent, Ohio. Each potential participant was informed about the purpose of the study and was given information about the interview beforehand. The author indicated to the young men that their parents' or guardians' consent were needed in order for them to participate if they were younger than eighteen years of age. Some cases occurred in which the author had the opportunity to speak with the parents about the study before speaking to their sons. Upon obtaining the written consent of the parents or guardians, the author proceeded to obtain the written consent of the participants.

The fathers were told that participation in the study was voluntary and that the information they provided in the interviews would be kept confidential. This was not the case, as was explained to them, if their parents or guardian did not waive their right to listen to the taped interviews. In one case, a parent did request to listen to a tape but later changed her mind. This was the only parent or guardian who did not waive his or her right beforehand to listen to the taped interview. In this case, the teen parent was aware that his mother had requested to listen to the audiotape. In reviewing this particular transcript and comparing the responses given by others, it did not appear that knowing his mother's request affected his answers. At any rate, none of the

52 VOICES OF AFRICAN-AMERICAN TEEN FATHERS

participants or parents or guardians objected to having the interview with their sons audiotaped.

Before beginning the interviews, I briefly discussed with the fathers what they would be doing and how the interview would be structured. I pointed out that I was interested in their views and perceptions and that I would not make any judgments about the comments they made or the positions they took on the issues that were discussed. Basically, I informed them that my job was to listen, ask questions, and to obtain as much information as possible about their fatherhood experiences and views without imposing any preconceived notions, opinions, or ideas of my own. Unfortunately, due to my inexperience, this did not happen in some of the earlier interviews in which I may have appeared to challenge the views expressed by the young fathers. One example of such an occurrence is in the following passage:

INTERVIEWER: Are those the only types of jobs you foresee them doing if they try to find a job?

PARTICIPANT: Yeah. What else you expect? They can't get a job in a plant or anything. You gotta have a high school diploma or a GED or something. Plus, you still gotta know the right people. And they sure in hell ain't going to get a job in an office or something right?

INTERVIEWER: I don't know.

PARTICIPANT: Ahh, you're bullshitting. You know I'm telling the truth.

INTERVIEWER: I'm sure it's different for different people.

PARTICIPANT: Right. Only if they have the right education and the right connections.

In this interview I probably should have accepted the participant's reality about individuals not being able to get jobs or simply asked him to elaborate on his views. However, exchanges as the one offered previously were avoided in subsequent interviews. For instance, instead of emphasizing or suggesting that all African Americans experience the same racist or parenthood experiences they discussed, I learned to acknowledge their views, ask them to elaborate on their perceptions, and provide my opinions only when asked.

The Interviewer's Role and Influence on the Process

I was cognizant of my role and position as an interviewer and researcher as well as of the impact that these roles would have on the project as a whole and on the respondents in particular. My socioeconomic status, personal experiences, theoretical perspectives, political views, and personal biases and assumptions would influence the entire research process (Andersen 1993; Denzin 1994; Reinharz 1992). For example, these factors influenced the topic I chose to study, the research questions asked, and my analysis and interpretation of the data collected.

The fathers in the study might possibly have disclosed different information to another interviewer depending on the interviewer's gender, race, age, and so on. However, this possibility does not diminish the "truth" or validity of the fatherhood accounts shared with the current interviewer. It merely represents another "truth," another aspect of their experiences, and therefore should not be discounted (Andersen 1993).

Although perceived social distance by the participants might have influenced the interview process, I do not believe that this difference had a negative effect on the interview processes. In fact, my social location may have served to enhance disclosure on some issues. For instance, some discussions about race and racism occurred that might not have taken place, or not have taken place in the same context, had the interviews been conducted by a white interviewer. Still, the participants appeared to discuss some topics with caution because of my race and sex. For example:

INTERVIEWER: You've mentioned a couple of times that his wife is white. What do you think about that?

PARTICIPANT: Oh that's cool. One of Sean's last girlfriends was white, too. I'm seeing a black one right now, but I'm peeping one right now [dating or engaging in predating activities with a white young woman]. I'm not saying that the white ones are better or anything. . . But. . .

INTERVIEWER: But what?

PARTICIPANT: I don't know. I mean, they do more for you, you know. I hope I'm not disrespecting you as a black woman and all. But . . .

VOICES OF AFRICAN-AMERICAN TEEN FATHERS

INTERVIEWER: No, I don't feel any disrespect. Can you tell me what you mean when you say they do more for you?

In this example the participant did not want to offend me because of his preference for white women. His awareness of my race and gender probably shaped or framed the way in which he presented this information and proceeded with the interview, although he appeared to be very frank and open overall.

In other instances the participants acknowledged a social distance between themselves and me. Although I did my best to downplay any educational or cultural barriers (mainly regional language and terminology used), it became apparent to the participants at times that these differences existed. This can be seen in the following exchange in which I interpreted the term "sisters" in one way, calling into question my insider status in the African-American community. I had asked the participant about the two mothers of his two sons:

INTERVIEWER: I was going to ask you earlier, but are Mitsy and Kim black? White? Or of another race?

PARTICIPANT: They're sisters.

INTERVIEWER: What? Really? No ... earlier you said that ... Oh, you mean that they're black? *[Laughs]* I thought you meant they were relatives. Related. Oh, my gosh. *[Laughs]*

PARTICIPANT: Oh, I'm sorry. I guess I was talking ebonics to you.

INTERVIEWER: *[Laughs]*

PARTICIPANT: They're *African Americans.*

INTERVIEWER: *[Laughs].* I'm sorry. I wasn't thinking. Okay. Do you think teen parenthood is more prevalent in black communities?

PARTICIPANT: Can I ask you where you're from?

INTERVIEWER: I live here in Wichita.

PARTICIPANT: You don't live in a black neighborhood or anything, huh?

INTERVIEWER: Yeah. I live in a racially mixed neighborhood.

PARTICIPANT: Hmmm. All right.

Although I thought that my misunderstanding of the participant's definition of "sister" was amusing, I also felt that it shifted the flow of

Research Methods 55

the conversation, and to some extent the rapport I had built with the participant, because of his cynicism or skepticism (illustrated by his question, "You don't live in a black community or anything, huh?"). Even though I did not believe that the quality or content of information the father divulged would have changed much, I was thankful that this interchange occurred near the end of the interview.

I mentioned my graduate-student status and work (at that time) in the community at a local college to each participant. A few of the respondents asked me questions about my social class, where I lived, and whether I had children, demonstrating that their perceptions of me were important to them. These perceptions might have shaped both the content and style of their responses. The following is a passage from a transcript of an interview conducted with a participant who was curious and surprised about my parenthood status:

INTERVIEWER: Now earlier before I started the tape, you told me that he's one year old right?

PARTICIPANT: Yeah. His birthday was on June eleven. I guess, if I was a woman I would be saying he's thirteen months old or something. Why do women do that?

INTERVIEWER: Do what?

PARTICIPANT: Say their child is twenty-four months old instead of just saying he's two years old. They break it down into months and days, when all they have to say are the years.

INTERVIEWER: *[Laughs]* I'm not sure.

PARTICIPANT: Do you do that, too?

INTERVIEWER: Well, no, I don't have any children.

PARTICIPANT: You don't?

INTERVIEWER: No.

PARTICIPANT: You don't?

INTERVIEWER: No.

PARTICIPANT: Why not?

INTERVIEWER: My husband and I just don't want any right now.

PARTICIPANT: How old are you?

INTERVIEWER: *[Chuckle]* Hey, this interview is about you, not me. But I'll answer that question. I'm thirty-four.

PARTICIPANT: Wow. And you don't have any children?

VOICES OF AFRICAN-AMERICAN TEEN FATHERS

INTERVIEWER: No.

PARTICIPANT: I don't know if I know one black woman that old who doesn't have any children.

Of course many African-American women postpone having children, choose not to have them, or are unable to bear them, but the participant was not aware of many (or any) in my age category who had not given birth to (or perhaps adopted) any children. The passage illustrates the fluid, unstructured nature of the "active interview" and the sharing of information, feedback, meanings, and perceptions between both the interviewer and the interviewee. For instance, perhaps my "novelty" status as child free challenged his preconceived notions or realities about African-American women and children and says much about the different social worlds we inhabit.

Selection Bias

Usually when data are gathered from voluntary participants, selection bias may play a role. For instance, bias raises the question as to whether the young men in this study held different views on fatherhood than those who declined to participate or who were not selected to participate. Nine of the fathers in this study had participated in a community-based or school-based organization that provided services such as parenting classes and counseling. These fathers might have been more likely to volunteer for this study than were fathers who had not participated in such services in part because they had already thought extensively about the topic of fatherhood and their roles. Their fatherhood views or experiences might have been influenced by their experiences with the organizations. Therefore, I attempted to minimize the number of fathers who had participated in such services. Furthermore, six of the participants were interviewed in a church, and out of those six all but one of them were referred from another church member or were attending church when an announcement was made about the project. Because of their ties to formal or organized religion, the possibility exists that selection bias may have existed with this group as well.

Most of the teen fathers ($n = 25$) were in high school at the time they were interviewed, and one was in college. Thus, some of the adolescent fathers that were not included in this study were those who were no longer attending school (although this was the case for two of the participants who had graduated from high school), those who had dropped out of school (only one participant had dropped out of school), young fathers who were part of the criminal justice system (one teen participant had been recently arrested and was awaiting trial, however), and teen fathers who were in gangs (although one teen participant was a gang member). The perceptions and experiences of fathers that I was unable to reach may have been different from those that were interviewed.

RELIABILITY, VALIDITY, AND GENERALIZABILITY

Reliability and validity are limited since this study was conducted by a single researcher. My interpretations and perspectives influenced the entire study from the topic chosen, to the sample selected, to the questions asked, to the interpretation of the data. Nonetheless, reliability, validity, and generalizability should be understood in the context of the study. For instance, it was not my intent to provide explanations or descriptions of the experiences of the entire population of African-American adolescent fathers, although the information provided in this book might aid in understanding them. The purpose of this study was to obtain from African-American adolescent fathers their interpretations of fatherhood in their own voices and to position these stories in a broader social context. This study also aims to gain more in-depth understanding than is possible with surveys and close-ended questions as well as to raise questions for further studies.

TRANSCRIPTION

In accordance with the policies of Kent State's Human Subjects Review Board, written consent of the participants and their parents or guardians to audiotape the interviews was obtained. All of the tapes were transcribed verbatim. Although this part of the research was very time-consuming, listening to the tapes provided the opportunity to develop some initial thoughts on the data analysis and a chance to capture some important points in the interviews I failed to notice as they occurred.

58 VOICES OF AFRICAN-AMERICAN TEEN FATHERS

I assured each participant that during the transcribing process (at this point, I explained to him what transcription was in case he did not know) that his actual name or the names of those mentioned in the interviews would not be used. Therefore, each participant was assigned a pseudonym, as were the individuals they mentioned or discussed in the interviews.

DATA ANALYSIS

Qualitative data analysis is based on an inductive process of organizing the information or data collected into categories and identifying patterns and/or relationships among the categories that emerge from the data (Strauss and Corbin 1990). Coding has been described as the process of categorizing and sorting data and providing important links among data and the conceptualization of them (Bryman and Burgess 1994a, b; Dey 1993). It is the breaking down, examining, comparing, conceptualizing, and categorizing of data (Bryman and Burgess 1994a). According to Bryman and Burgess (1994a), two types of coding exist: open or initial coding and axial coding. I first employed open coding in analyzing the data since it represents the gradual building up of categories. According to Christina Hughes (1994), categories should be broadly grouped. Judith Okely (1994) also suggested that categories be broad headings and that nothing should be rigidly preestablished. Okely further stated that classification should be made *after* the fieldwork. Nonetheless, I followed the lead of Dey (1993) who argued that qualitative researchers could have preexisting categories, although they must, at the very least, be confirmed by the data (Patton 1990) since precoded or preestablished categories are inadequate for capturing the phenomena that may emerge from the open-ended interviewing format (Holstein and Gubrium 1995).

Therefore, I sorted and organized the data by establishing a few preconceived categories deemed broad enough to allow me to sort the data. At the same time, I attempted to eliminate "irrelevant" data, or more accurately, to ignore that data that were not needed in the analysis (Wolcott 1990). Both during and after the fieldwork process, notes and transcripts were read and reread, and the categories and subheadings were revised according to the emergent codes and themes of the data. The Non-Numerical Unstructured Data Indexing, Searching and Theorizing (NUD*IST) computer software program was very helpful in sorting and organizing the data. The following questions were continually assessed: What do these categories mean? Are they important to the purpose of my study? Is this list sufficiently refined? (Dey 1993). An attempt was made to avoid becoming overwhelmed by superfluous data and categorizations that were irrelevant to the goal of the project. For example, although information concerning the fathers' experiences in school was interesting, it did not have direct relevance to their fatherhood status, and neither did it present recurrent patterns; therefore, these categories were discarded. Likewise, information given about a summer trip or church activity, for instance, may have been bracketed or discarded as "irrelevant" as well.

After the initial coding process, the question "What relationships exist *between* the categories?" was asked (Dey 1993). At this point I began axial coding in which I attempted to identify relationships and important connections between the categories themselves, between the categories and the study's research questions, and between the categories and some of the positions or findings found in the literature review.

Procedures in Analyzing the Data

Since I transcribed the interviews, I was able to identify a few analytical leads during that process. For instance, I noticed that the participants tended to describe ideal fatherhood in terms of provider roles but their own fatherhood behavior did not reflect such. I also observed that they had distinct ways of categorizing their relationships with the mothers of their children and used terminology that reflected this. Thus, the transcription process enabled me to think in analytical terms prior to the formal coding process.

The second step in the analysis involved reading through the transcripts once completed and coding each individual sentence or paragraph in them. Many patterns were detected and I started to notice themes at this point in the process. Many of the established categories were influenced by the interview questions. For example, knowing that I was interested in how the participants defined themselves as fathers, I looked for information that would help me address that question, and appropriately coded the information as such. Strauss and

60   VOICES OF AFRICAN-AMERICAN TEEN FATHERS

Corbin (1990) mentioned that researchers do not begin the analytical process without preexisting ideas, and that was found to be the case during this coding process.

I tried to look for both patterns and diversity in the responses in the interviews. This became easier once the NUD*IST software program was utilized and was able to combine and list all of the participants' responses to a particular question or category. For instance, I was able to code the respondents' initial reactions to the pregnancies of their children's mothers, and was then able to determine whether any similarities or divergences existed in the responses.

After completing this stage of the analysis, I moved on to interpreting the data. For example, I concentrated on linking the data from the initial coding process to the research questions and linking the initial coding data to the insights provided in the literature review. I wanted to know, for example, how different the data were from what was in the literature, and whether what was found could contribute new insights and understanding to that literature.

In the following chapters, the data obtained from the teen fathers will be discussed. First, the perceived factors that precipitated their parenthood will be addressed. Second, their parenting experiences, particularly exploring their involvement with their children, both perceived and actual behavior, will be discussed. Chapters 5-7 will focus on their relationships with significant persons in their lives, including the mothers of their children, family members, and peers. Finally, the challenges they perceive and experience as African-American teen fathers will be examined. The data presented in these chapters are based upon the teen fathers' own perspectives and the experiences they chose to share.

Chapter 3

How and Why African-American
Teens Become Fathers

Much attention has been focused on the causes of teen pregnancy; however, the role of teen fathers and their views about pregnancy and childbirth have been largely overlooked. The teen fathers in the current study were asked how and why the pregnancies occurred, whether any form of contraception was used when their children were conceived, the reasons for not using contraception if such was the case, and for those using contraception, why it failed in preventing pregnancy. The themes that emerged from the data point to disregard for potential consequences of unprotected sex and lack of communication between the sexual partners about contraception (prior to the pregnancy). Furthermore, the fathers' attitudes toward abortion as an option were explored. This chapter addresses the reasons that teens gave for how and why pregnancy and childbirth occurred.

CARELESSNESS: "IF IT HAPPENED, IT HAPPENED"

Twenty-six of the fathers (74 percent) did not use condoms during the time period in which conception occurred. Almost all of the fathers discussed why they did not use condoms. This discussion was usually preempted by a direct question on my part about the issue. Although most of them stated that they were aware of the dangers of not using condoms (e.g., pregnancy and disease transmission), many deliberately chose not to use them. Malik indicated that sometimes he used protection but was not always consistent. Dangers existed in this unsafe practice, he admitted, but stated:

Voices of African-American Teen Fathers
© 2006 by The Haworth Press, Inc. All rights reserved.
doi:10.1300/5477_04

62 VOICES OF AFRICAN-AMERICAN TEEN FATHERS

MALIK: If any girl asks me to use a condom, I do. I'd rather not, but I will if she asks. But if she doesn't ask or anything then I just assume she doesn't care what happens, or that she's on the pill. So if anything happens to her, then she's the dummy to let it happen.

Malik accepted no blame or responsibility if a future pregnancy should occur. He said that he had sex with women no more than sixteen years old because he believed they were less likely to "have a disease." That is, he assumed that they were less sexually experienced. Lack of respect for women and double standards about sex were more evident as the interview continued. He explained:

MALIK: I mean I look at it like this: girls know that guys are going to want to do one thing with them—at least guys around my age. We ain't looking to be serious or anything. We just want . . . well you know. And if they're that dumb to think we want anything more than that, well, that's on them.

Fourteen-year-old Malik experienced relationship problems with the mother of his child both before and after the pregnancy. He felt she was too "clingy" and wanted too much of his time. Although he is still in a relationship with her, he has had intercourse with other women.

The choice to use condoms was perceived as a man's prerogative in many instances, not just in the case with Malik. For example, fifteen-year-old Tyreese had negative views about women, African-American women in particular, that reflected racist and sexist stereotypes. During the interview he discussed how African-American women were too independent, materialistic, and self-centered. He viewed white women more positively. They were less independent, materialistic, and self-centered according to Tyreese. His views on relationships were based on male entitlement to be the center of male-female relationships, especially in the realm of sexuality. This entitlement shaped his decisions about condom use:

TYREESE: I wore a rubber most of the time, but not all of the time. I wore one if I felt like it. Most girls will still have sex with you even if you don't use something. Even if they ask about it, they still leave the decision up to the man. So if I felt like wearing it, I did, and if I didn't, I didn't.

Tyreese's statement "Even if they ask about it, they still leave the decision up to the man" addresses his (and other young fathers') control over their sexual encounters. However, at the same time, women were seen as responsible for pregnancy and sexually transmitted diseases.

This notion was also illustrated in interviews with other fathers. For example, seventeen-year-old Darrius shared similar views and stated that women were at fault if they became pregnant. Darrius was very direct in talking about how he had used the mother of his child for sex. Similar to the double standards expressed by many fathers, he talked condemningly about her promiscuity while feeling that it was acceptable for him to be promiscuous. This masculine notion of privileged sexual behavior is also seen in Darrius's negotiation of condom use. Although he continued to have sex with the mother of his child, he did not use condoms even though he knew she was not on birth control. With indifference he stated, "She'll probably end up getting knocked up again." When asked how would he feel if that happened again, he replied:

DARRIUS: I don't care. If she has another one, I'm going to keep on doing what I'm doing. I'll do what I can, but she knows better, so if she ends up pregnant, it's going to hurt her more than it's going to hurt me. In the end she's going to have to bear the burden, as they say.

Simply put, Darrius did not see pregnancy as his concern or responsibility. He believed that he would make financial provisions if he was able to do so, but the children were not ultimately his problem. Thus, having a second child was not going to make a difference to him and would do little to change his circumstances or his efforts to provide. Therefore, if the mother of his child "foolishly" got pregnant again, he felt that she would be the one to suffer, not him.

The self-focused nature of the teens' sexual relationships with women was based, in part, on the perceived quality of their sexual encounters. In short, condoms decreased their sexual pleasure, therefore they did not want to use them. Their pursuit of self-pleasure and gratification took precedence over protecting against pregnancy and disease. For instance, eighteen-year-old Brandon talked about how he did not use condoms with the women with whom he was currently having sexual intercourse. He was no longer in a relationship with the mother of his child because he thought she got pregnant on purpose.

64 VOICES OF AFRICAN-AMERICAN TEEN FATHERS

Although he did not use condoms with her, he thought she was trying to "trap" him because he was "popular" and he did not "know one woman that didn't want [him]." Brandon was a senior in high school and planned to attend a community college upon graduation. He explained why he does not use condoms, saying "I don't use them because they don't feel natural." In Brandon's case, his control over the use of condoms was evident. When I asked him whether any of the women asked or insisted on his using condoms, he replied, "A couple of them did, but I told them I wasn't. So I didn't." According to him, they still had sex with him anyway. Brandon said he could not explain why the girls "gave in," only that they did. Some of the literature indicates that "doing gender"(acting out expected gender roles) is an issue here. Young women have sex when they do not wish to, and they do not push condom use for fear that they might offend the men and/or that they might put their relationships in danger if they do not give the men what they want (Luker 1996; Wingwood and DiClemente 1998).

LACK OF COMMUNICATION:
"WE JUST DIDN'T TALK ABOUT IT"

Power, control, and masculine entitlement were not always at the center of the young men's refusal to use condoms. Sixteen-year-old Clayton, who was no longer in a relationship with the mother of his child and was having intercourse with others, stated:

CLAYTON: The times we had sex, we just did it. To be honest with you, I didn't give any thought to birth control or anything at the time we were doing it. In the back of my mind, I did though, but I was just hoping that she was taking care of things.

It appeared that lack of communication and assumption of female responsibility for "taking care of things" was at the root of what happened in this case. Similar to the other fathers, Clayton indicated that he made the decision about condom use. Since he did not like to use them (he did not like how they felt), he did not use them all the time. The choice to use condoms was his, and the blame for pregnancy belonged to his female partners.

How and Why African-American Teens Become Fathers   65

Lack of communication about contraception was a consistent factor associated with many of the pregnancies. For example, seventeen-year-old Carl said that he initially used condoms with the mother of his child even though she used birth control pills. At one point in their relationship he stopped using condoms, assuming that she was still using birth control pills. When she got pregnant, Carl never confirmed his conclusion that she had stopped taking them without informing him. He regretted that they did not discuss this situation prior to the pregnancy. He was not in a relationship with her at the time of the interview, although he sees her when he visits his child.

Nineteen-year-old Jermaine, father of two children by two different women, also revealed that lack of communication about contraception was part of his story. He said the following about the "decision" not to use condoms:

JERMAINE: I don't think it was a decision per se. We just didn't [come right out and] say we weren't going to use it. We just didn't talk about it, that's all. I guess we had that attitude though, but we just didn't talk about it.

The longer the fathers had been in the relationship and/or the stronger their feelings for the mothers, the more likely they were to have discontinued the use of condoms. This supports prior research that indicated that the more deeply involved the relationship, the higher the tendency for discontinued use of contraception (Franklin 1987; Wingwood and DiClemente 1998). For example, eighteen-year-old Bill felt he was in love with the mother of his child and would have liked to have eventually married her. However, he reported the feelings were not mutual. Although he had relationships and sexual intercourse with others prior to his relationship with her, he said that this was his first serious relationship. When asked about condom use in this relationship, he stated:

BILL: I started off using a condom whenever we had sex, but after a few months I think we both felt comfortable enough with each other to stop using it. I don't think we planned not to use birth control; it just happened. We weren't being very responsible, and I'm the first to admit that.

66 VOICES OF AFRICAN-AMERICAN TEEN FATHERS

Bill accepted some responsibility for the pregnancy, as some of the fathers did. He used the pronoun "we" (e.g., "We weren't being very responsible . . .") as opposed to language that indicated his partner's responsibility and fault for the pregnancy. However, he could not articulate why they stopped using contraception, only that they "felt comfortable enough with each other to stop using it." Bill's explanation suggests the possibility of some sense of commitment and trust in the relationship.

Likewise, seventeen-year-old Craig said he was in a serious relationship with a young woman who had been his girlfriend since seventh grade. In fact, Craig said he planned to marry her after he graduated from school and joined the military (he was in twelfth grade). Similar to Bill, Craig had stopped using condoms after some time passed in their relationship.

CRAIG: We used [condoms] earlier in our relationship, but after a while we just stopped. I can't tell you exactly why. I guess we just got too comfortable with each other or something. We didn't even discuss it. We just sort of stopped . . . but then about a year later she stopped having her period, and the rest is history.

Both Bill and Craig used similar language. For example, Bill stated, "I think we both felt comfortable enough with each other to stop using it." Similarly, Craig stated, "I guess we just got too comfortable with each other something." The length of the relationship facilitated this "comfort" that led to the discontinued use of contraception.

In almost all cases, pregnancy was unintended. They were not trying to get their girlfriends pregnant. Neither did most of them believe that the mothers of their children got pregnant on purpose. However, because of lack of concern for the consequences of their actions, they became teen fathers.

GETTING "TRAPPED": "I THINK SHE GOT PREGNANT ON PURPOSE"

Although the majority of teen fathers did not believe that the mothers of their children intentionally became pregnant, a few believed the opposite and thought that the young women tried to "trap" them with

How and Why African-American Teens Become Fathers   67

pregnancy. For example, Eric resented April, the mother of his child, for getting pregnant. He believed she got pregnant on purpose in order to secure a long-term relationship with him. Because he was an excellent football player, he had no doubts that he would be offered college scholarships to play. He believed professional football was in his future, as he claimed others, including the mother of his child, also felt. He felt this was motivation for April's pregnancy. Interestingly, Eric claimed that his mother and grandmother supported his views, which may have worked to further fuel his resentment. He accepted no blame for the pregnancy, even though he did not use condoms, because she claimed to be taking birth control pills, which he thought should have been sufficient. Even after this pregnancy he had not taken measures to prevent further pregnancies with other women. In fact, he stated, "When it starts feeling good, I might take it off [condom]."

Likewise, nineteen-year-old Keith thought the mother of his child got pregnant on purpose. Unlike Eric, however, Keith accepted responsibility for the pregnancy. He mentioned that he used condoms, but not consistently. About the pregnancy, he said:

KEITH: I love my son and I wouldn't give him up for nothing in the world. I wouldn't do anything to hurt him either. So, I try to respect Jackie because she's his mother, but if I had to say whether I believe she got pregnant on purpose, I'll have to say yes. Yes, I do.

INTERVIEWER: Why do you think that? Did she ever say that?

KEITH: No, she didn't, but before she got pregnant she used to say she was joking when she asked me how would I feel if I was a father, or if she had a baby. I didn't think she was playing. I told her that I wouldn't like it, and that I would be upset, but that I would still take care of my responsibilities. I think she was trying to feel me out.

INTERVIEWER: Why do you think she would want a child?

KEITH: I don't know. I think she just wanted a baby. A lot of girls do. I think Jackie wanted one because she wanted someone to love. She has a family and everything, but I think she wanted something special. And she probably thought that it would make things better between us, but it didn't. I'm there for Todd [his son], but I'm not in a relationship with her. We're just friends now.

68   *VOICES OF AFRICAN-AMERICAN TEEN FATHERS*

As previously mentioned, a few of the fathers thought the mothers of their children deliberately tried to get pregnant, either in hopes that the relationship would last or in search of deeper meaning and purpose in their lives.

INTENTIONAL PREGNANCIES: "WE WANTED TO HAVE A BABY"

Most of the young men did not seek to become fathers, although they came to accept it. Two teen fathers, however, did seek fatherhood. Roman, an eighteen-year-old father of a three-year-old son, was motivated to become a father and expressed that he had a child in order "to pass down [his] genes." As a gang member, he wanted to ensure that he left behind his legacy in case he was incarcerated or killed. He perceived his life span to be relatively short and/or his freedom potentially limited; therefore, he wanted a child in order to leave behind a part of himself. This was his way of remaining in the world despite not being able to control being eliminated—"I don't know how long I'm going to be around, so I want someone to carry on my blood."

Another teen father, William, discussed how he and his girlfriend planned for her to get pregnant because he wanted a family. In this particular case, too, a deliberate choice was made to start a family. William was a nineteen-year-old father whose own father had left his family when William was three years old. Although William technically lived with his mother, she was rarely physically present. According to William, his mother usually stayed overnight, sometimes a week at a time, with male friends and spent very little time with William and his younger brother when she was at home with them. He talked about his dream of having a "real family" and how he attempted to create a family with his girlfriend, at that time, of eleven months (at the time of the interview they had been together for two-and-a-half-years). Unfortunately, William and his girlfriend had a very rocky relationship, and having a child seemed to further complicate it. The birth of his daughter did not give him the dream he thought he would attain. In fact, at the time of the interview, William's girlfriend had not spoken to him in almost a week, and he had not seen his child for almost two weeks. William felt that he was mostly to blame for their relationship problems.

WILLIAM: I wanted a family, but I didn't know it. I didn't understand it. I didn't have the concept. Like I told you, I didn't have a good childhood or a good family. As a matter of fact, I don't think I had one friend whose parents were married. But I knew what I wanted in a family . . . But how could I do and make what I never knew?

LIMITED ALTERNATIVES:
"ABORTION AND ADOPTION WERE NOT OPTIONS"

Once confronted with pregnancy, some of the teen fathers hoped their partners would abort the pregnancy. For instance, eighteen-year-old Brandon was extremely nervous about having a child when he found out about the pregnancy. He reported feeling very upset and asked the mother of his child to consider having an abortion. Thus, he was not opposed to abortion, and in fact, encouraged it. However, when she refused to have one, Brandon distanced himself from her and "the situation." Since his one-and-a-half-year old son, Keeshawn, has been born, Brandon had seen him twice.

Similar to Brandon, others had secretly wanted the mothers of their children to have an abortion. Sixteen-year-old Mark was very nervous about being a father when he found out that Sherry was pregnant. He did not have a romantic and loving relationship with her at the time and did not want a child. He was requested to explain how he felt after hearing about the pregnancy. He replied:

MARK: Well, I was kind of scared at first. I admit that I was hoping that Sherry would have an abortion or something. I mean, I feel sort of guilty feeling that way now, but that was how I felt then. I thought I was too young to be a father, and I didn't want that kind of burden. I wasn't ready for that.

Regardless of the relationship they had (or did not have) with the mothers of their children, the fathers expressed their feelings about pregnancy in self-centered terms. Noticeably lacking was concern for their partners. For example, when asked about the "burden" he

70 VOICES OF AFRICAN-AMERICAN TEEN FATHERS

discussed and anticipated, Mark talked about pressures from Sherry to spend more time with her. He stated:

MARK: I know she was about to have my baby, but we didn't have a real relationship or anything, and as far as I was concerned we weren't about to start one just because of the baby. I just wanted to have my space . . . it was too much pressure.

Fathers who did not want their partners to have an abortion objected to "allowing a part of myself to be killed," as one father stated. Once their female partners became pregnant most of them wanted their genes "to be passed down," as Roman, the eighteen-year-old gang member explained. The African-American teen fathers in this study were not opposed to abortion or adoption in general, but many had strong objections when the situation applied to themselves and their offspring.

Jermaine, a nineteen-year-old father of two children by two different women, had strong feelings about abortion as it concerned his own offspring. Initially in favor of abortion, his views changed after his first child, two-year-old Cornell, was born. When the mother of his second child, Raeshawnda, became pregnant, he strongly opposed abortion.

INTERVIEWER: Did you try to convince Melinda [mother of his first child] to have an abortion or something?

JERMAINE: No, but honestly at the time, if she had said she was going to, I would have been relieved. But you know, that was a different time. Now, I wouldn't want anyone to do that. Not with my child.

INTERVIEWER: You don't believe in abortion?

JERMAINE: It's not that I don't believe in it. I think it's a personal decision. And it's best for a lot of people. But I don't want to see any kid with my bloodline killed, you know.

Again, the fathers did not generally disapprove of the concept or idea of abortion in itself, but had negative views of it when applied to their own "bloodline" or potential children.

Whether the fathers opposed or hoped for abortion, in most cases the topic was never broached by the mothers of their children, they stated. Some felt there was an "understanding" that abortion and adoption were not options to consider (at least not for their children), or they wanted abortions but believed that the decision was ultimately

How and Why African-American Teens Become Fathers 71

up to the women. Still, their failure to discuss options demonstrated the general lack of communication between the couples. For example, Darrius, a seventeen-year-old father of a two-year-old son, was asked about abortion or adoption when he discovered that his girlfriend, Kelly, was pregnant:

INTERVIEWER: Did she ever consider abortion or adoption?

DARRIUS: Abortion or adoption?

INTERVIEWER: Yes.

DARRIUS: No.

INTERVIEWER: Why was that not a consideration?

DARRIUS: I guess she doesn't believe in it. We never talked about it.

INTERVIEWER: What if she had brought up abortion, how would you have felt?

DARRIUS: I wouldn't have liked it.

INTERVIEWER: Why not?

DARRIUS: Because if she did get pregnant—and she did—I wanted my child.

INTERVIEWER: Do you have some religious views on abortion?

DARRIUS: No, I mean, I think some people need to get it, but I wanted my child.

Darrius's position on abortion, in particular, is typical of the African-American teen fathers in the study. Although their views about abortion varied, their reasons for supporting or opposing abortion were self-centered. In the end, however, the fathers expressed that they had little influence or involvement with the final decisions made by the women. This was demonstrated in the situation of seventeen-year-old Russell. Russell was a junior in high school and lived with his mother and two brothers. He had a close, intimate relationship with the mother of his child, Brenda, both prior to the pregnancy and at the time of the interview. However, when Brenda told him that she was pregnant, similar to many of the fathers, he felt afraid and concerned. Unlike the other fathers in the study (with the exception of Brandon), Russell did discuss abortion as an option with Brenda and, in fact, tried to encourage her to get one.

72 VOICES OF AFRICAN-AMERICAN TEEN FATHERS

RUSSELL: Yeah, I tried to talk her into having one [an abortion]. I've never really supported abortion before, but when you're in that situation, it's different, and I'm not going to lie, I was scared. I was just fifteen years old then, and I asked her [Brenda] how could I be a father? I couldn't even support myself, so how was I going to support a child? So, I was scared. I didn't want her to go through with it [the pregnancy]. But, she did. So, here I am.

Adoption as an alternative was not mentioned often, but when it was the fathers generally expressed opposition to the idea. Similar to their views on abortion, they did not oppose adoption in general, but were opposed to the idea when it came to their own children. This was the case even with fathers who initially hoped that their partners would seek an abortion. For example, although seventeen-year-old James had hoped that his partner would have an abortion, adoption was not an option he would have wanted her to consider. He stated:

JAMES: Oh, adoption was definitely out of the picture. No way. We didn't talk about it, but that just wasn't going to happen. If she didn't want to have it [the child], that was one thing, but if she was going to have it, then nobody but one of us was going to raise it.

INTERVIEWER: So abortion is okay, but adoption is not?

JAMES: With *me,* adoption is not okay, but it's not a bad thing either. One of my boys [friends] is adopted, and he's cool with it. I'm just saying nobody is going to raise *my* child except me if my woman can't.

In a similar vein, sixteen-year-old Tevin had negative feelings about people who gave their children up for adoption. Generally, he opposed the concept of adoption, and stated, "I can't understand how parents can give up their children to strangers." Tevin's family had a strong extended family and kinship support, and the idea of allowing nonfamily to raise one's children was unfathomable to him. Tevin lived with his mother, aunt, older male cousin, and siblings. Their family was very close and supportive of one another, he stated, and helped each other financially and emotionally. Tevin's family resembled the type of "kin" system (versus fictive kin) observed by Carol Stack (1974), although in Tevin's case he focused on blood ties. Many times African-American women have found assistance in extended

How and Why African-American Teens Become Fathers 73

family or nonfamily support systems (Stack 1974; Billingsley 1992; Collins 1994), as Tevin's mother did.

Seventeen-year-old Carl discussed how abortion and adoption were not as acceptable in the African-American community. Adoption (which he perceived to be worse than abortion) was considered an indication of failure. The idea of adoption seemed to contradict their conceptualizations of appropriate masculinity. For men it meant they could not provide for their children, and therefore they were not "real men." For instance, according to Carl, by "giving up your child," you are an incompetent, bad parent.

INTERVIEWER: Why would [adoption] have been worse than abortion?

CARL: I don't know. I guess black people just don't do that. I know I would have been more embarrassed to have done that because it's like saying that you don't want your kid, and that you can't take care of it. Don't get me wrong, I know that's not how everybody feels when they give up their child, and I know that people have all kinds of reasons for giving up their children, but for me, even though I wanted her [the mother of his child] to have an abortion, I would have felt less of a man if we had had Robin [his daughter] and just gave her away.

INTERVIEWER: So you said black people just don't do that?

CARL: Maybe I shouldn't have said just black people. But if you think about it, it's just not our thing . . .

Carl felt that African Americans do not generally support adoption.

Based on this study, African-American teen fathers are generally not opposed to abortion, but do not see adoption as a desirable alternative for the African-American community. When it comes to their situations, they may initially hope for termination of the pregnancy, but ultimately value the birth of "their" children. Similar to other studies in which African-American and Hispanic fathers have expressed opposition to abortion (see Sullivan 1989), these young men did so as well. It was apparent that religion did not seem to be a factor among those that opposed abortion, but rather that they did not want the pregnancies aborted because they wanted their children to carry on their legacy. In response to racism, alienation, poverty, and other adversities, the African-American family has learned throughout history to become adaptable and resilient (Billingsley 1992). The development of family support systems is just one example of adaptation to structural change and adverse challenges (Stack 1974; Collins 1994). The opposition to abortion (to preserve their "bloodline") by the fathers in this study may yet be another example of survival in the African-American community.

Chapter 4

How Teen Fathers Think About and Do Fatherhood

In this chapter the ways that African-American adolescent fathers think about and enact fatherhood is explored. Many of the fathers provided some economic assistance for the mother of their children, and some were involved in their children's lives. The extent to which they provided for their children and the frequency and nature of their interactions varied. They cared, worried, and thought about their children and had distinct ideas about what constitutes the role of father. More often than not, however, their fathering behaviors were inconsistent with their conceptualizations of these roles and responsibilities. Drawing on the work of Kathleen Gerson (1997) on adult fathers, the data from the adolescent fathers in the present study were broadly grouped. The following categories for African-American adolescent conceptualizations of fatherhood behaviors were derived from the data: provider, involved nurturer, and independent father (see Table 4.1).

The conceptualization of fatherhood was further examined by the fathers' ages to see if any differences existed. The categories that were used for the teen fathers' conceptualizations of fatherhood (provider, involved nurturer, independent father) were not mutually exclusive (see Table 4.1). These conceptualizations and the behaviors that characterized them were grouped according to what teen fathers indicated were the primary or the most important roles of fathers.

Within two age groups, fourteen to fifteen and sixteen to seventeen, more than half of the teen fathers conceptualized fathers as providers. However, in the older age group, eighteen to nineteen, an equal number of fathers defined fathers as providers ($n = 6$) as those who conceptualized them as involved/nurturing parents ($n = 6$).

Voices of African-American Teen Fathers
© 2006 by The Haworth Press, Inc. All rights reserved.
doi:10.1300/5477_05

VOICES OF AFRICAN-AMERICAN TEEN FATHERS

TABLE 4.1. Primary conceptualizations of fatherhood.

Category	14-15 years old	16-17 years old	18-19 years old	Totals
Providers	$n = 4$ (57 percent)	$n = 8$ (57 percent)	$n = 4$ (44 percent)	$n = 16$ (53 percent)
Involved nurturers	$n = 1$ (14 percent)	$n = 3$ (21.5 percent)	$n = 4$ (44 percent)	$n = 8$ (27 percent)
Independent fathers	$n = 2$ (29 percent)	$n = 3$ (21.5 percent)	$n = 1$ (11 percent)	$n = 6$ (20 percent)

FATHER AS PROVIDER: "I'M NOT RUNNING FROM MY RESPONSIBILITIES"

More than half of the African-American teen fathers in the sample defined fatherhood primarily in economic and provider-role terms. Being a good provider was synonymous with being a good father. They wanted to provide financially for their children and were willing to become "good" fathers (defined as good providers), but they encountered barriers to fulfilling this responsibility. To explore what fatherhood meant to them, the following questions were asked: How do you define fatherhood? What does being a father mean to you? What is your ideal notion of fatherhood? What does being a good father mean to you? Their answers included the following: "being able to take care of my child," "providing for my kid," or "being able to support my child." When asked to elaborate, they discussed how taking care of or supporting their children meant being able to provide financially for them.

A recurring theme in the data was that of being a "real man." The concept of a real man meant being masculine, which was directly tied to being a provider—the traditional notion of fatherhood. For example, fifteen-year-old Jarrod described what being a father or a real man meant:

JARROD: Being a father means being a real man. A real man will do what he has to do. He takes care of his own.

How Teen Fathers Think About and Do Fatherhood 77

INTERVIEWER: What do you mean by that? What is it that he has to do, and what does he take care of?

JARROD: He gets a job. He goes to work. He provides for his kids. He pays the bills. He takes care of his children. He do what he has to do. He takes care of his. That's what a real man does. That's what a father will do.

INTERVIEWER: And what does that mean for you as a father?

JARROD: I'm going do what I have to do.

Although Jarrod referred to getting a job in order to support his child when he stated, "I'm going do what I have to do," he was just fifteen years old and had not provided financial support to his child. Jarrod's father, who works as a store clerk, did not have money to assist either, according to Jarrod.

In so many words the fathers defined manhood as "doing what they have to do" as fathers and vice versa, and for most teen fathers this meant being responsible for and accountable to their children. The phrase connotes providing for and taking care of their children financially. The notions of being self-sufficient and being a provider are concepts closely associated with traditional masculine values.

The relationship between fatherhood and masculinity was important to nineteen-year-old William. William worked full-time at a telemarketing company, and conceptualized father as provider, the traditional notion of fatherhood. The phrase *real man* emerged in his discussion as well, and he stated, "Anybody can make a baby, but a real man will be there for his child." William's enactment of fatherhood was consistent with his primary conceptualization of a "real man" as provider.

Important to note is that teen fathers do not equate being a provider with being a breadwinner. Providing for their children meant supplementing the children's economic welfare, or "helping the mothers out." Providing for their children did not implicate intention to become the sole providers for their children, nor did it mean that they planned to become the primary source of income for their children or to their children's households as they, the teen fathers, matured into adults. For example, sixteen-year-old Tevin provided some financial assistance to the mother of his child. His source of income was money given occasionally to him by his mother, cousin, and aunt who all resided in the same household. Tevin explained that the financial

78 VOICES OF AFRICAN-AMERICAN TEEN FATHERS

burden involved in raising children ultimately fell on the mother, and that women were lucky if the fathers assisted at all.

TEVIN: Take me for example. My father basically doesn't have anything to do with me or my brothers. He helps out zero. My mom doesn't receive any money or anything from him. But me, one day I'll be able to help out Charlene by myself, but even then, she's the one going to really have to take care of Tracie. If the man and woman aren't together, that's just how it is.

Tevin was in the eleventh grade at the time of the interview and planned to become a music producer and rapper. His views on financial responsibility were shared by many fathers who used the same terminology of "helping her out." Therefore, being providers meant providing economic assistance, not being a breadwinner or sole source of financial support.

These findings contrast with Hamer's (2001) research in which she found that the majority of the adult, nonresidential African-American fathers did not define fatherhood in provider terms. Instead, these adult men felt that being involved in their children's lives by spending time with them and giving them emotional support was more important than being a provider. Being involved fathers, as defined by being nurturing and emotionally supportive, is an increasing trend, according to Gerson (1997), and it is the second most often cited definition of fatherhood by adult fathers in the general population. Although fatherhood is defined in economic terms by child support systems and welfare reform policies, low-income, low-skilled African-American men find it increasingly difficult to provide economically for their children. It is possible that because African-American adolescents in the present study have not had the opportunity to perform in an adult capacity nor experienced the challenges that the adult African-American fathers experienced in trying to provide for their children, their conceptualization of fatherhood tended to reflect the dominant, traditional conception of father as provider.

Most African-American teen fathers in the present study provided some type of tangible goods (e.g., diapers, clothes, baby food) for their children, and sporadically gave economic support to the mothers of their children. This assistance came primarily from their own parents. Although less common, some teen fathers failed to provide anything.

How Teen Fathers Think About and Do Fatherhood   79

Those young men that thought of fathers as providers were apt to experience role strain because they thought it was appropriate and expected of them to provide more than what they were able to. Inconsistencies in how they defined fatherhood and how they enacted fatherhood were problematic to many. Some age differences existed in this regard, too, with younger fathers accepting their inability to provide (due to perceived age limitations) more than did the older fathers who were old enough to work.

Fifteen-year-old Michael primarily defined fatherhood as providing economic support for children. He was the father of two children (a two-month-old girl and an eleven-month-old boy) by different mothers, but did not consider himself as being "in a serious relationship" with either of the mothers. His relationships with them were amicable, however. Michael maintained that both pregnancies were accidental and were caused by his condom tearing during sexual intercourse in both cases. As a father, he provided very little, in fact, almost no support at all for his children although he conceptualized father as provider. His concerns about providing for his children were expressed as follows:

INTERVIEWER: How do you feel about being a father?

MICHAEL: I was kind of down, but you know, what's happened has happened.

INTERVIEWER: Did you feel like that in both cases?

MICHAEL: Pretty much.

INTERVIEWER: Did you want to become a father?

MICHAEL: No. Because they're [the mothers] going to hit you up for money, and they're going to want you to see the kid. So, it's not that fun right now.

INTERVIEWER: Do you want to see the kids? You said they're going to want you to see the kids.

MICHAEL: Yeah, but on my time. Everybody want you to do stuff on their time.

INTERVIEWER: Are either of the girls making any demands on you right now?

MICHAEL: More so from my new baby's mom, but the other one, I guess she's more mature, so she's not too demanding. And she's out of school, too, so . . .

INTERVIEWER: So what kind of demands is the younger one making?

MICHAEL: She's still in school, and she doesn't know how she's going to finish school. She's worried about all kinds of stuff.

INTERVIEWER: Is she asking you to do specific things?

MICHAEL: Just want me to spend some time with her and the baby.

Spending time with his children and payment of child support were responsibilities that complicated life for Michael. He explained that he did not want to become a father, "Because they're going to hit you up for money." His lack of maturity emerged in some of his comments such as the one made about fatherhood not being "that fun right now," and in the remark about wanting to see his children "on his time." Similar to most of the fourteen- and fifteen-year-old fathers in the study, Michael fell back on his youth as an explanation for not providing or attempting to provide for his children. He later said about acting responsibly, "I'm young. I'm just fifteen." He was able to reconcile the discomfort of not being able to provide (at first he "was down" about being a father) by rationalizing his inability to provide, which was due to his youth.

Many of the fathers believed that they lacked the resources that would enable them to fulfill their roles as father roles. As McAdoo (1990) noted, choice and exchange theory suggests that the greater the economic resources, the more likely adolescent fathers are to provide economic and emotional support. The adolescent fathers in this study occasionally provided clothes, money, diapers, and other child-related supplies for their children when they could, and stated that they would give more if they had greater resources. The resources provided for their children came from assistance from their families (namely their mothers), working part-time jobs, or obtaining money from illegal activities (such as selling drugs).

Some of the adolescent fathers in the present study were determined to provide for their children but were unable to do so through legal channels. As a result, a few engaged in illegal activities to provide for their children. This was the situation with seventeen-year-old Darrius, who was raised by his grandmother. His mother lived in Chicago with two other children, and his father lived in Gary, Indiana with Darrius's three other half or stepsiblings. Neither of Darrius's parents assisted him in supporting his son, Alex, who was two years

How Teen Fathers Think About and Do Fatherhood   *81*

old at the time of the interview. His grandmother worked as a cook at a hotel and did not have much to provide. Darrius was proud of his ability to provide for his child, even though he earned money by selling drugs. In the following passage I asked him about his conceptualization of fatherhood.

INTERVIEWER: How would you define fatherhood?

DARRIUS: Hell, I don't know. That's a hard question. I don't know. [silence] Let me see. I guess, it means taking care of your responsibilities.

INTERVIEWER: What types of responsibilities?

DARRIUS: Giving them money for food, clothes, house, or apartment. Stuff like that.

Darrius conceptualized fatherhood as provider and rated himself as "a pretty good father" because he was able to provide money and support for his child (although through the illegal means of selling drugs). He did not indicate how much he gave to the mother of his child, and this question was not asked. As mentioned, he lived with his grandmother, who was unable to provide any financial assistance for his child.

Role theory suggests that it may be difficult to claim a particular identity because of the inability to adequately perform in that role (Warner and Feltey 1999). Thus, role strain may partially explain why some teen fathers have problems identifying themselves as "good" fathers. Their age makes it inherently difficult to provide as the role demands. When asked how they rated themselves as fathers and whether they thought of themselves as good fathers, many of their responses indicated that they felt that their performances were acceptable but "middle line." For instance, their answers included phrases such as "I'm okay," "pretty good, I guess," and "I could be a better." Furthermore, their struggle with assuming their new identities as fathers was evident in their accounts about themselves. Their focus was usually on their personalities and favorite activities or passtime actions (without mentioning their children in these activities).

The difficulties associated with assuming an identity that includes traditional masculine fatherhood roles when one cannot adequately carry out those responsibilities were apparent in an interview with a seventeen-year-old father, James. James grew up in a single-parent household and lived with his mother, two younger sisters, and his mother's boyfriend who had been living with them for more than a year. James did not see his own father very often even though he resided in the same city. Adult male figures in his life included his mother's boyfriends (present and past), two uncles, and a male friend of the family. He described the emotional struggle of dealing with fatherhood as a teen:

JAMES: A lot of people think we're [teen fathers] just running from our responsibilities because we don't want to take care of our children. There might be some like that, but I know that I'm not one of them. I want to be a good father, but there's only so much I can do. I know I need to be able to buy Kenis what he needs, but I'm just fifteen. I know I need to get a job, but I'm in school. Should I drop out? I know they don't want me to drop out. Then how would I support Kenis, or myself for that matter, later on down the road? You asked me how would I rate myself as a father, or how I feel about myself as a father or whatever, and I can only tell you that I'm not doing real good. I almost feel like I'm an uncle or something—you know someone that just drops by or gives you something every now and then. I don't feel like a good father, or a real father for that matter.

How teen fathers define fatherhood has implications for their behavior in that role. Because James's definition of fatherhood centered on being a provider, he felt more like an "uncle" than a "real father" because he was not able to provide what he thought he should. Youth was a factor that partially accounted for the role strain the young fathers experienced. Being young, teen fathers did not fit the expected image of father, and this awareness affected their identity as "real" fathers, but also got them off the hook (or excused them) as providers.

Although most teen fathers expressed concerns about not being able to adequately provide for their children, some did not experience this. These fathers were older and worked at least part-time jobs to supplement their children's economic welfare. Six fathers were working part-time, with an additional one who was about to start a part-time job. Their places of employment included a dry cleaners, a hardware/lumber store, a fast-food restaurant, a telemarketing company, a night

How Teen Fathers Think About and Do Fatherhood 83

shift job at a factory, and the army reserve. In the case of pending employment, the young man was going to work part-time in a warehouse. In one case, a nineteen-year-old father had been fired from a full-time job as an assistant manager with a fast-food restaurant. Overall, the young fathers that were employed felt that it was their duty to provide as much money and support as possible for the mothers of their children, and they devoted some of their income to that purpose.

Five out of seven working fathers (here the one who was about to start a job is included) had intimate, romantic relationships with the mothers of their children and expected to maintain them. They were involved with their children, spent an average of four days a week with them, and engaged in such activities as playing with their children, holding them, showing affection, and some caregiving activities. The lengths of time they spent on these visits varied, ranging from as little as ten minutes to several hours.

Seventeen-year-old Craig, father of two-year-old Joy, worked part-time at a factory and did seasonal work at stadium concession stands as well. He attended an alternative high school and planned to join the military upon completion of school. Unlike most teen fathers, when Craig was requested to discuss something about himself, the first thing he mentioned was being a father. Readily acknowledging this identity may partially explain why Craig assumed behaviors (getting a job and providing financial support) that were consistent with his definition of fatherhood. It might also be the case that by being able to provide meant Craig more readily identified with being a father. Craig was asked whether he experienced changes since becoming a father:

CRAIG: Well yes. Other than having less time to myself, I guess the biggest thing is just feeling I have to be more responsible, which I should. Like, I had to start working. I work at "Coleman's" part-time. Plus, I do some work at the university during basketball season; I work at the concession stands. So, I do what I can to earn money to keep things flowing smoothly.

Craig discussed the following about working in order to assist the mother of his child:

VOICES OF AFRICAN-AMERICAN TEEN FATHERS

CRAIG: That's the point. Otherwise, I wouldn't be working while in school. Well, I would probably be working since I didn't stay at North [High], in a regular school. But I would have been working just for myself. I wouldn't have to work for someone else or feel like I have to.

INTERVIEWER: Because you have a responsibility now?

CRAIG: Right. Before, working was optional, but now it's not.

According to Craig, he gave Deborah, the mother of his child, approximately half of the money he made. He stated:

CRAIG: I would say about half of the money I make goes to her. About a quarter goes to my mom, and then the other quarter goes to keeping up my car, gas, stuff like that.

Craig's mother, a custodian at a hospital, was unable to provide economic assistance to her grandchild. However, she occasionally bought toys or some clothes for the child, Craig stated.

In summary, most of the fathers in this study conceptualized the role of a father as provider. Ironically, they stated this in terms that they could not meet as teen fathers. They understood the limitations their age brought to their responsibilities as fathers. Their adolescence partially accounted for their lack of desire or ability to work and their lack of commitment to fatherhood. Hamer's (2001) study found that African-American adult fathers primarily defined fatherhood in terms of being involved and nurturing. Because the adolescent fathers in the current study were not able to provide for their children, one may wonder at what point the teens (if they do) change their notions of what makes a successful father. Because paternal choices are neither innate nor unalterable (Gerson 1997), the question then is whether they will transform their conceptualization of fatherhood and their actions as they confront the harsh realities that make it difficult to fulfill the ideal. Gerson (1997) asserts that certain social factors transform men's commitments as fathers. At this juncture in the teens' parenthood, however, they have not undergone many experiences that have transformed their commitments, although such experiences will probably come with age and time.

THE INVOLVED NURTURER:
"I'M BEING THERE FOR MY CHILD"

Responsibility and involvement were the most frequent responses to the question asked about what it meant to be a father. Being emotionally involved, physically present, and nurturing were attributes that made good fathers, according to one-fourth of the teens. Allen and Doherty (1998) characterized these qualities as "being there," and found that they were most commonly expressed by the African-American adolescent fathers they interviewed. They wrote that "being there" might have been most important to the African-American teen fathers in their study because the fathers did not believe that they could reliably provide for their children in traditional ways. Being there encompassed fatherhood in two related contexts: being there physically and emotionally for their children, and being present at the time of birth. In the present study, "being there" was further reported as a state in which they provided emotional support to their children, spent "quality time" with them, and were involved in care-giving activities.

The teen fathers in this study that primarily defined fathering as being involved and nurturing, sometimes cited "being a provider" as a fatherhood function as well (and vice versa). Again, the established categories for the teen fathers' primary conceptualizations of fatherhood (provider, involved nurturer, independent father) were not mutually exclusive, and were grouped according to what teen fathers' indicated were the primary or the most important roles of fathers. That these categories are not mutually exclusive is captured in the interview with Tevin. Although defining fathers primarily as providers, sixteen-year-old Tevin, father of a six-month-old daughter, Tracie, described the importance of being there for his daughter also:

TEVIN: [Being a father to me also means] spending quality time with my girl. Being a key part to her life. When she gets older, I want her to know that she can count on her daddy. I don't want her to think that I'm just there to give her money whenever Charlene can't. I want her to know that I'm there for her when she needs someone to talk to, and to tell me her ups and downs, and her problems and her joys. I want to her to know that I'll be there.

86 VOICES OF AFRICAN-AMERICAN TEEN FATHERS

Keith, a twelfth grader and nineteen-year-old father of a thirteen-month-old son, Todd, stated the following about being involved with his child:

KEITH: What I mean by that is that I want to be a part of my son's life. I don't want him to think that he has an absentee dad. I want him to know I'm there. I want to be there when he hits his first baseball or makes his first basket. I'm going to be there when he needs to know about women. I'm going to be there when he's having problems at school and when he's being pressured by his friends to do things he knows are wrong. I'm going to be there when he graduates from school. He's going to know that he can come to me and talk to me about anything, because I'll be there.

The fathers in this study did not discuss "being there" in the context of being present at the time of birth. This issue was mentioned only if directly addressed by the interviewer. Many of the fathers were not present during the births of their children, but among those who were, they found the experience to be profound and gratifying. For example, sixteen-year-old Clayton described the circumstances of his child's birth and how he felt when she was born:

CLAYTON: I was kind of nervous. When it happened, I was over to my Uncle Nate's house and mom called and told me that Quendasha was in the hospital and was about to have the baby. So my uncle took me to the hospital. I was real nervous, you know. I didn't think I was going to feel that way, but I did. I just felt scared. To tell you the truth, I didn't really want Quendasha to have her at first, but after she was born, I was like "man."
INTERVIEWER: Sounds like you were proud. Amazed?
CLAYTON: Yes, both. When she was born, I thought she looked funny and all, but I thought she was beautiful at the same time. I was real happy. Very proud I would say.

Clayton described fathers as involved, nurturing parents. He saw his daughter about twice weekly, sometimes more, and engaged in some caregiving activities such as changing her diapers and feeding her.

Some fathers were not, however, present during childbirth, sometimes because they were not told, or sometimes because they were not

How Teen Fathers Think About and Do Fatherhood   *87*

interested. For example, sixteen-year-old Mark stated that he did not want to become a father and had wanted the mother of his child to have an abortion. He was very resentful, and described the following about the day his child was born:

MARK: I wasn't there when it happened. That might sound bad. But I just didn't want to deal with it. I found out about it because her mom called to let us know that Sherry was in the hospital, about to have the baby. But still I just didn't want to be there. So I didn't go and mom wasn't home when they called, so she wasn't there to make me [go].

Fathers who defined their role as "being there" performed this function through a range of behaviors. The "involved" behaviors included visiting their children, spending "quality" time with them (e.g., spending extended periods of time with children and engaging in various activities such as play), showing affection and love by holding them and playing with them, and performing caregiving activities (e.g., feeding their children, changing their clothes, and putting them to sleep). The teens' fatherhood activities in the current study also differed by age, with older fathers making more visits during a one-week period and spending more time with their children than did the younger teens. It was the older fathers who were most likely to think about fathers as nurturers. Within the two younger age groups, forteen to fifteen and sixteen to seventeen, very few fathers defined fatherhood as being involved and nurturing.

Some who defined their role as being an involved nurturer engaged in what they called "babysitting." The term *babysitting* was used when they discussed keeping their children, whether briefly or overnight. This description captures the separation and distance the teen fathers felt in their roles in raising their children. Watching, keeping, and taking care of their children were viewed as primary responsibilities of the mothers. Because the teen fathers did not live with the mothers or their children, their own care was considered supplemental, such as "babysitting" when needed. They babysat their children; the mothers of their children did not. This view was articulated in the interview with nineteen-year-old Keith. Keith's primary conceptualization of fatherhood was as nurturer and caregiver. However, these duties were characterized differently for the man and woman, with

88 VOICES OF AFRICAN-AMERICAN TEEN FATHERS

men providing assistance rather than being responsible for these activities: "Men help out. We babysit sometimes. We might feed the baby, change her clothes, rock her to sleep—stuff like that. I know I do. When I have her [his child] I do those things."

Although being involved and nurturing were the second most often cited definitions of fatherhood, most teen fathers did not consider the involved or caregiver role to be an appropriate *primary* role for fathers. However, among those that did consider this their primary role, gender differentiations were enforced. Even though the role of the involved, nurturing father was similar to the traditional role of mother, what distinguished the father's role from that of the mother was that the mother was still considered the primary caregiver. Not surprisingly, the young fathers felt that the mothers were primarily responsible for their children's overall welfare and well-being. Even though several of them provided some type of caregiving activities at one point or another as involved nurturers, many of them considered caregiving and other involved activities as "bonuses" when given to their children or as "favors" they gave to the mothers. These findings are somewhat similar to Gerson's (1997), who found that only a minority (about a third) of the "involved" adult fathers in her study actually became equal or primary parents.

The idea of "doing her a favor" when providing caregiving activities is illustrated in an extreme example by Calvin, the sixteen-year-old father of eight-month-old Denae.

CALVIN: I like being a dad, but I'll just be honest, I think it's her [referring to the mother of his child] responsibility to take care of Denae. I mean, she's lucky that I come around at all. Most fathers my age wouldn't spend the kind of time I do with my child.

INTERVIEWER: What kinds of things do you do with her, Calvin, when you're with her?

CALVIN: I play with her and stuff.

INTERVIEWER: Do you feed her, or . . .?

CALVIN: No, I ain't doing them types of things. That's not my job. I ain't changing no Pampers, and feeding her and stuff like that. To me, that's what Bianca should be doing. That's what she should do.

INTERVIEWER: Have you ever performed those types of activities . . . feeding her, changing her, dressing her?

CALVIN: Yeah, I'll do it every now and then. Every now and then I'll help Bianca out, you know. I'll give her a hand. Like I said, she's lucky. Most women don't have a man that'll come around like I do and help her out sometimes.

As an "independent" or autonomous father, Calvin actually spent very little time with his daughter and performed relatively few caregiving activities. He saw his child about once a month for approximately one hour.

Unlike Calvin, the caregiving and nurturing activities (including time spent with children) that were performed by involved/ nurturing fathers were mostly done out of love for their children and were performed in greater magnitude. In comparison to the mothers' responsibilities, however, these activities were barely significant in frequency and in quality. For example, whereas the mothers were with their children every day, the involved/nurturing fathers saw them about three times a week. Gender was re-created and reproduced in all of the enactments of fatherhood, but varied with intensity and form depending on the individual father, his conceptualization of fatherhood, and other factors (such as relationships and structural barriers) that will be discussed in the following chapters.

Overall, however, fathers in this parenting category spent more time with their children than those fathers who conceptualized fatherhood primarily as a provider. Involved fathers in the present study spent approximately three days a week with their children, and the time spent ranged from one to four hours per visit. Sometimes the fathers kept their children overnight at their own homes, even though they turned over the children to their own mothers. Their mothers were most often the primary caregivers when the children were kept overnight or longer. The child's paternal grandmother babysat the child if the teen father "had other things to do," fed and dressed the child, and put the child "to sleep."

According to eighteen-year-old Byron, spending time with one's child is the most important role of a father. Byron, father of an eleven-month-old daughter, Asia, lived with his mother and sister and said that his family "gets along pretty good." He liked that his mother respected his manhood at eighteen (she allowed him freedom and did not treat him "like a child"). Byron had signed up to join the air force when he graduated from high school, and planned to marry the mother of his child, Anita, who was white, seventeen years old, and still in school. Although Anita's pregnancy was an accident, both were happy when they found out she was pregnant. Byron worked at a hardware/lumber store in order to provide for Asia, but he believed that spending "quality time" with her was more important. After asking Byron what makes someone a good father, he explained that it has to be something more than just being a biological father. He was then asked where being a provider fit into his conception of fatherhood, and his response was the following:

BYRON: It's important to provide for your child, because that's part of being a good father, too. But not all fathers are able to give to their children in a material sense, but that doesn't mean that he's not a good father. Take my dad. I don't care that he never tried to give me anything; he might not have been able to. But if he had just came around every once in a while and tried to spend some time with me, well that would have been doing his job, his obligation as a father. So, I think spending quality time with your child is more important than being a provider.

Byron's conceptualization of fatherhood was consistent with his behavior. He saw his daughter almost every day and spent most of his time playing with and holding her "because she likes to be held." Byron also provided financial support for his child. Soon after he found out that his girlfriend was pregnant, he got the part-time job at the lumber store. Although he did not specify the amount he gives her, he said that he gives her money every other week when he is paid.

Many of the teen fathers who were involved/nurturing fathers were excited about parenting and intended to participate in their children's lives over time. Spending time with their children was seen as a priority. Clayton, a sixteen-year old father of an eight-month-old girl, fondly described his daughter and mentioned the pictures of her that he had at home. In addition to babysitting his daughter, Clayton also did such activities as change Kierra's diapers and feed her. He described how he felt about being a father:

CLAYTON: I look forward to seeing Kierra. When I'm at home or hanging out or something, I just have a good feeling knowing that

I'll be seeing her later that day or the next day or something. So to me, being a dad is a plus.

Although many of the fathers visited their children two or three times a week, Paul, a seventeen-year-old father saw his eleven-month-old daughter on a daily basis. Right after school, for instance, Paul visited Brianna for about thirty minutes to an hour, occasionally spending a couple of hours with her. Although he did not economically provide for his daughter, he believed that the time he spent with her was more important.

INTERVIEWER: Well, what makes someone a good father, in your opinion, and what makes someone a bad father?
PAUL: When they don't spend time with their kids.
INTERVIEWER: So you rate that as being the most important factor in being a father?
PAUL: Uh hmm. [yes]
[Later in the same interview]
INTERVIEWER: How important is being a father to you?
PAUL: It's real important, because I didn't have a dad like I said earlier. So, I want to be a good dad.
INTERVIEWER: Hmm. How do you define fatherhood? What does it mean to you?
PAUL: Being able to take care of the baby.
INTERVIEWER: And for you that means . . .?
PAUL: Being there for her.

An interesting spin on what constituted an involved, nurturing father was captured in an interview with Roman, an eighteen-year-old father and gang member. Roman discussed the importance of spending time with his three-year-old son and providing him guidance and proper life lessons and teachings. He felt his own mother neglected him in this regard, as did his father who had been in prison for as long as he could remember. Roman had no siblings, and although he lived with his mother, he considered himself financially and emotionally independent since she provided no direct support. The following illustrated how his mother was neglectful to him:

ROMAN: Everything that I had to learn from gangbanging is something she [his mother] should have tried to teach me. She should have spent time with me, taught me something about being a man. Something. She should have tried to take care of me a little instead of leaving me at eight or nine years old to find my own way, [to] feed my ownself . . . All she was concerned about was that pipe [crack cocaine addiction] and anything else she could get her hands on. She just should have been there, you know.

Roman's concept of a father's responsibility is partially constructed in contrast to his own mother's behaviors, and is also related to the sense of "family" he experienced in a gang he joined four years previous to the interview. Completely trusting his fellow gang members, depending on them for protection, and being taught "everything you need to know to make it in this world" by them, Roman was greatly influenced by them. He desired to reproduce his position, status, and experience in the gang by passing down the gang membership to his three-year-old son, Jamal. For Jamal's own good, this intergenerational membership and status were needed, Roman felt. The most important thing a father could do for his child, he stated, was "teaching him what he needs to know to survive." Therefore, according to Roman, Jamal will one day be a member of his gang, or his "family" as he called it. The likelihood of this occurring was strong since the mother of Roman's son was also in the same gang.

THE INDEPENDENT FATHER:
"IT'S NOT MY RESPONSIBILITY!"

Some African-American teen fathers consciously detached themselves from their father status—both conceptually and in behavior. They absolved themselves from all fatherhood responsibilities or roles for various reasons, and identified with their parenthood status in terms of biology or paternity only. Although they had ideas about what a father should be or how he should act (e.g., provider, nurturer), they did not associate themselves with those roles or responsibilities. What separated them from other teen fathers in this study was their

How Teen Fathers Think About and Do Fatherhood 93

deliberate choice to opt out of fatherhood and their feelings of justification in doing so. This type of fathering was expressed by one-fifth (six) of the fathers in this study.

The reasons for their detachment from fatherhood were complex, yet recurring themes were their beliefs that the mothers of their children "trapped" them by getting pregnant on purpose, or that the mothers had shown irresponsibility in not preventing pregnancy. Consequently, the responsibilities for raising the children did not belong with them as fathers since the pregnancies were not their fault. Therefore, they did not feel an obligation to be involved. Furthermore, their children presented a threat to their sense of freedom and to their identities as teenagers as well as representing potential obstacles to their personal goals and dreams. The reality of being a father could not coxist with their identities as teenagers since the two were mutually exclusive concepts to them. For instance, eighteen-year-old Brandon, father of one-and-a-half-year-old Keeshawn, prioritized his own needs, desires, and goals before those of his son. Brandon believed that he could not be a father and a teenager at the same time:

BRANDON: I love my child, I really do, but I got to be true to myself. How am I going to be a good father for him if I don't do what's right for me? How am I going to do right by him if I don't do right for myself?

INTERVIEWER: What does doing right for yourself mean?

BRANDON: Being right for me means not letting this situation get me down and doing what I got to do.

INTERVIEWER: Do you mean being a father when you say not letting the situation get you down, or what do you mean by that?

BRANDON: Yes, I'm talking about being a teen father. I can't let that situation get me down. I want to go to college and become a lawyer one day. I can't let what's happened with Tisha stop me. I can't quit school, or get a job, or give up my life over what's happened. I want to spend more time with Keeshawn, but I can't. I want to provide for her, but I can't stop doing what I have to do and give up my dreams. Should I? Why should I throw away everything I want to achieve because of a mistake her mom . . . okay, we, made?

Even though Brandon was considered a teen, in many respects his eighteen-year-old status could be construed as an adult. Still,

94 VOICES OF AFRICAN-AMERICAN TEEN FATHERS

Brandon did not view himself as an adult ("I'm talking about being a teen father. I can't let that situation get me down."), and therefore saw his "situation" as a parent as daunting.

Role conflict may explain how their youth served as justification for their parental detachment. The fathers felt overwhelmed with the idea of being a teen father and did not know how to deal with their expected fatherhood roles. Therefore, instead of adopting the identity of father, this group of young fathers chose to maintain their identities as teenagers exclusively. As teens they had freedom from responsibilities, and their subsequent rejection of paternal responsibility reflected their commitment to that role. For example, sixteen-year-old Calvin justified why he saw very little of his eight-month-old daughter Denae and why he did not provide economic assistance to her. Calvin explained that the mother of his child, Bianca, an eighteen-year-old woman, should take on full and sole responsibility for raising Denae because he believed she got pregnant on purpose. Moreover, as a legal adult, Bianca should bear the responsibility, he felt. Again, this view reflected how being a parent meant being an adult, therefore, some fathers felt relieved from responsibilities of fathering because they were still minors. Although Calvin expressed love for his daughter in the interview, he stated the following about his role as a father:

CALVIN: I'm just not ready for it. I'm just telling you the truth. I'm not ready to be a father. I'm too young. I don't want those kinds of responsibilities right now. I don't want to be a father, and I'm not going to act like one.

Fathers who rejected paternal responsibility saw their children infrequently (at most once a week). Less time was spent with children from fathers in this category relative to others, and the time spent was usually less than one hour.

Despite their behavior, in some cases the parents of the teen fathers did their best most of the time to provide economic and emotional support for their grandchildren. Occasionally they reprimanded the teen fathers for what they perceived to be egregiously poor parenting and lack of concern, according to the young fathers. However, in about half of the cases (three), the parents of the young fathers did not make efforts to provide economic or nurturing support for their grandchildren. Similar to their teen sons, they did not believe that

How Teen Fathers Think About and Do Fatherhood　　95

they should be responsible for their grandchildren. These attitudes and behaviors by the paternal grandparents of the children seemed to further fuel the teen fathers' justification for not accepting responsibilities as fathers. According to the literature, one of the conditioning factors necessary to move toward accepting responsibility as fathers is social support (Billson 1996). When parents of the teen fathers do not encourage their sons to accept responsibility for their fatherhood, the young fathers may use this to support their negligent actions. This was apparent with fifteen-year-old Jeremy, who explained that he should be relieved of parental responsibilities. Jeremy lived in a single-parent household with his mother and older sister. He resented being a father and felt as if parenthood was forced upon him. He stated:

JEREMY: I don't have to do it [act as a father] if I don't want to. Even my mom said she [the girlfriend, Crystal] just got pregnant on purpose. She doesn't even believe that I should have to suffer because of what Crystal did.

INTERVIEWER: Does your mom help out with Jasmine?

JEREMY: Nope. Why should she?

INTERVIEWER: Does she spend time with her?

JEREMY: Nope. Don't get me wrong, she's not heartless, and neither am I. We do care about Jasmine. I just hate someone ruining my life because of their own selfishness. Because of what they wanted.

INTERVIEWER: You mean Crystal?

JEREMY: Right.

INTERVIEWER: And so you believe that you shouldn't have to assume any parental responsibilities because you weren't responsible for the pregnancy?

JEREMY: I'm not dumb. I know it takes two. But this half didn't try to do it on purpose.

INTERVIEWER: What makes you think Crystal got pregnant on purpose?

JEREMY: Because she didn't make me use a condom. She didn't use birth control. Obviously. And she didn't seem like she minded being pregnant when she told me that she was. That's why.

Jeremy not only denied responsibility for the pregnancy but also failed to accept any responsibility as a parent, a decision supported by his mother who was also a single parent. Interestingly, she (Jeremy's mother) did not receive any emotional or financial support from Jeremy's father. Perhaps most interesting in Jeremy's abdication of responsibility is his claim that Crystal "didn't make" him use a condom.

In summary, the fathers' sense of manhood and masculinity were mostly validated by their actual enactment of fatherhood. One was being a good father if he actually provided economic and/or nurturing support for his children. As William stated, "Anybody can make a baby, but a real man will be there for his child." With the exception of independent fathers, being responsible and "being a real man" were very important to the fathers, yet enactment of such did not always take place. Sometimes their enactment of fatherhood was influenced by the type of relationship they had with the mothers of their children and by the experiences they had with their parents. In the next chapter, the relationships that teen fathers have with their families of origin and how these relationships shape and influence their fatherhood experiences will be explored.

Chapter 5

Teen Fathers
and Their Families of Origin

Environmental influences and social expectations shape fathers' ideas about, and behaviors in, the role of father. It is in the family, a primary agent of socialization, that children usually construct their first notions of what roles are expected of a mother and father. Their parents, whether intentionally or not, influence the children's future perceptions, expectations, and behaviors. In this section, the African-American adolescent fathers' relationships with their parents and how these relationships may have influenced their fatherhood experiences will be examined.

RELATIONSHIPS WITH THEIR FATHERS

The majority (58 percent) of African-American households with children are matriarchal (Chadwick and Heaton 1998). Similarly, the majority of young fathers in the present study lived in single-parent, matriarchal households. Just 20 percent ($n = 6$) lived in households with both parents, and one teen lived in a household in which the father was the only parent. Many of the adolescent fathers had never personally known their own fathers, and their feelings toward their fathers ranged from being respectful and affectionate, to being neutral and nonchalant, to being angry and resentful, with many of these feelings overlapping. This section will address what these African-American teen fathers said they felt about their fathers, their experiences with them, and the impact their fathers had on their adolescent fatherhood experiences. It became clear that their fathers were an important factor in their construction of fatherhood.

Voices of African-American Teen Fathers
© 2006 by The Haworth Press, Inc. All rights reserved.
doi:10.1300/5477_06

98 VOICES OF AFRICAN-AMERICAN TEEN FATHERS

When discussing their nonresidential fathers, the teens' views of their fathers were not positive ($n = 19$), and these views tended to fall into three broad categories. In the first category, the young fathers conveyed the impression that no hurt or pain was caused due to their fathers' absence ($n = 4$). They came across nonchalantly when they explained how their fathers were not involved in their lives—as if this absence or noninvolvement did not affect them, or that it was not a "big deal." They had accepted the state of their relationships, or had accepted the situation. In the second category, the teen fathers dejectedly spoke of their experiences with their fathers ($n = 5$). The pain was obvious either in their stories or in their voices. They did not appear to be angry with their fathers or harbor extreme animosity, but they certainly appeared to be injured emotionally by their fathers' behaviors. Finally, some teen fathers expressed anger about their fathers ($n = 10$) and used derogatory words to refer to them. Their pain was apparent; they revealed both hostility and resentment. This reaction was representative of the majority.

Nineteen-year-old William illustrates the first category—nonchalance. He and his former girlfriend had made a conscious decision to become teen parents because they wanted a "family." William worked full-time at a telemarketing company and provided financial support for his child, even though he and the mother had recently stopped seeing each other. William's own father left their family when he was three years old, and William had not seen him since. When he spoke about his father, he sighed and stated nonchalantly, "He's never been around. I don't know him, and I don't care to know him. He hasn't been a part of my life all these years, so why sweat it? It's not worth it."

Tevin, a sixteen-year old father, grew up in a single-parent, female-headed household with his mother and three brothers. At the time of the interview, he had an aunt and an older male cousin living with him and his family. He expressed pain and disappointment about his relationship with his father who was minimally involved in their family's life and did little to provide money and other necessities for their poverty-stricken household. Tevin's mother supported them by working part-time at a grocery store and by receiving public assistance. When the interviewer asked Tevin about his father, his first words were, "He's no good." His father was worthless to him and his family, he explained. Over time, he and his mother had gotten to the point where they simply did not expect anything from his father—time, money,

Teen Fathers and Their Families of Origin 99

concern, or love. Tevin had become resigned to the fact that his father may never be involved in his life and he talked nonchalantly about this experience. However, he did have one concern: he feared that the mother of his child, Charlene, held similar views and had low expectations of him as a father.

INTERVIEWER: How do you think Charlene feels about you as a father?

TEVIN: She doesn't expect much from me.

INTERVIEWER: What do you mean by that?

TEVIN: She doesn't ask me for anything. If I don't give her anything, say for a few weeks or whatever, she won't say anything. Maybe every now and then she might ask if I could give a little something, but the only time she'll say something is when I haven't seen Tracie [his daughter] in a while. Then she might say something about that. Well, I don't mind her asking me to see Tracie, but I kind of wish she would ask me to give her something sometimes, too. Something. Even just a little money. I can't do much, but I still want her to think I can give it to her, you know.

INTERVIEWER: Why does it bother you so much that she doesn't hassle you about it? Or rather ask you about it?

TEVIN: [pause] I don't know. I don't know why it bothers me. It makes me think . . . it makes me think she feels like I'm less of a man, you know. It makes me feel like she doesn't expect much out of me. Like I said, I know I can't do much, but. . . . I don't know. I guess it makes me feel a little bad. It's like she doesn't expect the basics out of me, you know? As if she doesn't think I can do better. She's never said that, but that's how she acts. I don't know. It . . . it just disturbs me. Because I don't want to be looked at by her, like me and my mom look at my dad, you know.

INTERVIEWER: And how was that?

TEVIN: Like he's not a bit of count. He's no good. So me and mom were like, why bother with him? But I don't want Charlene to think it's going to be like that with me.

Tevin's notion of a man was tied to his conceptualization of father as provider. Because he was unable to provide very much for his daughter he felt as if he were "less of a man" when he perceived that the

100   VOICES OF AFRICAN-AMERICAN TEEN FATHERS

mother of his child felt the same. Furthermore, similar to most of the teen fathers, Tevin seemed to repeat the cycle of fatherhood experienced by his own father despite his repugnance for his father's behavior, and what his ideal of fatherhood should be.

Fifteen-year-old Jeremy is one of the youth whose responses portrayed rejection, hurt, and disappointment, but not the anger felt by some. His father lived in the same city with him but was not involved in Jeremy's life. Indeed, until just two years before the interview with Jeremy, they had not spoken a word to each other. He described an emotional, first-time encounter with his father:

JEREMY: The last time I saw my father? I see him around all the time. But if you want to know the last time I spoke to him, which was also the first time and will be the last, I can tell you that. I remember everything about it. I was thirteen years old then. He was, my father was, at one of my friend's house. I knew who my father was. I've always known. And he knew who I was. My mom told me he's always known. But he ain't never said anything to me though. We had only seen each other around. . . . But I've caught him sometimes looking at me. Anyway, I was hanging out at my friend's house, and he was outside with my friend's dad and some more men. When he got off by himself for a moment, I just went up to him and asked him how he was doing. He said he was doing okay. And he just kept looking at me, but he didn't say anything. . . . Then I worked up my nerves, and then I just said it. I said I'm Jeremy. I'm your son. And he just nodded his head and kept looking at me. Just kept staring. I didn't know what to say or what to do, because he didn't say anything or do anything. Then he just turned around and walked off to where the other men were, and just started laughing and talking to them. I didn't know whether he was talking about me or something else, but I just felt *[pause]*. I just felt mad. *[pause]* Real mad. And hurt, too, I guess. So, right after that I just went back into the garage where my friend was and tried to play it off.

INTERVIEWER: You played it off? Then how did you really feel? You said you felt very mad?

JEREMY: Yeah. But I really just felt like . . . Well, I'll just say it. I felt like being a punk and just breaking down and crying. But I didn't. I held up. But I didn't stay there long.

At the time of the interview, Jeremy had not spoken with his father since the incident he described, although he has seen him in passing. During those times, Jeremy says that he looks away and does not speak to his father. When I asked him why he reacts like that, he just shrugged his shoulders. Perhaps he did not wish to experience the rejection he felt from his father on the first day he "worked up his nerves" to speak to him. Jeremy's tale clearly displays classic male gender socialization. Despite the hurt and rejection at that moment with his father and his desire to cry, he "held up." Masculinity and being male demand that these guys "save face" and "be strong." Showing vulnerability is not traditionally viewed as manlike or masculine (Thompson 1989).

Although most of the teen fathers stated that they made concerted efforts to avoid the parental neglect or abandonment they experienced with their own fathers, some were still concerned that the cycle would continue. They wanted to be better fathers to their children than their fathers were to them, yet the fear of repeating the parenting behaviors demonstrated by their fathers remained. This was the case with seventeen-year-old Russell who, similar to Jeremy, described the pain and rejection he felt from his father's noninvolvement. Russell feared that he was in danger of following in the footsteps of his father who was neglectful and who had never provided economic or emotional support to Russell and his two brothers. Their relationship improved because of his changed attitude, as he explained:

RUSSELL: Growing up, I always wished I had my father in my life. But he's never cared anything about me or my brothers. He's never been around. Never did anything with us. Never gave us anything. That hurt, I'm not going to lie. And so I don't want to be like him. I don't want to do to my son what our father did to us.

INTERVIEWER: Do you fear that's a possibility?

RUSSELL: Yes. I know how painful it feels to think your father doesn't love you. And while I don't want to be like him, I almost feel like I am to a certain extent.

INTERVIEWER: Why do you say that?

RUSSELL: Because I'm not seeing Brenda as much as I should, and I'm not giving her the support she needs either. So, I don't know. It's not that I don't love Brenda. It's not that. But I don't know what it is. I just have to try harder.

102 VOICES OF AFRICAN-AMERICAN TEEN FATHERS

Finally, some discussions about their fathers were laden with anger and resentment, as Mark's story illustrates. Mark was a sixteen-year-old father of a four-month-old son, Marquise. He discussed his anger at his father:

MARK: I don't know my dad. I mean I know his name, and we have a couple of pictures of him, but I don't know him.

INTERVIEWER: Does he live here in Wichita?

MARK: He used to, but I think my mom said he moved to Oklahoma City or somewhere.

INTERVIEWER: Is your father also your older brothers' father?

MARK: No. Their dad is in the military. He used to be stationed at McConnell [air force base]. My mom was with him for a few years, before he moved on. He's at some base in New Jersey now.

INTERVIEWER: Does he stay in contact with your brothers?

MARK: Yeah, he sent Kevin some money and a birthday card last week. He sends them the usual on their birthdays and on Christmas. But that's better than what I get from mine. I get nothing.

INTERVIEWER: How does that make you feel?

MARK: Well, it just makes me angry sometimes, you know? I mean, he'd better stay away, because I'll probably curse him out if I saw him.

INTERVIEWER: For the way he's neglected you?

MARK: Exactly. I know I'm not the best father I can be right now, but at least I'm there, you know? Plus, I know that I'll give my son what he needs later when I'm able to. My father, my biological father, is a punk.

INTERVIEWER: Is that how you look at him?

MARK: How else can I look at him? He's a punk. But I ain't worried about it. That's all right.

Mark's parenting behavior was similar to his father's. Mark acknowledged that he was "not the best father" he could be, but stated, "at least I'm there." In his view, he had at least attempted to father his child, whereas his father made no attempt to do so with him. Displays of masculinity were also demonstrated in the previous passage with Mark. When Mark discussed his father not being in his life, he stated,

"But I ain't worried about it. That's all right," when clearly he felt hurt and vulnerable, characteristics considered traditionally unmasculine (Thompson 1989). Mark's feelings about his father did not fit the demeanor he "put on."

Anger and rejection about his father's noninvolvement were also expressed by Keith. Although earlier in the interview nineteen-year-old Keith stated that his relationship was fine with his father, he later revealed that it was tumultuous and complicated by his father's alcohol abuse. Keith was twelve years old when his parents divorced. Although he continued to see his father until he was fifteen years old, his father was emotionally abusive toward him, especially when he drank. Keith mentioned that everything he thought negatively about himself, both physically and mentally, his father thought twice that, and he felt as if his father didn't care about him. He had always tried to earn his father's approval by working hard to please him. For instance, he earned very good grades at school, "stayed out of trouble," and excelled at both basketball and football in school. However, none of his efforts pleased his father, he stated. Not only did his father tell him that he needed to work harder at everything, but sometimes he would tell Keith that no matter what Keith did, he would "still never amount to anything." Keith saw his father only during some of the holidays. When asked how he thought his father influenced him as a father or as a man, he responded:

KEITH: My first instinct is to tell you that he hasn't taught me anything. He hasn't taught me nothing about being a man or about being a father. But that's not true because he's taught me what a man isn't, and what a father shouldn't be.

The sentiment expressed in Keith's statement was typical of many of the teen fathers with nonresidential fathers. They felt that their fathers failed as adequate providers, nurturers, and as men, and they did not feel loved by them, nor did the teens love them in return. Most of the teens deliberately constructed fatherhood in opposition to what they experienced with their biological fathers. However, at the same time they enacted similar behavior. This contradiction appeared to be lost on the teens, and when acknowledged it was rationalized away.

Tevin believed that masculinity and manhood roles (including fatherhood) could be taught only by a male role model. Although his

104 VOICES OF AFRICAN-AMERICAN TEEN FATHERS

mother had taken on two jobs to raise him and his siblings after their stepfather left them, he did not believe that she could teach him to be a "man":

TEVIN: People don't understand, it's a challenge trying to be a man or a father without having a man or a father to show you how to do it. My mom worked hard to teach me everything I needed to know, but she couldn't teach me how to be a man.

Similar to some of the other adolescent fathers, Tevin believed that gender-specific expectations and practices needed to be modeled by a same-sex parent. Gender was very important to the fathers in constructing their sense of manhood and fatherhood. Although they vowed to refrain from becoming fathers similar to their own fathers, either consciously or unconsciously, they enacted similar behavior.

Again, for the most part, the teen fathers did not have father figures to demonstrate the practice of fathering. One of the factors that encourages the decision to accept a new identity is having models to demonstrate appropriate behavior for a particular identity (Billson 1996). When African-American adolescent fathers do not see what they perceive to be "appropriate" fatherhood behaviors demonstrated by their own fathers or significant others, then it is less likely that they will assume fatherhood responsibility. Although the young fathers in this study articulated a vision of fatherhood against the modeling they saw, they also demonstrated that they are not likely to enact it.

Although their biological fathers might not have been involved in their lives, some teen fathers had other male figures that were influential in their lives, such as grandfathers, uncles, family friends, etc. It is unclear as to how these men influenced the teen fathers' parental attitudes and behaviors.

Sometimes other father figures were not just grandfathers or uncles, but were also what I refer to as "serial dads" or "serial father figures." These multiple father figures (who were often the boyfriends of the teens' mothers) had varying effects on the youth, but for the most part contributed to a sense of instability and insecurity. If anything, it appeared that these serial father figures negatively impacted the teens' conceptualizations and enactment of fatherhood, quite similar to the way the young fathers' own nonresidential, uninvolved fathers did. Calvin (an independent father, using previous

Teen Fathers and Their Families of Origin 105

categorizations) discussed how he had always wanted an involved father in his life—someone who would spend time with him and "teach [him] what men are supposed to know." Nevertheless, what he desired most was "someone who would just stick around." The experience of having serial fathers is captured in his story:

CALVIN: The first dad I knew beat on my mom and he beat on us [the children], too. She divorced him about . . . about three months after they were married [they were living together prior to their marriage]. That was my real dad. The second dad I knew didn't stick around much. He could do everything though, like fix on cars, fix things, like stuff in the house. But we hardly ever saw him when he was living with us. Moms said he ran around on her. She wasn't married to him but we called him dad because he was cool with us and stayed for a while. For about two years.

INTERVIEWER: Why did you like him?

CALVIN: Because he was good and he brought us stuff we needed and did things with us. One time he took us to a concert, and to Kansas City to see the Chiefs play. Stuff like that. But then he just up and left without telling none of us good-bye. I don't know where he is or what he's doing now. The last we heard he was in Dallas somewhere. After that we didn't have no one around for a while. Then there was Joe for a bit. I liked him, too, but he had a family already, and he went back to them. Then Mom up and married this other man. We didn't like him. He was pretty mean. He always called Mom out of her name [he called her a derogatory name], and knocked her around a little. He didn't like us kids either, but he didn't touch us. She finally kicked him out.

INTERVIEWER: How long was your mother married to him?

CALVIN: About a year.

INTERVIEWER: How do you feel about not having a father right now in your life?

CALVIN: Well . . . I've gotten used to it. It's not a big deal. I guess it wasn't in the cards.

Although many of the teen fathers (namely those who had non-involved, nonresidential fathers) conceptualized fatherhood in opposition to what their own fathers did as parents, the enactment of these conceptualizations was not consistent, as previously stated. They seemed determined to be different from their own fathers, and reported that the abandonment by their own fathers increased their motivations to be involved with their children, either financially and/or emotionally. They wanted to provide for their children because they felt that their own fathers had neglected them, and they wanted to "be there" for their children because their fathers were "not there" for them. Furthermore, they wanted their children to feel loved by them, because they did not feel loved by their own fathers. When asked what they anticipated their future relationships to be with their children, they mentioned that they wanted their children to respect them and to feel as if they could depend on them as fathers because they did not have respect for or reliance on their own fathers.

Yet, in actuality, most of the parenting behaviors of these teens reflected what they experienced with their own fathers. They admitted to not being very involved in their children's lives as providers or as emotionally involved parents or nurturers. However, they explained that their actions or inactions resulted from their age. Some claimed they would become better parents later as adults. They believed that they were for the most part performing adequate father behaviors as adolescent parents, and that they were "being there" for their children as much as their adolescent status would allow. Their own fathers, however, "didn't have an excuse" for not being better parents in their opinions.

Some exceptions were found to the types of experiences previously described. Most of these teen fathers were raised in homes in which the biological adult father was present. As earlier stated, teen fathers who had adult residential fathers in their homes tended to have positive attitudes about their fathers (as did a few who had nonresidential fathers who stayed in contact with them). These young men did not construct fatherhood against what they experienced; instead, their construction of fatherhood reflected their experiences with their own fathers.

One of these examples was with fifteen-year-old Jarrod. Jarrod and his older sister Elise were removed from his mother's custody when he was eleven years old. His mother was a heroin addict and eventually became addicted to crack cocaine. When he lived with his mother, he and Elise were often left home alone with very little to eat. He discussed how his mother was so despondent or high at times that they would often stay home from school, watch television, and play for days at a time. As a result of excessive absences in school, Jarrod ended up repeating both first and third grades. After he and his sister were removed from his mother's custody, they stayed in a foster home for almost a month until his father moved them to Wichita with him. Elise is not the biological daughter of Jarrod's father, yet his father assumed care for her as well. Although missing his mother and worrying about her constantly (at the time of the interview Jarrod reported that his mother was living between his grandmother's house and "the streets"), he said that moving in with his father was the best thing that ever happened to him.

Although he was fifteen years old at the time of the interview, Jarrod was in the seventh grade and made average grades in school. He did not like school but had learned to deal with it. He believed his father provided a wonderful example of what a "good father" was supposed to be. Jarrod's primary conceptualization of fatherhood was described in provider-role terms, but it also consisted of being an involved, nurturing parent as discussed previously. As described in a previous chapter, Jarrod was not able to financially provide for his child (his own father worked as a store clerk and had limited means); however, Jarrod did attempt to see his child whenever he could. He discussed the impact his parents had on his own parenthood:

JARROD: I was always scared I was going to end up like my mom.

INTERVIEWER: What do you mean by that?

JARROD: End up being a drug addict, or something just as bad. And being someone who doesn't care about no one or nothing but himself. Like mom, she didn't care about us. She cared more about getting a "hit" than she cared about us. That was the thing I hated most: just feeling like she didn't love us or that nobody did. I soon got to the point where I didn't care either—about me, about school, about nothing.

INTERVIEWER: Was your father involved in your life then?

JARROD: No, my dad wasn't around then. I didn't really know him much before he took us to live with him. But I have to give it to my dad, when he did step in, he did it in a big way. He showed me and Elise that he didn't just care about us, he loved us. . . . I feel like he saved us.

108 VOICES OF AFRICAN-AMERICAN TEEN FATHERS

INTERVIEWER: How did he save you?

JARROD: He saved us from ending up like my mother, or just from ending up lost . . . lost to the streets. He saved us from being people we didn't want to become. I used to be scared that I would end up like my mom and become the kind of person or parent she is. But now I think about my dad and how I hope I can be half the dad to my son that he is to us.

In summary, most of the teen fathers did not bring up their fathers in the interviews unless I addressed the topic. However, when the teens discussed their fathers, their stories were compelling. If any individual was most influential on the teen fathers' experiences, it was probably their adult fathers. Teen fathers who had biological, residentially residing fathers in their homes tended to have positive experiences. Yet when nonresidential fathers were involved even minimally, there appeared to be a positive impact on the teens' notions and attitudes about fatherhood. When the adult fathers did not reside with the teen fathers, they were usually emotionally unavailable and economically nonsupportive. The adolescent fathers reported that they did not see their nonresidential fathers very often, and when they did see them their interactions were usually bereft of emotion and feelings of love. Economic support was not regular or substantive in the opinions of the teen fathers, and it was usually provided through informal means.

RELATIONSHIPS WITH THEIR MOTHERS

The mothers of the teen fathers mainly reacted to their sons fatherhood status in the following four ways:

1. Did not approve of their sons' paternity
2. Encouraged their sons to become responsible fathers
3. Became the primary source of economic support for their sons in providing for their grandchildren
4. Demonstrated both traditional masculine and feminine parenting attributes, and these parenting behaviors were significant to the young fathers because they influenced the teens' conceptual-

ization of motherhood, which in turn may have impacted their own fathering behaviors.

Almost all of the teen fathers had positive relationships with their mothers. Growing up as sons in single-parent, matriarchal households, the teen fathers' primary sources of support when providing for their children, and their primary confidants when dealing with parenting issues and concerns, were their mothers. Although the teen fathers generally reported feeling supported by their mothers, this was not always the case. When the mothers found out that their sons' partners were pregnant, this information was generally not well received. They did not like that their sons were about to become adolescent fathers, and thought it would bring additional hardship and challenges to their sons and to them. Yet after accepting their sons' imminent teen father status, the fathers reported that their mothers often provided the social and economic support they needed to provide for their children. For example, Paul, who lived with his mother and grandmother and is the father of eleven-month-old Brianna, discussed how his mother did not like the idea of him becoming a teen father, but later came to accept the idea of having a grandchild. Although Paul said that his mother could not financially provide any means of support to the mother of his child, she did see his daughter about twice a week.

INTERVIEWER: How does your mom feel about your daughter?

PAUL: She didn't like it. She thought I would just end up like her [his mother].

INTERVIEWER: What do you mean by that?

PAUL: Not working, you know. Just having another obstacle to overcome, you know. She didn't like it.

INTERVIEWER: How does she feel now?

PAUL: She's warmed up to the whole thing. I mean she loves Brianna. That's her baby now.

INTERVIEWER: Your daughter?

PAUL: Right.

INTERVIEWER: How often does she see your daughter?

PAUL: A couple times a week. Sometimes I bring Brianna by the house.

110 VOICES OF AFRICAN-AMERICAN TEEN FATHERS

Similarly, Carl, a seventeen-year-old twelfth grader and father of a four-month-old girl, spoke about his mother's negative reaction to hearing about the pregnancy of his girlfriend, Rachel:

CARL: She didn't flip out or anything, but the disappointment and concern was all over her face. I felt like curd after I had talked to her. I just hate I disappointed her. But she's adjusted to the idea now, and she knows things will work out. Plus she loves Robin, probably more than she does me *[laughs]*.

According to the teen fathers, their mothers' initial negative reactions were usually related to their limited economic resources. The mothers discussed with them the long-term consequences, including financial struggles and loss of freedom their young fatherhood would likely bring.

Even though the mothers may not have initially been receptive to their teen sons' paternity, most encouraged their sons to be responsible fathers and to take care of their children. According to the teen fathers, the mothers attempted to instill in them what they thought they should be and know as fathers, which was often the opposite of what their own fathers demonstrated. For example, James discussed:

JAMES: Mom has taught me that now since I'm a father I have to be responsible. I have to support my son and do what's right.
INTERVIEWER: What's right?
JAMES: I have to take care of Kenis. Provide for him. Spend time with him. Mom told me I can't be like my father and not handle my responsibilities. I have to be better than that.

James's own father was not presently involved in his life. His mother had a boyfriend that resided in their household. As previously stated, James provided very little economic support for his son, Kenis—approximately twenty to thirty dollars a month, and did not visit with his son very often (approximately once a week). His mother had stressed to him the importance of doing more, and she occasionally gave him money or gifts to provide for his child, including occasional money, diapers, and other supplies. James did not work and was still in high school.

Teen Fathers and Their Families of Origin 111

Likewise, Brandon's mother impressed upon him the importance of providing for his child. He stated:

BRANDON: She told me, "Don't you be no good-for-nothing-son-of-a-bitch like your dad, now. You better take care of your kids." I just laughed at her. I'm not going to have any more [children]. This is it.

The eighteen-year-old twelfth grader, Brandon, was categorized as an independent father because he deliberately chose not to assume a fatherhood role with his one-and-a-half-year-old son, Keeshawn, despite his own mother's encouragement. Virtually no economic or nurturing support was provided. Brandon's own father had not been a part of his life since he was five years old, and he refused to discuss his father in the interview, except to say that he could provide no comments, "because I don't know the man."

The mothers of the adolescent fathers usually provided some form of support for their sons' children. Their provisions ranged from giving an occasional gift (such as clothing or diapers) to providing money on a regular basis. Since their mothers made financial contributions to their grandchildren, the teen fathers were able to define themselves as providers, or at least to "enact" these roles via their mothers. For instance, Carl, who conceptualized fatherhood as being a good provider and "being there" for his child, stated this about being a father to his daughter, Robin:

CARL: I'm spending quality time with her. Plus, I may not provide money to her, but my mother does for me. So, even though the money and other things are not coming directly from me, they're still getting to her on my behalf. So, yes I think I'm meeting both obligations at this time.

The mother of seventeen-year-old Alinius made it possible for Alinius to enact his primary conceptualization of father as involved nurturer. Alinius had a three-month-old daughter and attempted to see her and spend time with her when possible. They had one family car, but his mother, who must use the car to go to work, drove him to visit his daughter as frequently as possible. Furthermore, Alinius's

112   VOICES OF AFRICAN-AMERICAN TEEN FATHERS

mother was his primary source of economic support for his child since he did not work. When asked about providing economic assistance, he stated:

ALINIUS: I thought about [working], but I don't have a car or anything, so I wouldn't be able to get to work, you know. I can't depend on my mom because she has to use her own car to get to work. And it's not like I can depend on someone else either, you know. . . . My mom has given me some money to give her [the mother of his child], but it ain't much. It's not like she makes a lot of money or anything.

Although fathers who are considered minors in the state of Kansas are not required to pay child support, and neither are their parents, the adult mothers of the fathers in this study usually provided some assistance. However, because of their low socioeconomic statuses, as with Alinius's mother, many were not in a position to provide very much. Even so, they remained their son's primary source of economic support (albeit little) in providing for their sons.

The teen fathers tended to speak of their mothers with love and reverence. This was especially interesting given the way they viewed the mothers of their children. Furthermore, their mothers were considered almost to be superwomen who assumed the traditional masculine and feminine parenting roles in raising them. Several fathers commented that their mothers were "my mother and my father" because their mothers were not only their nurturers but also their providers, and in many cases their friends. Again, the notion of provider was associated with the traditionally perceived masculine role of fathers, thus their mothers functioned as their "fathers" also.

Nineteen-year-old Keith discussed how important his mother was to him because of the sacrifices she made as a parent.

KEITH: She does everything, and all by herself. She works two jobs, raise four kids plus a niece, and she helps me out all she can with Todd. I mean as busy as she is, she still finds time to give me what I need.

INTERVIEWER: What types of things do you need from her?

KEITH: Her time. I just need her to talk to me and keep me on track.

INTERVIEWER: How does she help you take care of Todd?

KEITH: She helps me take care of him when I bring him home, and she gives Jackie money about once a month. Not much, but she gives her what she can. Plus, she's taught me how to change diapers, burp Todd, feed him—all that good stuff.

Similar to many of the fathers, Keith was able to talk to his mother about his concerns as a parent. In addition to being someone he could communicate with about his challenges, his mother was also his provider and nurturer. Seeing their mothers as superwomen—or as a "supermom" as one teen father referred to his mother—may *partially* explain why double standards exist in regard to what they perceived as their responsibilities as fathers versus their perceived responsibilities of the mothers of their children. The adult mothers may have influenced their sons' views of the roles of mothers (which included taking on the responsibilities of fathers) despite the opposite of what they were trying to teach their sons. Perhaps the young men unconsciously thought that if their own mothers (similar to many other women around them) could enact both provider and nurturing roles without significant assistance from the adult fathers, then they probably felt that the mothers of their own children should or could do the same. Subsequently, their behaviors as fathers took on auxiliary or supplementary functions, not very unlike their own fathers. These behaviors, as stated previously, were created by and/or reinforced by other factors (e.g., joblessness, racism, poverty) that will be discussed later in the book.

Similar to Keith, fourteen-year-old Malik described similar views about the responsibilities of mothers. When he was asked what made someone a good mother, he responded:

MALIK: The same thing like with a father. But a mother has to make sure the children are taken care of even if the dad isn't there for the child or if he can't help out. The mom has to make sure that's done if he doesn't, and if she doesn't do that, then she's a bad mother.

In Malik's opinion, mothers were expected to provide economic and nurturing support for their children. These responsibilities were primarily the mother's, and solely the mother's if the father was unable or unwilling to "help out," as he said. Malik discussed how his own mother had done this in the absence of his father. Although the father of a six-month-old son, Malik did not assume any responsibility for his daughter's care.

Seemingly, responsibilities for taking care of and providing for the children largely fell on the teen mothers and on the teen fathers' adult mothers. Either way, the responsibility became a woman's. The question becomes, what does this do for the teen fathers' conceptualization of fatherhood and to their parenting behaviors? In a sense, the fathers were unknowingly socialized by their mothers and biological fathers to assume parenting behaviors similar to their fathers. The teens' responsibility as fathers became to "help out" the mothers. Their definitions of fatherhood, although resembling the traditional notion of fatherhood as provider, become altered. This tendency toward modification and inconsistency in conceptualization and behavior were created and/or reinforced by the challenges and difficulties they experienced from their youth, growing up in poverty, and being black and male as will be discussed later in the book.

Atypical of most fathers in this study, Bill was employed and contributed substantial support for his fifteen-month-old son. Eighteen years old and in the twelfth grade, he worked part-time at a fast-food restaurant in order to provide economic assistance for his child, Justin. Sometimes he provided an entire check to the mother of his child, Heather, and he tried to see his child whenever he could. Even though he considered himself to be "friends" with the mother of his son, he thought she fell very short of his expectations as a mother. Although his conceptualization of father was provider, his conceptualization of mother was similar. First, he compared Heather to his own mother who had experienced many challenges and hardships in raising Bill and his two sisters. His mother had once been married to Bill's father, who left her for another woman. Shortly thereafter, because of the pain from his abandonment and the poverty she incurred because of it, she became extremely depressed and had a "nervous breakdown," Bill described. However, his mother eventually "pulled herself together," moved their family to Wichita, worked during the day as a clerk in a convenience store, and went to school at night to train to become a licensed practical nurse. Bill stated that he admired her for her strength to overcome her problems, to improve their financial circumstances, and to remain a good parent.

On the other hand, Bill felt that Heather, the eighteen-year-old mother of his child, was neglectful of their child because she did not spend what he considered enough time with Justin and did nothing to provide economic assistance. He felt that she acted heedlessly because she still liked to go out and have fun, as opposed to acting "responsibly." This neglectful behavior Bill perceived of Heather could have been related to the abandonment he felt from his father's desertion. Regardless, Bill considered himself to be a responsible parent and expected Heather to behave more similar to his mother (as a nurturer, provider, and a woman with high ambition and drive). He stated the following about Heather and being a good mother:

BILL: A good mother may not actually do her best by other people's standards, but she's someone that tries to do her best. She actually tries. That's why I don't think Heather is a good mother, because she's not trying to be a good mother. It's time for her to grow up. She's eighteen. She needs to get a job and try to stay home and take care of Justin.

Bill expected Heather to obtain employment and still "stay at home and take care of Justin."

The difference between Bill's enactment of the fatherhood role of involved nurturer and of other fathers was that Bill did more than just "help out." He provided significant financial support and spent time with his child. Perhaps Bill's parents played a part in his conceptualization and enactment of fatherhood. Bill's mother was a stay-at-home mother and his father was the breadwinner before deserting their family. Bill's mother ended up performing, as did many single mothers, the roles of provider and nurturer. Maybe Bill's conceptualization of motherhood would have solely been that of a nurturer or homemaker had his father and mother not divorced. His conceptualization of motherhood may have shifted to the "superwoman" notion after his mother "pulled herself up" and enacted traditionally perceived masculine and feminine parenting behaviors—which incidentally he expected Heather to demonstrate or to attempt to do as well. His own fathering behavior and conceptualization of fatherhood may have been different from many of the other fathers in the study because he was raised by a father who enacted the provider status in their family at one time.

In summary, the mothers of the teen fathers were influential in these teens' lives, and partially set the foundations for what their parenting behaviors became. First, the mothers enabled their sons to enact fathering behaviors by providing the economic support needed for the young men to "provide" for their children. Although they did not approve of their sons' teen parent status, they were supportive in general and encouraged their sons to be "good fathers," according to the young men. Still, even though most fathers wanted to be good fathers and expressed intentions of becoming so, their behaviors were not consistent with their conceptualizations of fatherhood. So, despite their mothers' encouragement, they provided very little for their children on their own and visited them infrequently. Because the teens talked so admirably about how their mothers provided for them and raised them as single mothers, they may have expected similar behaviors from the young mothers of their own children. Therefore, through necessity on the adult mothers' part to enact nurturing and providership roles, the mothers modeled behavior that the young fathers probably expected from the mothers of their children. Furthermore, the lack of involvement from the teens' biological fathers helped create and maintain this socialization process. As a result of these and several other factors that will be addressed later in the book, the teens' conceptualization of fatherhood deviated from the traditional ideas of fatherhood (breadwinner/provider), and adapted a modified version in which provision of economic and nurturing support were perceived as supplementary parenting that "helped" the mothers.

Chapter 6

Teen Fathers and the Mothers of Their Children

Little is known about the relationships between African-American teen fathers and mothers. Among the few previous studies, Hendricks and Montgomery (1983) and Dallas and Chen (1998) found that African-American teen fathers described the mothers of their children in loving terms, viewed their relationships as positive, and expected to maintain these relationships. Contrary to their findings, in the present study, the teen fathers expressed a range of attitudes **about** the mothers of their children. This chapter will examine the fathers' views of these relationships and how they impacted their fatherhood experiences.

The relationships adolescent fathers had with the mothers influenced their fatherhood experiences and behaviors. Following Hamer (2001) and her categorizations of African-American adult "live away" fathers, I was able to code the teen fathers' descriptions of their current relationships with their children's mothers. Teen fathers described various relationships with the mothers of their children. For example, some of the young fathers expressed feelings of love toward the mothers, whereas others indicated strong dislike or resentment. Most of the teen fathers considered the mothers of their children to be friends and did not have romantic, loving relationships with them. Moreover, some relationships deteriorated after the birth of the children, whereas others improved. Three categories emerged from the data that described the quality of these relationships: friendly and amicable, romantic and loving, and hostile and distant.

Voices of African-American Teen Fathers
© 2006 by The Haworth Press, Inc. All rights reserved.
doi:10.1300/5477_07

VOICES OF AFRICAN-AMERICAN TEEN FATHERS

AMICABLE ASSOCIATIONS

"She's Just a Friend"

African-American teen fathers talked about their relationships with the mothers of their children in very specific terms. They were very certain and specific about the types of relationships that existed. The type described most often by the adolescent fathers (n = 17 or 52 percent) was friendship. This was the case within the fourteen- to fifteen-year-old age group (n = 4 out of 8 relationships), and within the eighteen- to nineteen-year-old age group (n = 7 out of 11). In the sixteen- to seventeen-year-old age group, relationships reported as positive and friendly (n = 6 out of 14) were equal to the number of relationships reported as romantic and loving (n = 6) (see Table 6.1).

Fathers who depicted the mothers of their children as "just friends" were adamant that their relationships were not romantic or "serious." In fact, I was corrected a couple of times when inaccurately referring to the mother of a child as a "girlfriend." Friendship was distinguished from relationships that were romantic and loving (which, to the fathers, also implied a level of commitment). Usually when the mother was viewed as a friend, the child was conceived under circumstances in which the mother and father had casual sex but did not consider themselves "in a relationship." Yet sometimes the term "friends" seemed loosely used by fathers who also used it to describe relationships that were based primarily on sex. Fathers in this cate-

TABLE 6.1. Relationships with the mothers of their children.

Fathers	Friendly	Romantic and loving	Negative and antagonistic
14-15 years old	4	1	3
16-17 years old	6	6	2
18-19 years old	7	2	2
	N = 17	N = 9	N = 7
Totals	(52 percent)	(27 percent)	(21 percent)

gory described their relationships with the mothers of their children by using such phrases as "we're just friends," "we were just kicking it," and "we were just hanging out and messing around." They perceived this "friendship" to be mutually understood.

Alinius was a seventeen-year-old father of a three-month-old daughter, Starr, who described the nature of his relationship with his daughter's mother, Crystal, as one of friendship. At one time, Alinius had doubts about his child's paternity. Although he initially felt nervous and financially unprepared to be a father (because he felt he was too young to be a father and could not support a child), he was relieved and happy when the blood test confirmed his paternity and erased his doubts about being Starr's father. Alinius and Crystal were no longer having sex or "seeing each other" intimately at the time he was interviewed. However, Alinius maintained that they were still friends and that he cared about Crystal as the mother of his child.

What is significant about these types of relationships was that most of the fathers liked and cared about the mothers of their children. For instance, even though little commitment existed in the relationships, they used such terms as "We get along real good," "We're just friends," "I care about her," or "I do like her." As the interview with Alinius indicated, the friendships between the parents often continued after the children were born. The children were usually conceived and born in relationships that were positive and friendly.

Generally, the teen fathers who thought about the mothers as friends did not believe that they would eventually marry the mothers of their children. On a practical level, they felt that they would always be involved with the mothers because of the children. Although they did not plan to become "seriously involved" with the mothers, some suspected that the mothers desired romantic and loving relationships. They believed the young mothers had problems distinguishing their fatherhood roles from their relationships with them as partners. The mothers wanted them to expand these two roles simultaneously not only by enacting fatherhood roles but also by becoming romantically involved with them, they thought. This emotional struggle is seen with nineteen-year-old Jermaine. He is the father of two children by two different women and has a friendly relationship with one of the mothers of his children. Still, he believed that she desired a romantic, loving relationship with him—which probably should not have been a surprise to Jermaine since he still had sex with her:

JERMAINE: Raeshawnda is real cool. She's good people. But I don't want a relationship with her.

INTERVIEWER: But you're still having sex with her, right?

JERMAINE: Right, but I don't want to get serious with her. She does though, and it gets to me sometimes. Because I want to stay cool with her, and I don't want any problems. Yes, we're parents to Cornell, but we're not married or anything. She seems to think that because we have a baby together that we should be together. But that's not how it is.

Jermaine felt that his relationship with Raeshawnda was in jeopardy because of her desires to become romantically involved. Similar to some of the fathers, he felt uneasy about this expectation. Jermaine seemed to easily separate his sexual relationship with Raeshawnda from an emotionally intimate one. He was unconcerned about how continuing to have sex with her probably encouraged her expectation of a romantic, loving relationship.

Regardless of some of the mothers' expectations for romantic, loving relationship, the fathers did not believe that the young mothers were confused about the status of their involvement, which were friendly and casual. Alinius's remark, that Crystal had "never expected more out of our relationship—not to my knowledge anyway," indicated he believed they were on the same page with the state of their involvement. This unspoken agreement between them may have helped them be friends.

Sixteen-year-old Mark, who was in the tenth grade at the time of the interview and father to four-month-old Marquise, discussed the relationship with the mother of his child. According to Mark, his relationship with Sherry deteriorated during her pregnancy, but to his surprise improved after childbirth. He stated that he and Sherry were now friends. However, because of his paternity, Mark felt that Sherry wanted more out of their relationship, but he preferred to maintain it as casual. The following excerpt illustrates as well how distinct and categorical the teen fathers perceived their relationships with their children from that with the mothers of their children.

MARK: I thought I was going to have all kinds of pressure on me from Sherry. I thought she was going to be hassling me. When she was

Teen Fathers and the Mothers of Their Children 121

pregnant, she did though. And so I dreaded the baby coming. I just didn't want to deal with her and that kind of stuff.

INTERVIEWER: Are things different now?

MARK: Yeah, they're different. She doesn't hassle me much anymore and things have calmed down.

INTERVIEWER: What kinds of things did she do to hassle you?

MARK: She called me all the time. I mean all the time. She was getting on my nerves. Then she always wanted me to come over and see her and stuff. I mean I know she was about to have my baby but we didn't have a real relationship or anything, and as far as I was concerned, we weren't about to start one just because of the baby. . . .

In general, the fathers did not consider themselves as "being in a relationship" because of the children. They separated their relationships with their children from their relationships with the mothers.

What was problematic with fathers who thought about the mothers of their children as friends was how the term *friends* was used. Sometimes fathers used this term to describe relationships that seemed based on sex. In some cases, an underlying animosity appeared to exist on the father's part, even though the fathers maintained they were "friends" with the mothers. For instance, these "friendships" were sometimes rocky and laden with problems and concerns, but they were not defined as hostile and distant by the fathers. Some were marked by emotional intimacy and sex while still bearing resemblances of hostility and resentment. In short, many of these relationships were complicated.

For example, Darrius, a seventeen-year-old father of a two-year old son, Alex, admitted that although he did not love the mother of his child, Kelly, and did not consider her his girlfriend, he insisted that he still cared about her because she was the mother of his child. Even though he used derogatory terms ("bitch" and "ho") in referring to Kelly in the interview, he still had sex with her after the birth of their child. Their "friendship" seemed to be based on his abilities to put his resentment aside for the sake of sex. His disdain and sexual use of her was apparent:

INTERVIEWER: So, you're still having sex with her?

DARRIUS: You know it.

VOICES OF AFRICAN-AMERICAN TEEN FATHERS

INTERVIEWER: Do you consider her your girlfriend? You referred to her as your "girl" and "your baby's mama."

DARRIUS: Nope. She's not my girlfriend but she's my bitch.

INTERVIEWER: What do you mean by that?

DARRIUS: She's my ho . . .

Darrius went on to discuss how he usually had sexual intercourse with her whenever he saw her, which was usually once a week when he went to visit his son. I was unable to discern whether the primary purpose for these visits was to see his son or to have sex with the mother. His visits were usually brief (an hour or so) and depended on "Whether his [referencing the child] mom feels like an ass or not," referring to how argumentative and difficult she was at times. His child support provisions were irregular and depended on how much he made selling drugs. Moreover, Darrius believed that Kelly and other mothers similar to her were responsible for protecting themselves from pregnancy. While accepting no responsibility for further pregnancies, he called Kelly "hardheaded" for still refusing to use birth control since giving birth to their son. Another factor that complicated their relationship was his belief that she was an unfit mother.

INTERVIEWER: How is she taking care of Alex?

DARRIUS: Not good. Her mom does all the work and buys him whatever he needs. She ain't doing nothing but the same thing she was before she got pregnant. Ain't nothing stopping her.

INTERVIEWER: What kinds of things was she doing before?

DARRIUS: Running the streets. [Having sex with] me whenever she got a chance. Going out with her girls. Just getting up and doing as she pleased. I mean, you wouldn't even know she had a baby.

Double standards associated with parenthood emerged during the interview with Darrius. Although it was acceptable for him to hang out with his friends, go out to a club, and even sell drugs for money, he felt it was unacceptable for Kelly to go out with her friends since she was a now a mother. Likewise, while he used negative language to describe her sexually, the same did not apply to his sexuality.

How did relationships that were considered friendly and amicable affect fatherhood experiences? Unlike the next two relationship types

Teen Fathers and the Mothers of Their Children 123

that will be discussed, relationships in which the fathers described the mothers of their children as friends did not seem to influence their fathering behaviors. No significant patterns were noted. Fatherhood involvement was quite varied in this group. Many provided some form of support for their children, although the amounts were inconsistent, very little, and usually provided through economic assistance from their own parents. Some provided nothing, but this might have been affected by their conceptualization of father (i.e., independent). Sometimes their noninvolvement had to do with other factors, for instance, not being able to work, not having parents who were financially able to assist, or not having transportation. As previously stated, relationships in this category were amicable. Most saw their children about twice a week, yet they indicated that they were allowed to see their children whenever they wanted under most circumstances.

Two major concerns were expressed by fathers in this group—fear of being replaced by another male parent figure and fear of being forced to pay child support. Because of the unromantic and/or nonintimate nature of the relationships with the mothers of their children, these fathers expressed concerns about being replaced by another male parent figure. Unlike fathers who had more "serious," committed relationships with the young mothers, many in this group feared their father-figure role would be taken over or interfered with by a boyfriend or potential husband of the mother. In one of the first interviews I conducted, a sixteen-year-old father, Clayton, described this fear. His concern was echoed by many of the teen fathers.

INTERVIEWER: Has she dated anyone since having the baby?

CLAYTON: Not that I know of. No. I would say not, because she would make sure I know if she did. But she probably will one day.

INTERVIEWER: How does that make you feel?

CLAYTON: I know I'm not going to like it, because it'll mean my daughter being around somebody I don't know. I don't want her trying to call somebody else her dad. So that's on my mind a lot, and I think Quendasha will try to use that against me because I don't want to get serious with her. I don't know how somebody is going to treat my baby. So I think about all that sometimes.

INTERVIEWER: Are there other concerns you have about your daughter, or about being a parent?

CLAYTON: Well not really. I think that's my main concern. I know that Quendasha's mom and her grandmother is treating her [his daughter] right. I'm just worried about somebody else stepping in.

Similar to several other fathers, Clayton indicated possessiveness for his role as father, even though he did not do much to enact this role. The role of father was theirs to fulfill (if it was to be fulfilled)—not another man's.

Another major concern discussed by fathers who defined their relationships as friendships was the fear of paying child support. Most of the fathers indicated desire and willingness to provide future child support for their children; however, they feared demands to pay such. They did not want the mothers of their children or "the system" to force them to provide economic support. Interestingly, almost all of the fathers indicated that the mothers had not requested economic assistance from them. When further probed about the issue, it appeared that the requests the mothers made were for the fathers to spend more time with them and/or with their children. They did not ask for financial assistance. Nonetheless, these requests supported the fathers' suspicions that the mothers were trying to turn their relationships into romantic, loving ones.

Seventeen-year-old James, who had a friendly relationship with his child's mother, expressed his concern about paying formal child support. Although he was not employed at the time of the interview and was still in school, he discussed how he intended to work and provide for his child:

JAMES: I don't mind paying child support, but I don't want to be hassled about it. I'm not a child. I'm a grown man. If I want to make [formal] child support payments when I get a job, that should be my choice. If I want to give it [child support] on my own, that should be my choice.

The resistance to pay formal child support may be a perceived as an attack on their manhood or masculinity—James stated, "I'm a grown man." Most of the fathers conceptualized fathers as providers, and planned to become such in the future. However, being "made" or forced to provide instead of doing so on their own volition could have been seen as an attack on their manhood or role of authority. Providing for their children or participating in their welfare was viewed as a responsibility. However, the method (formal child support) was seen as a choice. Keith also expressed similar views to James's:

KEITH: Women got to realize that if they want their men to stick around and be in their kids' lives, then they shouldn't make them pay child support. Most of them [the fathers] are going to do it [pay informal child support] on their own anyway. But we don't like being made to do it.

Keith implied an association between being required to provide formal child support and involvement with children. Although the author did not find such a connection expressed by other fathers in the interviews and failed to ask about it in the interviews, Keith's views were similar to James's and others in that formal child support was met with resentment.

In summary, the majority of fathers in this study described their relationships with the mothers as friendly and positive. Although they liked the young women and cared about them as the mothers of their children, they did not want to build romantic and loving relationships with them. Many suspected such intent on the part of the mothers. This suspicion did not, however, seem to impact on their relationships negatively. Furthermore, the relationships with mothers described as "friends" did not seem to affect the young men's conceptualization or enactment of fatherhood. What distinguished the fatherhood experiences of fathers in these relationships from that of others was the concern about their fatherhood role (whether provider or involved emotional nurturer) being interfered with or being replaced by another male figure. This was their role to fulfill, and they feared it being performed by another. They also had concerns about being forced to pay formal child support; however, this concern was not specific to this group. Providing economic and/or emotional support was perceived as a responsibility, although how they enacted it was viewed as a choice. The idea of being forced to provide child support was met with resentment, even though none of the young mothers described as friends in this grouping had demanded or threatened such from them. The mothers' requests were namely that the fathers spend more time with them and/or with their children.

LOVING, INTIMATE AFFAIRS

"She's My Girlfriend"

The teen fathers in this study were very specific in defining their relationships with the mothers of their children. When they considered the mothers as girlfriends, they made this very clear. Fathers ($n = 9$, or 27 percent) who referred to the mothers of their children as girlfriends, or used other similar terms, described their relationships as romantic and loving. This was the second largest category for fathers overall. However, differences occurred by age. For instance, only one of the eight youngest fathers (a fifteen-year-old) considered himself to be in a romantic, loving relationship. The others either had relationships in which they considered the mothers to be friends ($n = 4$), or relationships in which they had negative, antagonistic ($n = 3$) feelings for the mothers, as indicated in Table 6.1. Sixteen- and seventeen-year-olds (6 out of 9) were far more likely to consider their relationships as romantic. These fathers described the mothers in positive terms, believed that the mothers cared about their children, and thought that the mothers were doing their best as teen parents. They used such phrases as "she's my girl," "she's my girlfriend," and "she's my boo" (a commonly used slang word of affection). Their relationships were established prior to the birth of their children and continued afterward. Thus, children born to teen parents with this type of relationship were usually conceived and born in loving relationships.

The impact these relationships had on their fatherhood behavior and experiences was positive. Fathers were more likely to provide more emotional and economic support for their children than were fathers who did not have romantic/loving relationships with their children's mothers. The relationship between the fathers and mothers was connected to the level of involvement with the children. For instance, fathers who had romantic, loving relationships with the mothers of their children were more likely to make financial provisions for their children than were fathers who described the mothers as friends. Five of the nine fathers who had romantic, loving relationships with the mothers also had jobs, which helped them provide for their children. They also considered themselves performing in emotionally involved and nurturing roles as fathers to their children, and reported spending more time with their children than did teen fathers who did not have these relationships with their children's mothers. Spending what they considered significant time with their children was probably a by-product of the substantial time spent with mothers they labeled as "girlfriends." Mere association with mothers with whom they were intimately involved meant they were more likely to spend more time with their children.

Unlike most of teen fathers, when seventeen-year-old Craig was asked to discuss something about himself, the first identity he mentioned was being a father. Craig worked part-time at a factory and planned to join the military when he completed high school the following year. His girlfriend, Deborah, was one grade behind him, and they had been a "couple" since he was in eighth grade. They planned to marry when she graduated from high school. By then all of his military training would be completed and she and their daughter, two-year-old Joy, would be able to join him. Craig was asked about his relationship with Deborah, and he discussed how he has spent more time with her since Joy was born. He explained that he went from seeing Deborah about twice as week to seeing her and the child almost every day of the week. Had the quality of the relationship between Craig and Deborah been different, it is unlikely that he would be seeing Deborah and the child almost every day. He enjoyed spending time with them, and he felt that it was normal to see them on a daily basis since he now had a "family." Therefore, the close, intimate nature of his relationship with the mother of his child influenced the amount of interaction with his child.

Dwayne, a nineteen year-old father of a two-year-old daughter and an eight-month-old son by two different young women, discussed how these relationships held different expectations and required different fathering behaviors on his part. Dwayne spent equal amounts of time with both of his children on the weekends (he would pick them up on Friday evenings and return them that Sunday morning or afternoon to their mothers). Although he was a college student at the time of the study, he discussed how he had the same visitation schedule when he was in high school. Dwayne's only independent source of income was from the army reserve. He paid his son's medical expenses and provided what economic support and assistance he could to his son's mother, Wendy, whom he eventually planned to marry. Dwayne had been involved with Wendy for two years prior to the birth of their eight-month-old son. Although the pregnancy was not planned, he explained that they did not mind if she "accidentally" became pregnant.

On the other hand, Dwayne said he did not provide much economic support for his daughter, his other child, because he did not have a close relationship with her mother, Teresa. Since they did not have an intimate relationship, Dwayne said that Teresa assumed the majority of their daughter's expenses. He was uncertain whether she would ask for child support in the future, however. To illustrate how casual their relationship was, he discussed how he did not find out that he was a father of her child until one month after his daughter's birth. Although Teresa, the mother, "did not shoot straight" about his paternity, Dwayne said that he and his parents promptly "took on the responsibility." His parents were supportive and provided some monetary support, and their involvement was mostly in the form of spending time with their grandchild. Likewise, Dwayne did the same.

Dwayne's fathering behaviors reflected the different relationships he had with his children's mothers. Although he felt an obligation to provide financial support to the mother of his son since he was in a long-term, romantic and loving relationship with her, Dwayne did not feel the same obligation for his daughter. Similar to the general population, the fathers' responsibility for their children was dependent on their relationships with the mothers; they are more likely to be involved with children when they are on good terms with the mothers (Hamer 2001).

Moreover, Dwayne did not define the relationship he had with Teresa and their daughter as "family," whereas with Wendy he did. The word "family" emerged frequently in conversations (brought up by the fathers in all instances) by fathers who described the relationships with the mothers of their children as romantic and loving. Their concept of family was not restricted to the traditional family in which the mother and father were married, but rather to the nature of the relationship itself. For instance, Steve, a seventeen-year-old eleventh grader and father of an eleven-month-old daughter, Shanelle, described the relationship with his girlfriend and daughter as family.

INTERVIEWER: What do you like most about being a dad?

STEVE: I like having my own family, even if it came earlier than I wanted. But that's okay. I'm making it through.

INTERVIEWER: So you look at you and your girlfriend and your baby as a family?

STEVE: Yes. We are a family.

For Steve, having a girlfriend and a child meant having a family, even though he was not married to the mother of his child. This modified traditional notion of family was further illustrated by his attempts to be a provider. He worked part-time at a dry cleaner's in order to assist his daughter's mother, Monique. He stated:

STEVE: Yep that was the whole point of getting a job. I give her what I can, minus gas money and sometimes lunch. It's not a whole lot, but I'm trying.

The concept of family for teen fathers meant having romantic, loving relationships with the mothers of their children. The relationships with the mothers went beyond just "being friends." It is the union (romantic and loving) with the mother, plus their child, that equals a family. Teen fathers who described the relationships with the mothers of their children as romantic and loving also viewed the mothers of their children as "working partners" in caring for their children for the most part. They did not feel that the mothers were "out to get" them, or would "put child support" on them. Rather, they believed that the young mothers appreciated what they were able to provide, and that the young mothers cared about their well-being as fathers and as partners. On the contrary, fathers who did not have romantically involved relationships with the mothers did not describe their trio (father, the child, and the mother of the child) as a family.

In summary, the relationship with mothers described as girlfriends or in similar terms had a positive impact on the fathers' experiences. For instance, those who conceptualized fathers as providers were more likely to work or make financial provisions for their children if they had romantic, loving relationships with the mothers. If fatherhood was conceptualized as involved nurturers, then the fathers were more likely to spend more time with their children. Overall, their behaviors tended to be more consistent with their conceptualizations of fatherhood than were fathers who had mere "friendships" with the mothers of their children. The fathers in loving relationships with their child's mother also tended to conceptualize their relationships

130 VOICES OF AFRICAN-AMERICAN TEEN FATHERS

with the mothers and their children as family. This term was not used by fathers who had other types of relationships.

ANTAGONISTIC RELATIONSHIPS

"She's a Pain"

Seven (21 percent) of the African-American adolescent fathers described negative, unfriendly relationships with the mothers of their children. Out of the seven fathers who categorized their relationships as such, three were in the youngest age group, and two in each of the others. Furthermore, out of the seven fathers who had negative, hostile relationships with the mothers, five of them conceptualized fatherhood primarily as independent fathers—perceiving no obligated responsibility for being involved with their children's lives unless it was something they wanted to do. These unfriendly relationships usually developed under "sexually casual" conditions, but became more negative and tumultuous after the pregnancies or births of the children. Hostility, resentment, and animosity were common feelings expressed by the fathers in this group. They used such phrases as "I can't stand her," "I hate her," "She's a pain," "She gets on my nerves," and "I wish I had never met her." Their fatherhood experiences were negative, and their fathering behaviors were practically nonexistent and appeared to be linked to the negative feelings they had for the mothers. From their perspectives, their antagonistic feelings were based on fear of paying future, legally enforced child support; belief that the teen mothers "trapped" them by getting pregnant on purpose; and belief that the young women were not good mothers.

As previously discussed, one of the main concerns of fathers who had friendly relationships with their children's mothers was that the mothers would eventually demand formal child support. The same was true for fathers who had negative relationships with the mothers of their children. These fathers were likely to feel "trapped." For instance, Eric, a sixteen-year-old promising football player and father of four-month-old Daniel, had family members who supported his views. Eric did not have a good relationship with sixteen-year-old April, who he believed got pregnant intentionally. Her reasons for doing so were twofold in his view—to become his "girlfriend," and to benefit from his future money and fame. Eric's mother and grandmother were also suspicious and supported his beliefs. Consequently, Eric did not provide any economic support for his son, and said he spent just ten to fifteen minutes a week with him by "dropping by for a quick minute."

He considered the greatest challenge of being a father dealing with April, whom he referred to as a "vulture" because she was "after his money." On the contrary, he admitted that April had never asked him for money. However, because he envisioned himself playing professional football after college (he stated that he was very good in football and had already been contacted by potential college recruiters while being only in the tenth grade), he believed that April got pregnant to ensure that she would be part of his future wealth and fame. Eric's mother and grandmother supported his views, and similar to Eric, were not involved in Daniel's life as a result. When asked what was the best thing about being a father, Eric stated that the only benefit was that his last name was given to his son.

Eric's case illustrated how the relationship with and feelings toward the mother of the child affect the teen father's parenting behaviors. Teen fathers who perceived the mothers of their children as adversaries believed the mothers had high expectations of them providing economic and emotional support for their children. According to them, the mothers wanted or would eventually demand that they spend more time with their children and/or "help out" as providers. Subsequently, perceptions of the mothers tended to become more negative over the course of the relationship. Still, although the fathers were concerned about providing legally enforced child support, according to the teen fathers, nearly all of the young mothers had not yet asked the teen fathers for financial support or assistance. Only two of the children's mothers had actually threatened the young men with child-support requests. The majority of the children's mothers were being supported by their families and/or by public assistance.

According to the laws of the state of Kansas, minors cannot be sued for child support, and child support payments can not be collected from the minors' parents or guardians. Young mothers are unable to file for child support under state laws if the fathers of their children are younger than eighteen years of age. Therefore, it is possible that some young mothers did not request the teen fathers to provide financial support because they could not legally place any demands

132 *VOICES OF AFRICAN-AMERICAN TEEN FATHERS*

on them until the fathers reached the age of eighteen. Once the father of the child turned eighteen, however, the mother is required to sue for child support if she has applied for public assistance. That claim would include retroactive payments, dating from the time of the child's birth, even if the father was a minor at the time of birth. Therefore, the young fathers in this study believed their concerns about being sued for child support when they "turn legal" were justified in their view because many of the mothers were receiving public assistance at the time of the study.

Jermaine, a nineteen-year-old father of two children, Nicholas (seven months old) and Cornell (two years old), used the strategy of maintaining a relationship with one of the mothers of his children under false pretenses in order keep her from filing for child support. Being of legal age, he felt particularly vulnerable to this possibility. Although he said he did not like this particular mother and had negative feelings towards her, he felt it necessary to pretend the opposite. Thus, his description of this relationship fell into a gray area because on one hand he described the mother of the child in negative terms and felt animosity toward her, his outward behaviors and external relationship with her were portrayed as positive or neutral.

INTERVIEWER: Is it difficult seeing them both [the children] because they live in different households?

JERMAINE: Not really, because both of the mothers try to stay close to me, so I end up seeing the kids in the process.

INTERVIEWER: What do you mean when you say they try to stay close to you?

JERMAINE: They want to maintain a relationship with me. They want to keep something going on with me.

INTERVIEWER: Do you see both of them in that way?

JERMAINE: With Raeshawnda, Cornell's mom, I do, but not with Melinda. I may lead her on a little just to keep her acting right so she don't cause no problems, but I don't see her like that.

INTERVIEWER: What do you mean to keep her acting right?

JERMAINE: Just to keep her in line. To keep her from doing something foolish, like not letting me see Nicholas. Or you know, I've always giving her money for Nicholas and for herself, but she might try to take me to court if I don't keep her satisfied you know.

I mean, I don't sleep with her, well, not since I've become serious with Raeshawnda. But you never know what a woman might do, you know. So I just try to lead her on so she don't do something stupid.

The passage above revealed Jermaine's mistrust of women ("but you never know what a woman might do"). It was also significant that he has manipulated this young woman to keep from paying child support. Interestingly, even though Jermaine did not personally like the mother of his two-year-old son (and in fact "used" her), he still provided some economic assistance to and spent some time with his child. Although antagonistic relationships were likely to negatively affect their fathering behavior (e.g., spending less time with their children than other fathers, providing less financial support than other fathers), it was a matter of degree. Most teen fathers provided some (albeit very little) economic and emotional support for their children regardless of their relationships with the mothers of their children.

As earlier stated, some fathers felt that the mothers had children in attempts to develop a relationship between them, and they resented the girls for this because of the consequences it had for them—the possibility of future forced child support payments, more responsibilities, and loss of freedom. They had negative feelings toward the young mothers because they felt they were "trapped." To them "being trapped" meant not only that they might one day be forced to pay child support against their will, as previously discussed, but also that a deliberate attempt was made on the young women's part to sustain a relationship with them by intentionally becoming pregnant. One father stated that he believed teenage girls in general think that having babies will make the fathers love them or make them "stick around."

For instance, eighteen-year-old Brandon felt that the mother of his child, Tisha, threatened him with child support to get revenge when he failed to become more romantically involved with her after the pregnancy. Brandon was in the twelfth grade and had no job. Similar to many of the fathers who had hostile, negative relationships with the mothers of their children, Brandon was also an independent father. He provided no support and saw very little of his son. Brandon had dated Tisha for approximately six months before she became pregnant, and during that time, he stated, she fell in love and wanted him

134 VOICES OF AFRICAN-AMERICAN TEEN FATHERS

to date her exclusively. He never committed to doing this, but during the course of their relationship she became pregnant while supposedly taking birth control pills. Although he admitted that he did not wear a condom (thus being responsible himself), he believed that she got pregnant intentionally. After accusing her of this, their relationship deteriorated and became even more hostile after the birth of Keeshawn, who was one and a half years old at the time of the interview. Brandon stated that Tisha had threatened to file for child support and had not allowed him to see his son. He believed her threat was a result of his refusal to commit to a monogamous relationship. He mentioned:

BRANDON: I've gotten to the point where I don't care nothing about her [Tisha]. I can't stand her. She's trying to pay me back because I won't go with her [commit to her in a relationship]. So she's making it her mission to make my life miserable.

The impact that these negative relationships had on the parenting experiences of these fathers was more negative and pronounced than the impact of other types of relationships. These fathers tended to have less contact with their children. Perhaps because the fathers did not want to be around the mothers, they ended up spending less time with their children. In comparison to other fathers, they also provided less economic assistance. Sometimes their resentment and animosity toward the mothers justified what they admitted to be inadequate economic and emotional support. Antagonistic relationships between the teen parents negatively influenced fathering behaviors because the fathers spent less time and provided less economic support than teen fathers who had positive relationships with the mothers.

Finally, some fathers claimed to feel dislike toward the teen mothers because they considered them "bad" parents. When these young fathers described what a "good" mother was, they usually did so by describing what a good mother was not—using the mothers of their children as examples. It was unclear when these negative opinions of the mothers of their children developed. As noted previously, Calvin, a sixteen-year-old father of an eight-month-old daughter, Denae, discussed at length why he abhorred Bianca, the eighteen-year-old mother of his child. In addition to believing that Bianca "wanted a child to love" at his expense, he also believed that she was an unfit mother. According to him, she "stays in the streets" by going out to clubs and "partying with her friends." He stated that their daughter was mainly being raised by Bianca's elderly grandmother. As far as his own parenting behavior, Calvin spent an average of one hour per week with his daughter and provided no financial support. Yet, as stated in a previous chapter, he did not feel compelled to do more because "it was her fault she got pregnant." Furthermore, because of his youth and Bianca's adult status as an eighteen-year-old, he did not feel it was necessary to assume a father role. It was difficult to determine whether Calvin developed his beliefs of Bianca's "unfit" parenting independent of his resentfulness toward her for getting pregnant. Either way, he had double standards about what he could do as a father and what he expected her to do as a mother.

Fifteen-year-old Jeremy also believed the mother of his child, Crystal, was an unfit parent. She was two years older than Jeremy, and their daughter was eleven months old. When I asked Jeremy about her parenting behavior, he observed:

JEREMY: She could be a better mother. She gets welfare [public assistance], I think, and then she just don't do nothing. She doesn't work. She doesn't go to school. All she does is smoke weed. All she wants to do is chill. She's not setting a good example for Jasmine [their daughter]. I don't think she's a good mother, but maybe she'll change. But until then, we're not going to get along.

Jeremy's behavior contradicted his expectations for the mother of his child. For instance, Jeremy expected her to work and to do something more than do drugs ("smoke weed") and hang out or "chill." However, his own behavior was very similar. In fact, I categorized Jeremy as an independent father. Nonetheless, he wanted their daughter cared for, expected Jasmine's mother to assume all responsibility for their child, and resented her for not acting accordingly ("until then, we're not going to get along"). Perhaps he felt that if his daughter was being better parented, he would have felt less guilt for not being a more responsible father himself. The next chapter captures this implication.

In summary, fathers who had antagonistic relationships with the mothers of their children suspected that the mothers would eventually require legally enforced child support. Unlike fathers who described their relationships as friendships, this concern had a negative impact on these relationships and caused further resentment. Furthermore, some fathers also suspected that the mothers had "trapped them" by getting pregnant in order to maintain a relationship with them. This suspicion created great resentment, and some fathers distanced themselves from both the children and the mothers. Finally, the fathers in this category tended to have negative views about the mothers of their children, perceiving them as bad or unfit parents. These relationships seemed to have a negative influence on their parenting behaviors, too. For instance, the fathers were less involved with their children as providers and as involved nurturers. The possibility still exists that these fathers may have used the negative relationships and their skepticism as excuses to avoid parenting.

Chapter 7

Teen Fathers and Peer Influence

How African-American teen fathers view relationships with their peers and how these relationships affect their fatherhood experiences will be examined. The interviews with the teen fathers in this study showed that most of the friends of the teen fathers were not fathers themselves. Nearly all of the teen fathers knew other girls who were pregnant or who had children, but they had very few male friends who had children or who had partners who were expecting children. The fathers usually discussed their friends when talking about their past-time activities and people who were important to them. However, their peers seemed to have little influence on their actual fatherhood behaviors or experiences. They did not go to their peers for advice on parenting or talk to them about their concerns and problems with the mothers of their children.

FATHERHOOD AFFECTING FRIENDSHIPS

The friends of the teen fathers appeared to have influenced the kinds of activities in which the fathers engaged (e.g., sports, "hanging out," drug activities), which may in turn have indirectly impacted how much time they spent with or how they provided for their children. According to the fathers, their friends did not attempt to change their fathering behaviors, although some of their friends were initially concerned that the teens' fatherhood would interfere with their friendships. All of the teen fathers were asked what their friends thought about their fatherhood status. They reported a variety of reactions by their friends: some expressed surprise and/or concern, and many jokingly teased the young men about becoming fathers. Some reactions involved calling their paternity into question. Overall, their

Voices of African-American Teen Fathers
© 2006 by The Haworth Press, Inc. All rights reserved.
doi:10.1300/5477_08

138 VOICES OF AFRICAN-AMERICAN TEEN FATHERS

friends were neither supportive nor strongly opposed to their fatherhood. After the initial surprise, it was not a big ordeal to them, according to the adolescent fathers.

In one interview, fourteen-year-old David discussed how his friends were concerned that his relationship with them would change because of his fatherhood status. David was in the ninth grade and was the father of a four-month-old biracial son, Damon. David lived with both of his parents and an older sister. The types of activities he enjoyed with his friends included playing baseball, basketball, and soccer, and going to the mall, bowling alley, and movies. Out of the six friends he had, he was the only one who was a father. His friends reacted to the news of his becoming a father in the following way:

DAVID: They were pretty shocked, as I was, at first. Some of them reacted negatively about the situation, and said that things will change. But they haven't [changed], and we're all cool now.

INTERVIEWER: Why did they believe things might change, and how?

DAVID: They thought I would be spending all my time with Sarah and Damon. But, logistically, I can't anyway. It's not like she lives nearby and I can just walk over there or something.

David's situation was significant in terms of adult versus child status. He felt that because of his teen or child status, it was reasonable to assume that he could not enact responsible fathering behavior. Overall, teen fathers said that their relationships with their friends did not change because of their fatherhood status. They were able to continue doing "teenage things," such as hanging out and having fun with their friends.

WARNING FROM FRIENDS

Although most of the fathers in the study loved their children and were content with being fathers, they did not plan to become fathers and did not believe that they had anything to gain by becoming parents; the pregnancies were unintended consequences of their sexual activities. In fact, many fathers were warned by their peers and other men about the dangers of being "trapped" by women. For example, Russell stated, "My boys [his friends] always told me to watch out.

They [his female partners] might try to trap you." After their fatherhood was made known, many of the fathers were jokingly teased by their peers for becoming young fathers, and some had warned them that they would have a high price to pay for their mistakes. These warnings usually centered on their beliefs that they would have to pay child support and may have tumultuous relationships with their children's mothers. This reaction was not the case with two of the three youngest fathers in the study, however.

FATHERHOOD AS STATUS SYMBOL

The two youngest fathers in the study experienced an elevation in status because of their fatherhood. Fourteen-year-old Malik did not want to become a father and resented the mother of his child for becoming pregnant. On the other hand, he enjoyed the attention his fatherhood brought from his peers who gave him accolades and "respect" for being a father at such a young age. Earlier research (Anderson 1989, 1990; Dash 1989) suggested that the African-American male adolescent has something to gain in terms of status from becoming a parent, although this does not necessarily indicate motivation to become one. In these situations, their parenthood becomes a source of status among their peers. In the case of Malik, his young fatherhood brought him admiration and "respect" from his friends. Although he was upset about the pregnancy and felt very nervous about becoming a father, he gradually became less anxious about his upcoming fatherhood status after accepting that he "couldn't do anything about it." However, he decided that he would not participate in raising the child because he was "too young to get caught up in all that. . ." Earlier in the interview, he discussed how some adolescents enjoyed being fathers, "Because they like being a man . . ." In the following passage he discussed this source of "manhood" that adolescent fatherhood provided him.

INTERVIEWER: How do your peers act when they hear that you are a father?

MALIK: They don't react no certain way. They just seem a little surprised. Some guys give me props for being one.

140 VOICES OF AFRICAN-AMERICAN TEEN FATHERS

INTERVIEWER: So they commend you for being a father—those that give you props for it?

MALIK: Yeah, I guess they do.

INTERVIEWER: They're sort of patting you on the back, so to speak?

MALIK: Yeah, they do. I guess I never thought about it like that. But it is something to be a father when you're young. One guy told me he didn't know I had it in me.

INTERVIEWER: How did that make you feel?

MALIK: I don't know. Sort of proud I guess.

Although experiencing an elevation in status among his peers for becoming a father at such an early age, Malik did not intend to impregnate the mother of his child in order to obtain the status; thus, no advanced commitment to fatherhood existed. Becoming fathers did not appear to be a deliberate strategy to "prove manhood." Furthermore, Malik had not mentioned or apparently considered his elevation in status among his peers until I introduced the topic. He stated: "I guess I never thought about it like that." Yet, to a certain extent, adolescent fatherhood for Malik served as a symbol of his masculinity and manhood among his peers, although this status change did not influence his fatherhood behaviors. Malik continued to be an independent father, providing hardly any support for his six-month-old daughter. His teenhood status and relationship with his friends remained unaffected as well.

Admiration and approval from peers were similarly felt by another young father in the study. Randy was also fourteen years old and was father to eight-month-old Brandi. He became sexually active at thirteen, and within that same year his daughter was born. According to Randy, his friends were very important to him, and he described their relationship as being so close that it resembled a gang. He stated: "I don't belong to a gang, but me and my boys, we're tight like one." Their favorite activities included playing basketball and video games, watching BET and MTV on television, and listening to music. He alluded to dealing with drugs, although he refused to elaborate on this topic when pressed for more information. The following excerpt picks up at the point in the interview at which Randy was asked whether any of his friends had children:

Teen Fathers and Peer Influence 141

RANDY: Yeah, one of them do.

INTERVIEWER: How old is he?

RANDY: I think he's about seventeen. I'm not sure.

INTERVIEWER: Do your friends know you're a father?

RANDY: Yes, we don't keep stuff like that from each other.

INTERVIEWER: How did they react when they found out you were going to be a dad?

RANDY: They thought it was cool.

INTERVIEWER: Were they surprised?

RANDY: Yeah, they were surprised.

INTERVIEWER: Did they think it was a good thing or a bad thing?

RANDY: I don't know. I don't think they thought it one way or the other.

INTERVIEWER: What did they say?

RANDY: They didn't say much. A couple of them said I was the man. They gave me props. But other than that they didn't think about it one way or the other.

Randy's views introduce the question of whether fatherhood (planned or not) in African-American adolescents creates a rite of passage to adulthood. Stack (1974), Dash (1989), and Anderson (1989, 1990) support this notion as it pertains to adolescent African-American young women. Based upon the stories of Malik and Randy, some indication exists that very young teen fathers (no such indication existed among the older fathers) may gain elevated status among their peers because of their fatherhood status.

Randy thought about fatherhood in terms of being involved and nurturing. He visited his daughter about twice a week, but stated that hanging out with his friends was not a factor in how much time he spent with his daughter. Most of the fathers indicated that the time spent with or the economic support provided for their children had nothing to do with their friendships. Likewise, their fatherhood did not impact their friendships very much. They continued to engage in the same activities with their friends as they participated in prior to their fatherhood and, except for the fathers who worked, indulged in the activities with similar frequency afterward.

PEER INFLUENCE BEFORE FATHERHOOD

Although fatherhood did not generally influence the fathers' relationships with their friends, and vice versa, a couple of exceptions were found. For instance, Byron, an eighteen-year-old father of an eleven-month-old daughter, Asia, described how he no longer had as much time to spend with his friends because he wanted to spend most of his time with his daughter. Getting along very well with the mother of his child, he did not feel reluctant to see the mother and their child. The following excerpt starts at the point at which the topic of the interview turned to his friends:

INTERVIEWER: What about your friends? Have they influenced your life in any way?

BYRON: Yeah, I'm sure they have.

INTERVIEWER: In what way?

BYRON: I don't know. Maybe in my choice of places to hang out, girls I've dated, things I do.

INTERVIEWER: Places you go, girls, and things you do. What types of places do you hang out?

BYRON: Mainly at the park, in the gym. We go bowling sometimes. Movies.

INTERVIEWER: What about your choice in girls?

BYRON: Hmmm . . . you know, I think everyone is influenced by people. If there was a girl that everyone wanted, even if you might not have thought she was that cute at first, you begin to think she must be fine if everyone else wants her. Then you try to go for her. Things like that.

INTERVIEWER: And what was the other thing?

BYRON: Things I do. Just, what I do in my spare time, I guess. Like we play a lot of video games. Stuff like that.

INTERVIEWER: Are any of them fathers?

BYRON: Nope. Not yet.

INTERVIEWER: How did they feel when you became a father?

BYRON: They weren't bothered. Everyone knows someone else who has a child, even if it's a sister or something. It's not that big of a deal, so they didn't say much.

Teen Fathers and Peer Influence 143

INTERVIEWER: Has your relationship with your friends changed in any way since you have become a father?

BYRON: The thing that's changed the most is that I don't hang out with them nearly as much as I used to, because most of the time I'm trying to see Anita and Asia.

This passage illustrates that friends may influence behaviors prior to becoming parents rather than impacting them later as fathers. For instance, Byron mentioned that his friends might have influenced his preferences in women, the places he frequented, and his free-time activities. This supports earlier research (Franklin 1984; Anderson 1989, 1990) that contends that young men are susceptible to peer influence in general. However, Byron's behaviors as a father were unaffected by his peers. In contrast, he spent less time with his friends *because* of his fatherhood. Similarly, seventeen-year-old Paul mentioned that he did not spend as much time with his friends since becoming a father. He described himself as a good father because he saw his eleven-month-old daughter, Brianna, almost every day. Although he does not spend time with his friends as often as he had in the past, he felt it more important to sacrifice that time in order to spend time with his daughter.

In summary, although their friends were important to them, the fathers said that their parenthood experiences were not influenced by their peers. Neither were their friendships changed much because of their fatherhood status. Some exceptions were found, however, and in these few cases the fathers spent less time with their peers because they were trying to spend more time with their children and/or at their new jobs. Finally, with the exception of the two youngest fathers in the study, their fatherhood did not create an elevation in status among their peers.

In the next chapter, the perceived challenges and difficulties that the African-American adolescent fathers experience will be addressed. These challenges ranged from gnawing fears and concerns they had about child support to their experiences with violence and racism.

Chapter 8

The Challenges and Concerns of Teen Fathers

African-American teen fathers in this study had trouble making the transition from being child-free teenagers to becoming adolescent parents. They struggled with expectations of behaving in roles traditionally occupied by adults. Some challenges they experienced related to their youth and emotional immaturity. Some concerns were the diminished freedom they believed that accompanied parenthood. Other salient factors they discussed included poverty (e.g., financial problems, lack of transportation, and poor, crime-ridden neighborhoods) and racism. Thus, adapting to their new roles as fathers and meeting the perceived expectations that were associated with parenthood were problematic. In short, their fatherhood status created stress for many of them.

The current literature indicates that African-American adolescent fathers experience several types of stress, such as financial problems, loss of freedom, and relationship problems (Hendricks et al. 1981; Allen and Doherty 1998). This chapter reviews the factors that African-American teen fathers said inhibited or negatively affected their fatherhood performances. The factors associated with why they became fathers and the attitudes and beliefs they had about parenting did not occur in a vacuum. For instance, African-American adolescent fathers' perspectives on personal dilemmas and relationships are influenced by income, household conditions, neighborhood settings, and cultural context, thus their individual experiences must be understood in the context of cultural and structural factors.

Voices of African-American Teen Fathers
© 2006 by The Haworth Press, Inc. All rights reserved.
doi:10.1300/5477_09

VOICES OF AFRICAN-AMERICAN TEEN FATHERS

YOUTH-RELATED ISSUES

"I'm Too Young to Be a Father; I'm Not Ready for All That"

Most of the adolescent fathers were surprised to learn of the pregnancies of their children's mothers. In nearly every case, the pregnancies were not planned; they were unintended consequences of their sexual activities. In fact, most of the teen fathers had negative reactions to the news of the pregnancies. They were confused about what to expect from their impending roles as fathers and felt unprepared for their new positions. Although a few initially doubted that they were the fathers, at the time of the interviews they had come to accept their paternity. Yet, even upon acceptance of their biological identities as fathers, they struggled with the perceived responsibilities associated with fatherhood. Most were not ready to be fathers.

Low fatherhood readiness may partially be attributed to the adolescent fathers' youth. Underlying many of the struggles and challenges that these young African-American fathers faced in dealing with their roles as fathers was their youth. They wrestled with being regarded in society as children or adolescents (and viewing themselves as teens) while also being expected to assume adult roles as fathers. The complexities that this social position presented were difficult for them.

Fourteen-year-old David revealed how complicated it was to take on the role of father and the pressure he felt to fulfill this obligation. David discussed the expectations he felt, but explained why he did not strive to meet them.

DAVID: While I do concern myself at times with the role I play or should play in Damon's life, it's not something that . . . consumes me. It's like . . . it's like something I can think of in an intellectual sense. As if I'm thinking of it as an experience outside of myself. But when I'm being me, I'm not thinking about it at all. Well, it's not like I don't care, because I do, but I think it's because I'm young that I don't feel all torn up about it or anything. I just know that it's going to get better, and that's that. Sometimes I think I feel more guilty about not feeling more for Damon and Sarah [the

The Challenges and Concerns of Teen Fathers   *147*

mother of his child]. I feel like I should love them. I mean I care for them a great deal. But I think love develops over time. Are you understanding me?

INTERVIEWER: Yes, I think I am. Can you elaborate?

DAVID: I think I understand what I need to do, but . . . I'm not feeling it. I'm not feeling the family thing with them.

As earlier discussed, many African-American teen fathers in the present study felt an obligation to make economic provisions to their children and attempted to do so, either by acquiring jobs or providing via their parents' contributions. Some were not old enough to work legally, and others were not emotionally mature enough to acquire and/or to maintain jobs. The youngest fathers in this study were fourteen years old. One of them, Malik (father of a six-month-old daughter) stated the following about his youth and being expected to perform as an adult father. He stated:

MALIK: Well, I do see him, but I'm just fourteen. I'm going on fifteen. I don't work; I just go to school. Now if a girl thinks a fourteen-year-old man is going to be able to take care of a child, she's a fool.

Interestingly, Malik acknowledged that he was too young to perform in the role of a father as he saw fit and according to what he believed was expected of him in that role; however, at the same time, he also referred to himself as "a fourteen-year-old *man*." Although he felt his age exempted him from parenthood responsibility, he did not believe it did so for the sixteen-year-old mother of his child. When Malik was asked to discuss what fatherhood meant to him, he stated that it was "pretty important." However, his age provided an excuse for him to not spend time with his child, which he defined as an important part of fatherhood. He shared the following about spending time with his child and potentially providing for him:

MALIK: Well, that's something I can't worry about right now. I haven't even been through high school. What can I do? I mean I want to see him taken care of. I can see him more . . . and maybe I will start doing that. But all that other stuff, working and stuff, I'm not doing that right now.

148 *VOICES OF AFRICAN-AMERICAN TEEN FATHERS*

Being chronologically and emotionally young went hand in hand. To many of the fathers, it was a challenge to simply know how to behave with and care for their children. Parenting, a learned behavior, was especially problematic when they had not been shown the fathering roles they conceptualized and/or when they felt they were too young to assume those roles. For instance, Randy, a fourteen-year-old father, expressed how he felt inept as a father. He felt very uncomfortable and lacked knowledge about how to handle his eight-month-old daughter, Brandi, when she was simply crying:

RANDY: Like I said, when she starts all that crying and acting fidgety and stuff, I just give her to Janae [mother of his child]. I don't like all that. I love her, but I don't know how to take care of her like that . . . I guess I don't like not knowing what to do when she's crying and stuff. . . I guess if I spent more time with her, that would help. Janae and her mom said that if I did that then I wouldn't be that— what do they say?—I wouldn't be that nervous around her. I'm not nervous with her, I just don't know what to do with her. I think I'll like handling her better when she gets older.

Youth tended to be a barrier in fulfilling fatherhood roles. The fathers in this study were aware of the limitations their age presented to their parenthood situations. In fact, in some way or another, youth was at the core of other factors that inhibited fatherhood performances among adolescent fathers. Gender could also be a factor in the idea that that males do not do child care work, and females tend to learn it early.

FEAR OF LOSING INDEPENDENCE

"I've Lost My Freedom"

The fathers most often cited the loss of freedom as their biggest fatherhood concern. This potential loss prevented some fathers (e.g., independent fathers) from accepting and enacting father behavior. In their views, adolescent parenthood meant loss of their own personal accountability since they were now responsible for another human

The Challenges and Concerns of Teen Fathers   149

life. This was an uncomfortable position for them. According to the perspectives of some of the teen fathers, loss of freedom meant that they no longer had as much time to spend with their friends and others. It meant a literal loss of time. Thus, spending time with their children and/or with the mothers of their children meant a loss of personal, "free" time. They also conceptualized loss of freedom as no longer having free will to make personal choices about their careers and education because of the responsibilities they felt in having to provide economic or nurturing support for their children. Finally, some fathers viewed loss of freedom as a loss of mental freedom and comfort because of the anxiety associated with worrying about one's child. Overall, the teen fathers felt as if they had lost an important part or function of their previous identities as teenagers when taking on the roles of fathers.

Loss of freedom in the sense of losing one's free time is illustrated in the case of seventeen-year-old Paul. Paul conceptualized fatherhood as an involved father, and as an exception to most fathers in this category, he saw his daughter almost on a daily basis. He described how his relationship with the mother of his child, Tina, suffered after they became parents. He felt that he has lost his freedom because of his fatherhood:

INTERVIEWER: Has anything in your life changed since you've become a father?

PAUL: My freedom like it once was is gone.

INTERVIEWER: Do you regret that?

PAUL: Oh yeah, sometimes. But I love my little girl so . . .

INTERVIEWER: So would you say that's been the biggest adjustment you've had to make, or were there other thing you had to change?

PAUL: No, that was the biggest adjustment—my time. You just can't pick up and go like you want to.

INTERVIEWER: How has having Brianna affected your relationship with Tina?

PAUL: We can't do a lot of things like we once could because we have a kid now. You know. Unless one of our parents babysit . . .

INTERVIEWER: You can't do things like what?

PAUL: You know, go out. Go to the movies, you know. Just have fun.

150   VOICES OF AFRICAN-AMERICAN TEEN FATHERS

Paul displayed responsible behavior, because although he regretted losing a measure of freedom, he adjusted his behavior to spend time with his child. Having a romantic and loving relationship with the mother probably influenced his behaviors as well. Again, this behavior was atypical of most fathers. Their concerns with loss of freedom were not consistent with their behaviors. Although they stated losing freedom as a major concern, the time spent with their friends, they stated, was unaffected by their fatherhood. In general, the time spent with their children was not very much, as earlier discussed.

Loss of freedom, in the sense that it meant losing the option to make certain career and educational choices because of parenthood, was illustrated in the case of eighteen-year-old Byron. Byron was categorized as an involved nurturer, although he stated that being a provider was important as a parent as well. He described how he gave up his carefree lifestyle and obtained a job after becoming a father to eleven-month-old Asia. Although willing to "step up to the plate," he felt that he had lost his freedom to attend college and had instead made the decision to do something that would generate the money he needed to provide for his child.

INTERVIEWER: What has been the biggest adjustment you've made since Asia's birth?

PAUL: Hmmm . . . I don't know. Let's see. Just knowing I couldn't play around like I did. I knew I had to find a job, and that my daily pattern of just going to school, hanging out, and not being worried about much was going to change. But it hasn't been as bad as I thought it was going to be. I think if I had regretted having Asia like some fathers do about their children, then I would hate doing what I do. But I don't. I do it for her because I want to do it for her. So, I would say that was the biggest change I've made. Just having to work while I'm in school, instead of waiting till I graduate.

INTERVIEWER: Did becoming a father affect your career plans, or have you always wanted to join the air force?

PAUL: Yeah. That's another adjustment I had to make. At first I didn't know what I was going to do. I thought about college, and I think I could have done all right in it. But having a child, I know I needed to do something that would bring in money. I just didn't want to work; I wanted to learn a trade or a skill or something. I wanted more than just a job. So joining the military was the next best thing for me. Since I wasn't sold all the way on going to college anyway, it's probably the best choice regardless.

Similar to Paul, Byron responsibly made adjustments in his life in order to enact the provider role for his child. Although losing freedom in the process of trying to enact fatherhood, Byron obtained a job in order to provide economic support for his child. Having a romantic and loving relationship with the mother probably facilitated his responsible behavior. Still, his sentiments about this change could be felt by any parent, regardless of age. However, these changes have dif ferent consequences for young people and mean different sacrifices.

Nonetheless, Byron's enactment of fatherhood was not found among most fathers. Although other fathers discussed the fear of losing freedom, their behaviors were not consistent with this concern. Even though most planned, when they become adults, to provide for their children, it appeared that the specific plans they made for their careers, including the plans a few had for attending college, were not hindered or influenced by fatherhood.

Another interesting but atypical example of the fathers' concern of losing freedom was found with seventeen-year-old Craig. Craig was among the minority who worked in order to provide financial assistance to the mother of his child. He worked part-time at a factory and did seasonal work at concession booths in order to provide economic assistance to the mother of his child. He experienced a very different kind of loss of freedom than the ability to go the movies, for example. He discussed how being a father was a "mental burden" because of the worries and concerns it produced.

CRAIG: Well, I would probably say that even though I love having a daughter (and I will definitely always love her), there is a part of me that regrets knowing that I will never be totally free. It's like I will always have a responsibility no matter where I am, no matter where I go. I will always have to take care of my daughter. I don't mean necessarily financially, but I'll always worry about her, you know. I'll always worry about taking care of her, giving her what

152 VOICES OF AFRICAN-AMERICAN TEEN FATHERS

she needs or wants. I don't know if I'm making myself clear. But some people don't know that when you have a child, that's going to be a responsibility of yours for a long, long time. Even if you love your child, you'll never be completely mentally free.

INTERVIEWER: Do you think a lot of people have a children without considering the long-term consequences?

CRAIG: Oh yeah. I don't think they look at a child in the type of responsibility it will be. They look at how they're going to have this little cute little boy or girl and how they're always going to love it and all that, but having a child is a mental burden, too. Do you have any children?

INTERVIEWER: No, I sure don't.

CRAIG: Well, you might not know what I mean. I wouldn't give my daughter up for nothing in the world. Nothing. But the truth is, there is a certain sense of mental freedom that you lose with having a child.

Interestingly, Craig assumed that because I did not have children that I could not relate to the burden he felt in being responsible for a child, and he proceeded to explain this weight he was bearing. He spoke in terms of experiencing a "mental burden" in relation to having a child, which he perceived to be an overwhelming responsibility for young parents. However, not all of the fathers felt that they lost their freedom as adolescent fathers. For instance, sixteen-year-old Clayton was asked whether his fatherhood kept him from doing anything he used to do. His response indicated that he did not look at fatherhood from a deficit perspective.

INTERVIEWER: Does having a child keep you from doing anything you used to do?

CLAYTON: Not really. I mean, I may go over there sometimes [to his child's home], but if there is something else I need to do, then I do it. A lot of people think you'll have to lose your freedom if you have a child, but I don't think that's always the case. At least not for me. To me it's almost a plus, because you always have something to look forward to.

RELATIONSHIP PROBLEMS

"It's Hard Getting Along with My Baby's Mama"

Among the challenges experienced by teen fathers are antagonistic relationships with the mothers of their children. Although the majority of teen fathers considered themselves to have positive relationships with the mothers of their children, it was evident that they were struggling with their dual roles of being a father to their child and at the same time being a partner and/or coparent with their children's mothers.

As discussed earlier, the mothers of the children did not attempt to prevent the fathers from seeing their children. In fact, the teen fathers expressed that they could see their children more if they could or chose to do so. However, a few believed that the antagonistic relationships with the mothers of their children prevented them from wanting to spend more time with their children, or from being able to do so. This situation created a barrier to visiting with their children. Calvin, a sixteen-year-old father of an eight-month-old child, discussed how his relationship with his child was affected by the mother of the child's attitude toward him. Calvin did not know the child's eighteen-year-old mother, Bianca, very long prior to her pregnancy. He stated that he was upset that Bianca used their child as leverage in attempts to enhance their romantic relationship, and that she had threatened to impose child support when he gets older. He felt that Bianca's actions and attitude were acts of revenge because of his reluctance to become more romantically and intimately involved with her. He explained how this antagonistic relationship prevented him from seeing or providing for his eight-month-old daughter, Denae:

CALVIN: I just got to the point where I don't want to see her or my baby. If seeing Bianca means I got to put up with that shit, then I'm not going to do it. She's not going to get anything from me.

INTERVIEWER: Anything? Like what?

CALVIN: Like nothing. She's not going to see me, and she's not getting any money out of me.

The adolescent fathers' youth was probably associated with their beliefs that these negative relationships prevented them from

154 VOICES OF AFRICAN-AMERICAN TEEN FATHERS

providing for or being involved with their children. For instance, the majority of these young fathers had not experienced steady hetero-sexual relationships, and only a few were in long-term relationships with the mothers of their children. Because of their inexperience with relationships and their emotional immaturity it may have been more difficult for them to overcome problems in their relationships with the mothers of their children and to not let them affect their fathering behaviors. It was challenging to separate the child from the mother and the responsibilities of a father from the relationship with the mother. Instead, they were more likely to allow the antagonistic relationships or the negative feelings they harbored for the mothers of their children to hinder them from providing economic or emotional support for their children.

CONCERNS ABOUT CHILD SUPPORT

"I Know She's Going to Hit Me Up for Child Support"

As previously discussed, African-American adolescent fathers were particularly concerned about how they were going to provide for their children, both at present and in the future. Because they primarily defined fatherhood in provider terms, this issue was a major concern for them. Although teen fathers currently had trouble providing economic support for their children because of their relatively poor socioeconomic conditions, they also perceived future problems in this area as adults. Although they planned to provide for their children when they became adults, many of them worried about being legally required to make provisions (or being "forced" to provide support) as well as about the amount of support they would be required to pay. The concern these fathers had about child support appeared to indicate awareness of the economic disadvantages incurred by early childbearing. For instance, eighteen-year-old Brandon discussed the financial obligations he may have to face as a father. At the time of the interview, he did not work and provided no economic or nurturing support for his one-and-a-half-year-old son. Although he was presently categorized as an independent father, he particularly resented the idea of having to pay child support in the future.

The Challenges and Concerns of Teen Fathers   *155*

BRANDON: All I know is that I shouldn't have to pay child support if I don't want to. Why do women *make* men do it? If they don't want to do it, they shouldn't try to make them do it. I'm not saying that I won't pay child support one day. Maybe one day I will. But if Tisha tries to go through the courts or whatever to get them to make me do it, then she might not get a dime [from me].

Brandon was one of two fathers who had reported that the mother of his child had actually threatened to enforce child support. He felt anger and resentment at Tisha for these threats, but already felt animosity toward her because he thought she had tried to "trap" him when she got pregnant. Regardless, Brandon disliked her "threats" and forewarned that "she might not get a dime" if she delivered on her promise.

Fifteen-year-old Jarrod also discussed his resentment about the idea of being forced to pay child support when he graduated from high school. Despite explaining earlier in the interview that he had every intention of providing economic support for his three-month-old son, Demaris, because he wanted to do what a "real man" was supposed to do, which meant providing for his child, Jarrod did not want to be forced to keep his obligations. About child support, he stated:

JARROD: You know, I spend time with my son. I do. A lot of time. And if I could give Amber [the mother of his child] some money or something to help out, I would. But, you know, it should be my choice if I want to do it. It shouldn't be her choice or anyone else's choice. Because if I'm made to do it, that means it wasn't coming from the heart anyway. If I want to be a worthless, good-for-nothing dad, then shame on me. But that should be my mistake.

Although Jarrod conceptualized fathers as providers, he was not able to fulfill this role. He discussed how he was unable to work since the family had only one car, and talked about how his father was unable to help him provide financially for his child (his mother lived in another state and was a drug addict). Still, Jarrod spent a great deal of time with his baby and did his best to see him whenever he could. His position on paying child support was shared by many adolescent fathers. Although most wanted and planned to provide economic

156   *VOICES OF AFRICAN-AMERICAN TEEN FATHERS*

assistance for their children, they did not want to be forced to do so by the mothers of their children nor by the legal system. As "men" they felt that this decision should be theirs to make. Although feeling that taking care of their responsibilities (whether that was as a provider or as an involved nurturer) was an obligation, they believed that how or whether they chose to fulfill that obligation was their choice to make.

SOCIOECONOMIC CHALLENGES

"It's Hard Providing for My Child"

Another big challenge that African-American fathers experienced was providing economic support for their children. In fact, this factor is the underlying basis for nearly all of the challenges and concerns discussed by the fathers. As previously stated, this study focused on fathers from poor socioeconomic backgrounds, and the findings demonstrated that their financial situations certainly impacted their perceived abilities to parent. The greatest challenge their low socioeconomic circumstances created for them was financially being able to provide for their children. For several reasons the teen fathers were not able to provide financially for their children by the standards they expected or by those they felt others expected. These factors included the following from their standpoints: they were too young to get jobs or to seriously consider getting them; they perceived a low pool of suitable jobs; their current household incomes were relatively low, which meant their parents were limited in what they could provide; or they experienced a combination of these factors.

Many of the young fathers provided some economic support or assistance for their children. However, the level of these resources and how regularly they were provided varied from father to father. They admitted to giving amounts that were small in relation to the actual needs of their children. Two main sources of income from the fathers were identified—money from their own parents and part-time employment. Most of the fathers were not employed; however, five of them had part-time jobs, one had a full-time job, one was about to assume a job, and another one had been recently released from a job. Although they articulated the importance of finding jobs because of their fatherhood responsibilities, they rationalized that they were either too young to work, too busy with school or other activities, and/or that work compromised their teenhood and its associated freedoms. Nonetheless, lack of adequate money and resources were perceived to create a significant barrier to performing, or "adequately" performing, their fatherhood roles and responsibilities as providers.

Sixteen-year-old Clayton primarily defined a father's role as being involved and nurturing. He enacted this role by providing some caregiving activities, such as changing his daughter's diapers and feeding her. Although he did not believe he saw his daughter, Kierra, as much as he should, he believed it was very important to do so. In addition to being involved and nurturing, Clayton also expressed the importance of making economic provisions for his daughter. One of the biggest concerns he had, in addition to not seeing her as often as he thought he needed, was that he had to rely on assistance from others in providing for her. He stated:

CLAYTON: Probably the worst thing for me is just not seeing her when I want and not having enough money to buy her what she needs. I mean she gets what she needs, but I wish I could be the one that gives it to her—not her grandma, or my mom, or Quendasha's mom, or Uncle Nate, or anyone else. I want to be the one, you know? Plus just not knowing if Quendasha is going to bring another man around bothers me, too.

Although Clayton primarily defined fatherhood as being involved and nurturing, he also defined it in provider-role terms. Yet, he did not feel he was adequately or fully providing for his child because others were fulfilling this role for him. Contrary to Clayton's conceptualization of his role as a father, he did not plan to get a job soon, in part because he wanted to "chill" that summer and just spend time with his friends.

Similar to Clayton, other teen fathers in the study were reluctant to fully take on the responsibilities they associated with fatherhood because they believed they had to compromise too much of the behaviors associated with "just being a teenager." Thus, although some structural obstacles existed, some young fathers simply chose to not get or try to get jobs. Although lack of jobs and economic resources impaired their abilities to fully perform in their fatherhood roles as teens, they reconciled the role strain they felt by postponing this re-

158 VOICES OF AFRICAN-AMERICAN TEEN FATHERS

sponsibility until they were able to do so in their future capacities as adult fathers.

In addition to not wanting to work because they perceived it as a loss of their current adolescent lifestyles, teen fathers were not able to provide adequately for their children because of the perceived lack of "suitable" jobs, lack of reliable transportation to jobs, and limited abilities of their parents to assist them in providing for their children. For example, seventeen-year-old Darrius sold drugs in order to provide financial support for his two-year-old son, Alex. He also mentioned that his friends sold drugs as well.

INTERVIEWER: Do your friends do it, too?

DARRIUS: Of course. We gotta make that buck. How else are we going to?

INTERVIEWER: You don't feel that there's any other way?

DARRIUS: Hell no, nothing that's gonna pay.

INTERVIEWER: Do any of your friends work?

DARRIUS: For what? So they can make minimum wage flipping a damn burger?

INTERVIEWER: Are those the only types of jobs you foresee them doing if they try to find a job?

DARRIUS: Yeah. What else you expect? They can't get a job in a plant or anything. You gotta have a high school diploma or a GED or something. Plus, you still gotta know the right people. And they sure in hell ain't going to get a job in an office or something, right?

Although just a few of the teen fathers in this study engaged in the drug trade, Darrius's views about it not being worthwhile to pursue low-paying, unskilled jobs were held by the several young fathers. Because of their youth, most had not yet obtained their high school diplomas, and many felt that the only jobs available to them were positions in fast-food restaurants and grocery stores. Their strong objections to working in jobs in which they "just flip burgers" indicates that such work has become demeaning in their culture. These are certainly not jobs with a future. Nonetheless, even when open to accepting such jobs, many of the fathers stated that they did not have reliable

The Challenges and Concerns of Teen Fathers | 159

transportation that would allow them to work regularly and dependably.

Nineteen-year-old Keith, who was in the twelfth grade, discussed the bleak future he perceived for most African-American fathers:

KEITH: A lot of people want to think of us [teen fathers] as irresponsible men who don't care about taking care of our children. But the fact of the matter is we can't get jobs even if we wanted to. Not jobs that will help us take care of children. When we finish high school, what are we going to do? The only jobs around here we're going to be able to get is flipping burgers or waiting on people in stores and restaurants. Unless you get on with Cessna or somebody, man, you're going to be making minimum wage. You can't support yourself on minimum wage, no less [doing it for] somebody else.

Keith was not sure what he was going to do when he completed high school. He had no plans at the time of the interview.

TRANSPORTATION ISSUES

"I Would See Her More if I Had Transportation"

For some of the young fathers the distance from their children's homes created barriers to fulfilling their fatherhood roles. Not having access to transportation or not having reliable or consistent transportation was a common complaint of fathers who primarily defined fatherhood in "nurturing" and "involved" terms. Many did not own a car and did not have easy access to one. They either had to depend on their parents to drive them to their children's homes or had to depend on friends and other relatives to transport them. Coupled with the problem that city/bus transportation did not reach all locations within the city (or did not do so at convenient times for them), living beyond walking distance to their children's homes made it more difficult for them to become as involved in their children's lives as they otherwise would have, they reported.

160 VOICES OF AFRICAN-AMERICAN TEEN FATHERS

When fathers lived very close to their children's homes, they saw them more. For instance, seventeen-year-old Paul saw his daughter almost every day because she lived within walking distance of his home. Thus, it is possible that with better transportation or access to it, adolescent fathers would see or visit their children for longer periods. Fourteen-year old David described why he was unable to visit with his child for extended times:

INTERVIEWER: When you're with your son, how long do you usually visit?

DAVID: Sometimes for a couple of hours or so. Sometimes for less.

INTERVIEWER: What determines how long you visit?

DAVID: If my parents are with me, they don't like overstaying their visits, so we might just be there for an hour or less. If I'm there by myself, I stay for much longer. Then I'd call them to pick me up when I'm ready.

Seventeen-year-old Alinius also discussed the frustration he felt in not being able to see his child as often as he wanted:

ALINIUS: The worse thing to me about being a father is not being able to see Pookie [nickname] when I want to, and not being able to spend more time with her when I do.

INTERVIEWER: What specifically prevents you from seeing her as often as you wish?

ALINIUS: Like I said, I don't live with Pookie, and I just can't pop over to someone else's house whenever I want. Plus, it's not like I live close to them either, so I have to find a ride over there.

Not being able to see their children as often as they liked was a concern for African-American teen fathers in this study. With poor transportation, those who conceptualized fatherhood as involved/nurturers were unable to see their children as often as they wanted—which, to them, meant not being able to perform in the role they conceptualized as fathers. Likewise, those who defined fathers as providers encountered problems fulfilling their perceived responsibilities when they were unable to drive to jobs that would enable them to provide economic assistance for their children.

The Challenges and Concerns of Teen Fathers   *161*

CULTURAL INFLUENCES

"I Don't Want My Child Getting
Caught Up in the Mentality"

African-American teen fathers in this study resided in relatively poor neighborhoods and communities. Many of them thought that the culture of their communities created stress and concerns for them as fathers. Their neighborhoods were a source of strain and anxiety because they were thought to create conditions that encouraged pervasive negative attitudes and behaviors. Adolescent fathers were concerned that their children were susceptible to adopting the two main negative attitudes and behaviors that prevailed in their communities: (1) drug use, abuse, and trade, and (2) being exposed to violence and potential harm. Unfortunately, these fears were not unrealistic.

The concern of his child being drawn into and influenced by his neighborhood's culture or "mentality" was expressed by seventeen-year-old Carl, who was also a twelfth grader and in an international baccalaureate program in high school. Although Carl had plans to become a lawyer and had applied for several college scholarships, he was concerned about his daughter, four-month-old Robin, being raised in a neighborhood and environment that promoted what he considered "substandard conditions" and mediocrity. He was asked about his neighborhood:

INTERVIEWER: Is your neighborhood a safe place to live and raise a child?

CARL: Yes, I think so. I've lived here all my life and I haven't had any run-ins. There's more trouble on specific streets, but most of them are not like that. There're no gangs on my street or within my block. There are some kids that do drugs sometimes, probably, but, I don't think they sell drugs or anything. We don't have any crack houses on our street or within close range. Just people trying to work, and some not. But it's not bad . . . As far as raising a child in it? I would prefer not to. It's not necessarily bad, but you can still get caught up in the mentality here, and that's not what I would want for a child.

162 VOICES OF AFRICAN-AMERICAN TEEN FATHERS

INTERVIEWER: What mentality?

CARL: Like I said, some people work, and if they are, they're mostly jobs that you can barely make ends meet. So you're either struggling or trying to work two jobs. Then there're the people who don't work and just live off welfare and don't do very much. So I would just . . . I would just rather not raise a child here if I could help it. Because a child living in my type of neighborhood would more than likely end up falling in one of those lifestyles. In a sense, they end up thinking that they're going to be like one or the other, and then by them thinking like that, they end up like that.

Carl attributed his ability to avoid the "mentality" to two factors: having a "strong mom" who expected much of him and his optimistic attitude. Some adolescent fathers did not talk about a negative "mentality" or culture in their neighborhoods and communities. They had positive views about their communities and considered them relatively safe places to raise their children. They believed that their neighborhoods were "not that bad." However, most wished their children could be raised under better social and socioeconomic circumstances.

DRUG ISSUES

"I'm Scared I'm Going to Try It"

Although most of the fathers did not use or sell drugs, high level of exposure existed nonetheless. Some fathers had close relatives who sold drugs or were addicted to them. Some had friends, schoolmates, and cousins who did the same. Seventeen-year-old James talked about how he wanted to live in a drug-free neighborhood.

JAMES: It really gets to me sometimes. I can't walk down the street without seeing someone who is either selling or using. I don't even like going out my door at night because of the drive-bys and the people that are trying to constantly get you to do it. One man on my street keeps telling me that he's going to get me one day.

INTERVIEWER: He's going to kill you?

JAMES: No. He's going to get me to buy some drugs from him.

INTERVIEWER: Wow. How did that make you feel? What do you say to that?

JAMES: I just usually shake my head and look at him crazy. Sometimes it makes me scared, because I don't want to try it, but I'm afraid I might.

James declared that he has never tried drugs. However, his mother's current half-time/live-in boyfriend abused drugs. Also James had friends who smoked marijuana and sometimes did "stronger" drugs, and he lived next door to a crack house. The pressure he felt was intense, he stated, and he hated his neighborhood and the constant pressure he felt to do drugs.

Fifteen-year-old Jeremy is another young father who was heavily exposed to drugs. Although he was living with his mother at the time of the interview, he had lived in a foster home (because of his mother's earlier neglect), with his grandmother (who later died), and with his father (who moved to another state and didn't want to take Jeremy along). His life had been very unstable and he feared that he and his mother might have to move to Baltimore. He had visited cousins who lived in a poor housing project in that city, and he was afraid that he would eventually end up similar to some of them and their friends: drug addicted, imprisoned, or killed. Life in Wichita was not much better, however. Similar to James, Jeremy had friends who smoked marijuana and did other drugs, and he knew many people in his community who either sold or abused drugs. At just fifteen, Jeremy had tried many drugs but stated that he "just smoke[d] marijuana now." He discussed his experiences and perceptions about drugs in his community:

JEREMY: I just do marijuana now. That's all I smoke. But many of my friends do other stuff like wet daddy, ecstasy, crack, you name it. I've done them, too, but I stopped after I almost overdosed. That scared me to death. I didn't end up in the hospital, but I was in bad shape.

INTERVIEWER: Why weren't you taken to the hospital?

164 VOICES OF AFRICAN-AMERICAN TEEN FATHERS

JEREMY: The dudes I were with were scared they might get in trouble, I guess.

[Later]

INTERVIEWER: Why do you think so many people do drugs?

JEREMY: We do it for several reasons. Sometimes to fit in. To try something. Sometimes to dull the pain. Sometimes to just forget about stuff. To feel good.

INTERVIEWER: What kinds of pain are they trying to dull, or what kinds of things are they trying to forget?

JEREMY: Money. Not having enough money. Not going anywhere.

INTERVIEWER: What do you mean?

JEREMY: Not going anywhere in life. Plus, bad relationships. Bad grades. School pressures. Babies you can't take care of *[chuckles]*. Like me.

INTERVIEWER: Is that why you do drugs?

JEREMY: I don't know. I do it because I want to do it. But what's behind that? I don't know. Maybe a little bit of all of what I just said.

Interestingly, Jeremy had been categorized as an independent father. Although he expressed no intentions of providing for his daughter, apparently not doing so (or not being able to do so) was on his mind, as he discussed taking drugs to forget about not being able to take care of "babies you can't take care of. Like me." Although he laughed when he said it, a sense of hopelessness was felt about the situation. Most likely, his chuckle was merely a front to hide his feelings of helplessness, just as the drugs he took to "dull the pain" over the other pressures he and other young African-American men feel. Perhaps some independent fathers were so not because of their attitudes about ideal fathering but because they could not meet expectations and it was easier to keep distance.

Jeremy was in the tenth grade, and he was asked about his plans for graduation. With cynicism he replied, "If I'm lucky, probably be a factory worker or warehouse worker." The alienation and hopelessness these fathers felt is depressing. That many were not being raised by their fathers, and fewer felt loved by them, and that too many were exposed to prevalent drug use and abuse as well as violence was very disturbing.

The Challenges and Concerns of Teen Fathers 165

DAILY SURVIVAL

"If I'm Going to Lose My Life . . ."

Violence or potential exposure to violence and harm was not uncommon for these fathers. Although Roman was the only father who was officially a gang member, several were exposed to them and to their ways of life. For instance, seventeen-year-old Russell was not a gang member but had been pressured to join one. His plans to do so were interrupted when a man in his church a couple of years ago convinced him not to do it after observing that Russell frequently hung around members of a particular gang. This man's concerns were further underscored for Russell after a harrowing experience. He and four other guys (three of them were members of the gang which he was around) were eating at a local McDonald's restaurant. One of the boys in the group approached another group of young men outside of the restaurant and came back inside to report to Russell's group that they were challenged:

RUSSELL: He said that we were challenged, and I was naive at the time, so I asked him, "challenged to what?" The other guys started laughing and said that we were challenged to combat. A fight. Well, I'm the first one to fight if there's going to be a fight. I don't back down from nothing. You're going to respect me. So, I told them that as far as I was concerned, it was on. Everyone else was in it, too, because they didn't say anything. It was like a given. So, Billy went out, came back inside, and told us that the challenge was scheduled for one a.m. that night. I thought that was pretty late, and I knew my mom was going to be tripping when I got in, but I couldn't just back out. I didn't want to be a punk.

Russell, the original group of boys, and additional gang members met the rival gang later that night (or rather early morning) at a park. Russell explained that his naïveté almost cost him his life. One of the boys who was killed was with Russell at McDonald's earlier that evening, and another guy from the rival gang was shot but not killed. Apparently, these challenges were not uncommon, he said, and the boys were aware that they could either get seriously hurt or killed. However, that was the last time Russell hung out with that group. He said,

166 VOICES OF AFRICAN-AMERICAN TEEN FATHERS

"I'm hard. But I'm not crazy. If I'm going to lose my life, it's going to be over something real. Not just a fight for the sake of fighting."

For Russell, doing gender/masculinity meant projecting a certain macho toughness: "I don't back down for nothing. You're going to respect me." For some, being masculine and tough means being willing to die, apparently, but not for Russell. That is where he drew the line. Were their life circumstances so bad and/or their feelings of hopelessness so strong that they did not place value in their lives? Russell commented that he believed that was the case with many of them. He added, "I think some of them feel like what's the point. Life stinks anyway, so what's the point?"

Roman, the eighteen-year-old gang member further illustrated the impact of a community and neighborhood on one's experiences as a man and as a parent. Roman was very much a part of the "street life" around him and had a profound, disturbing view of his future—very similar to what Russell described of the young men in the previous scenario.

INTERVIEWER: Why don't you think you're going to live past twenty-five?

ROMAN: Oh come on now. You know better than that. What's the likelihood that I will? I'll end up either killed or end up in the house. The big house. And I'm not talking about the one on Pennsylvania Avenue. Prison. You know that. I know that. . . . It ain't nothing that could be done. It's all scripted out. . . . There ain't no choice in the matter.

INTERVIEWER: What do you mean?

ROMAN: If you're raised in the streets, you gonna die in the streets.

INTERVIEWER: Do you feel like you were raised in the streets?

ROMAN: Feel like? I *was* raised in the streets.

INTERVIEWER: What happened?

ROMAN: Life is what happened.

INTERVIEWER: What do you mean by that?

ROMAN: I was born and raised by a crackhead. So what do you expect? . . . She ain't never been there for me and still ain't. She ain't no mother. I didn't have a dad. Like I said, he's in the big house and has been there for as long as I can remember. Nobody helped me. Nobody raised me.

The Challenges and Concerns of Teen Fathers

When Roman was asked whether he felt life was "scripted out" for his son, he responded, "probably," and said that there was nothing he could do about it. The hopelessness and the helplessness to change matters were evident. He felt that offering his son a "gangbanger" lifestyle was the best way his son was going to be able to deal with life and the challenges it would present him.

RACISM AND DISCRIMINATION

"It's Tough Being Black"

Racism was another theme that emerged from the data. Experiences with racism were an everyday occurrence for them—from the incidences they experienced with teachers to situations in which they were "followed" in department stores. They described being stared at in restaurants predominantly frequented by white patrons and experiencing the same when they went to local stores in which they were being "watched" by the Asian-American store attendees. They felt they were being judged more critically at their jobs even when they believed they were doing everything right. Although racism was experienced in many ways and in many forms, the most prevalent forms discussed included barriers or perceived barriers to employment and experiences with or perceptions of law enforcement.

Although nineteen-year-old William worked full-time at a telemarketing company to provide support for his child, he felt tremendous stress in trying to maintain his job. He expressed that his white supervisor constantly stood over his shoulders, monitored his phone calls, and deliberately stared at his watch every time, William came in to work, took a break, or went home for the day. He felt that he was being unfairly and constantly watched because of his skin color, and claimed that other African-American employees felt similarly. His supervisor did not exhibit these behaviors with his white employees, William stated.

WILLIAM: It's really tough being black. It really is. It's stressful. When we try to work, they want to cut us down or get us fired. When we try to go to school, they try to make it harder on us to succeed. When we try anything, we just get knocked back down. For

168 VOICES OF AFRICAN-AMERICAN TEEN FATHERS

example, I'm trying to do my best with this job. I wanted to move up—become a team leader, then maybe one day a supervisor. I work hard. I come to work on time. I don't leave early. I work overtime when they ask me to. I try to do everything right. But it's still not going to happen. They see to it that it doesn't happen.

INTERVIEWER: What do you mean?

WILLIAM: We're never moving up. We're not going to get the good jobs, the good positions. Yes, a few of us will. But most of us won't.

William was the only father who talked about his personal experiences with racism in the workplace, although many others shared similar views about jobs and work opportunities based upon the experiences of family members or of friends. Most thought that African-American men had the greatest struggle to overcome in the workforce. William further discussed:

WILLIAM: You know what you ought to do a study on? Black men in the workplace. That's what you ought to do. We have it badder than everyone. If it's one person they don't like, it's the black man.

None of the fathers discussed what role(s) that African Americans played in these perceptions or racist-related experiences, if any. They perceived that many of their problems were directly or indirectly related to long-term, institutionalized racism, to being denied access to jobs and education, and from individual encounters with racism.

The issue of racism and what it does to one's masculinity was captured in an interview with nineteen-year-old Jermaine. He had had "run-ins" with police officers who he thought were picking on him and his friends because of their skin color. Many fathers talked about similar experiences they or others had, especially concerning police "profiling." In Jermaine's case, he discussed a scenario (that had occurred several times, he stated) in which he and a group of friends would be hanging out as a group at a park or similar public location, and a squad car would pull over, come up to the group, and ask them to "move along." Jermaine was convinced that had they been a group of white young men doing the same thing, the incident would never have occurred. He felt particularly

The Challenges and Concerns of Teen Fathers 169

concerned about being stopped for racial profiling or something similar in the presence of his sons:

JERMAINE: Like racial profiling. I've been stopped before, by myself and sometimes with my friends. They found nothing because we didn't do nothing. But, what if I have my sons in the car with me one day and that happened? How is that going to make me feel, you know? I don't look forward to telling my sons that they're not going to get treated equally just because they have darker skin. And I don't like the idea that I can't keep them from having to go through all that.

Jermaine seemed concerned about racial profiling for three reasons: it is dehumanizing, his manhood is threatened because he is not able to defend himself from these unfair intrusions—such incidents threaten his masculinity by putting him in a position in which he feels defenseless or weak, and he felt stripped of his "right" as a man to protect his children ("I don't like the idea that I can't keep them [his children] from having to go through all that").

Even when race-related experiences were not discussed, the overwhelming impact of racism was found in the most unexpected discussions. For instance, sixteen-year-old Eric was a father of a four-month-old son. Eric was categorized as an independent father, and he did not plan to provide or be nurturing to his child. He had deep-seated resentment toward the mother, April, whom he accused of getting pregnant on purpose to become a part of his life. Even so, Eric believed, and seemed quite relieved, that his son would potentially experience less racism because of what he perceived to be an advantage: his son was biracial. He stated the following about his son:

ERIC: He's a mixed baby. April is white, so he should have a little better life, and he might get better accepted by the white man.
INTERVIEWER: Why do you think he'll be more accepted? Because he's biracial?
ERIC: Yes, he'll be lighter skinned, have better hair. His mom is white, and he come from a white family, so . . . he'll have more changes.
INTERVIEWER: You think he'll have more breaks?
ERIC: Yes.

170 VOICES OF AFRICAN-AMERICAN TEEN FATHERS

Likewise, eighteen-year-old Byron had similar views about his biracial daughter. Unlike Eric, Byron had a loving, romantic relationship with the mother of his child and planned to marry her after he joined the air force. Before knowing that Anita was white, I had asked Byron whether he was concerned about racism and discrimination for his daughter. He responded, "That's an interesting question. Because Asia is half white and she's a girl, I don't think she'll be discriminated against as much." It was interesting that Byron thought his daughter had two distinct advantages over an African American with no evident white heritage: her light skin color and her female gender.

In conclusion, Byron's position related to some of the statements from other fathers in the study who felt that the African-American male had the greatest racial barriers to overcome among all races and genders in the United States. They were very cognizant of color and gender as barriers in their lives. For example, Byron thought that his child would have less racism and discrimination to experience since she was biracial (more than likely with a light complexion) and female. Racism was a serious concern and a daily challenge that intersected with the fathers' sense of masculinity, which tied to their perceived abilities to provide, to protect their children, and to their everyday experiences. Supplemented by other challenges with which they dealt, including those that were related to their youth and their low socioeconomic status, they have much to experience and overcome. All of these challenges and situations affect their perceived abilities to perform as fathers, not to mention their basic sense of manhood.

In the next chapter, findings will be summarized and theoretical implications will be made.

Chapter 9

Discussion and Conclusion

RESEARCH QUESTIONS AND MAJOR FINDINGS

In this exploratory study with African-American teen fathers, several things were learned. First, I examined how and why African-American adolescent fathers, from their own perspectives, became fathers. The findings point to four main factors that contributed to the African-American teen's fatherhood status: intentional nonuse of contraception, lack of communication with their partners about contraception, intent to become parents, and negative views about abortion and adoption.

Furthermore, the young men became fathers not due to contraceptive failure, but mainly due to their failure to use condoms or other forms of contraception at all. The choice to use condoms was the fathers' prerogative according to the results of this study. For the most part, they had control over the use of condoms, and a couple of respondents even talked about how they could get women to "change their minds about using them." The reasons the fathers stated for not using condoms included not liking how they felt, not having them available, and believing the women were using other forms of birth control. The fathers also discussed other factors that played a role in their becoming fathers. They included lack of communication about contraception, the condoms breaking, beliefs that the women deliberately became pregnant in order to "trap" them or to have a child to provide meaning and love to their (the women's) lives, and in two cases the deliberate act of a teen father and the mother to become parents.

Again, although a few of the adolescents wanted to become fathers, this was not the case for the majority. Pregnancy was an "accident." Lack of communication was a predominant theme in explaining what happened. This was linked not only to the circumstances that

Voices of African-American Teen Fathers
© 2006 by The Haworth Press, Inc. All rights reserved.
doi:10.1300/5477_10

172   VOICES OF AFRICAN-AMERICAN TEEN FATHERS

occurred before conception but also to what happened afterward. For the most part little communication occurred about whether to use contraception, and limited interfacing happened afterward about what to do once the pregnancy occurred.

Once pregnancy occurred, three options existed: the mother could choose to keep the child and raise it, give birth but put the child up for adoption, or have an abortion. The teen fathers expressed negative views about abortion. After finding out about the pregnancies, some had hoped the mothers of their children would have abortions, but most of them opposed the idea. Sullivan (1989) found that African-American fathers were culturally opposed to abortion—more so than the white and Hispanic fathers in the same study. According to Battle and Battle (1987), African-American adolescents are generally opposed to abortions because of religious values, family (the extended-family concept), and personal perceptions of abortions. However, the present study did not find that African-American teen fathers were particularly influenced by religion on this matter. Moreover, they were not opposed to abortion in general. For most of them, they were opposed to abortion when it applied to their own children; they were not in favor of it because they wanted to continue their "blood-line" once they were informed of the pregnancy. Generally, the issue of abortion was never discussed between the father and his partner, and the fathers perceived it to be the mother's decision.

Virtually no research exists on African-American adolescent fathers' views on adoption, but this study showed that the teens strongly objected to this as a personal alternative on the grounds that adoption insinuated poor, inept parenting. They felt adoption would be an indication of their personal failures as parents. Therefore, similar to abortion, they did not object to the idea of adoption in general but objected to it as a personal option.

Second, I explored how teen fathers conceptualized and practiced fatherhood. The teens in this study defined fatherhood in three major ways: provider, involved nurturer, and independent father. These categories were not mutually exclusive, and they were somewhat similar to what Gerson (1997) found with adult fathers. Adopting hegemonic norms, the majority of the fathers in the current study defined fathers primarily as providers. They conceptualized the role of a provider as a father who provided economic support for his children. However, providers were not necessarily breadwinners for these young fathers,

Discussion and Conclusion 173

although they believed that fathers should provide some economic support. In addition, masculinity and fatherhood were discussed in the sense that the teens frequently mentioned being "a real man." This phrase was brought up frequently and was tied to the fathers' traditional, masculine notion of being a provider and taking care of one's responsibilities. Being self-sufficient and being providers were concepts closely associated with traditional masculinity.

The involved nurturer was conceptualized as one who provided nurturing, emotional support and who engaged in caregiving activities with his child. This was the second most often conceptualized form of fatherhood. The most important characteristic of the involved nurturer was spending "quality time" with the child. Similar findings are supported in Hamer's (2001) study on adult African-American fathers who primarily described fatherhood in terms of the involved nurturer, and by Allen and Doherty's (1998) study with African-American teen fathers who stated that "being there" or being involved nurturers was more important than economically providing.

The independent father was one who deliberately opted out of fatherhood by not conceptualizing fatherhood as an important role or function and who did not accept fatherhood as a salient identity in his life. Many reasons for this were offered, namely that they felt they were too young to be burdened with fathering. Some felt that the pregnancy was the mother's fault and therefore her full responsibility.

Despite how teen fathers defined fatherhood, their fatherhood behaviors tended to be inconsistent with their conceptualizations. For instance, adolescent fathers who primarily identified the role of fathers as providers did little to make regular, consistent economic provisions for their children. Their sources of income were mainly from their parents or from part-time jobs, which very few held. Other sources of income were obtained through illegal means such as selling drugs. Some of the fathers experienced role strain because of their inability to perform as fathers. Similarly, fathers who conceptualized fathers as involved nurturers and emotional supporters did not spend regular, consistent time with their children, and very few engaged in caregiving activities such as feeding, bathing, and clothing their children. Although by their own standards they did not spend as much time as they could have, generally they did spend some, albeit little, time with their children. Independent fathers, however, were most consistent with their perceived responsibilities as fathers and their

174   VOICES OF AFRICAN-AMERICAN TEEN FATHERS

enactment of their conceptualized roles. Focusing mainly on themselves, they spent the least amount of time with their children and provided almost no economic support for them. This was consistent with what they thought they should do.

Many teen fathers were able to reconcile the inconsistencies in their conceptualization of fatherhood and their enactment of it by rationalizing their actions and/or by planning to improve their fathering behaviors as adults. For instance, most fathers rated themselves somewhat positively as fathers because they felt that they performed well in these roles considering their young ages, poor socioeconomic circumstances, and limited resources. Almost all planned to provide more for their children later in life, or planned to spend more time with them when they were able to afford transportation, for example. Although they admitted that their provisions were small in comparison to the actual needs of their children, they believed that they were doing their best considering the obstacles they faced, and most did not feel that they were "running from their responsibilities." Still, they placed most, if not all, responsibility for raising and providing for their children on the children's mothers. Of course, this was not true for several; African-American teen fathers are not a monolithic group, regardless of similarities in socioeconomic backgrounds. For instance, some young fathers were very caring, worked, and did their best to provide and spend time with their children. Yet, in most instances, the fathers considered their roles as supplemental and as "bonuses."

The third area of inquiry was the teen father's relationships with others. These relationships were examined in order to explore the impact, if any, they had on the young father's parenthood experience and vice versa. The author first examined the relationship between fathers and their families of origin. The frequency and intimacy with which one's family interacts provides the primary means by which culture gets transmitted (Seward 1991). In fact, a family's culture, or informal means of social control, influences a father's behavior more than governmental laws or formal means used by institutions (Seward 1991). For instance, Allen and Doherty (1998) surmised from their findings that the relationships the adolescent fathers had with the mothers of their children were influenced by the heterosexual relationships modeled in their families of origin. Also, eight of the ten participants in their study had fathers who were teen parents. In the current study, the stories told by the African-American teen fathers indicated that their families were instrumental in transmitting parenting values and behaviors. The teen father's parents influenced his expectations about how his position as father should be performed. In fact, the most influential persons in the teen father's life, in regard to his fatherhood, were his parents.

Most of the teen fathers did not have their biological fathers living in their homes; twenty-four of the thirty teens lived in single-parent, female-headed households. They discussed their fathers in feelings and behaviors characterized by nonchalance, pain and dejection, and anger and resentment. Most constructed fatherhood against what they experienced with their own fathers, which was most often marred by absenteeism and modest economic support. The pain and frustration these experiences brought them were evident in their stories. Thus, most of the young fathers resolved to become better parents to their children than their fathers were to them. This was similar to Allen and Doherty's (1998) findings. However, even with their resolve to be different, the behaviors demonstrated by them closely resembled the parenting behaviors exhibited by their fathers.

Adolescent fathers who lived with their adult fathers, and those few whose nonresidential fathers were involved in their lives, did not construct fatherhood against their fathers' behaviors. Instead, their views of their fathers were positive, and they intended to carry out parenting behaviors that were similar to those demonstrated by their fathers. These behaviors included providing economic and nurturing/emotional support for their children as well as discipline. Discipline was not mentioned as a fatherhood role by any of the young fathers who did not have adult fathers living in their households—it was discussed only by adolescent fathers who had fathers or father figures in their homes. This exclusion by the other fathers could be due to a number of reasons, including that the children were so young that discipline was not yet a concern. Also, since the teen fathers did not live with the children, perhaps this role was viewed as the responsibility of their children's mothers. Nonetheless, the omission of this role (disciplinarian) by the young fathers who were raised by single mothers may demonstrate how present fathers may impact the conceptualization of fatherhood in their sons.

The relationships that the teen fathers had with their adult mothers were mainly positive. Even though the mothers did not approve of their son's paternity, they were generally supportive and encouraged the teens to be responsible fathers. In fact, in most cases the teens reported that it was mostly with their mothers that they discussed fatherhood concerns and problems. Similar results were found in an earlier study conducted by Hendricks and colleagues (1981) who found that African-American adolescent fathers were more likely to go to their families for help with a problem. In the present study, the mothers were also the teens' primary sources of economic support for their children. However, some mothers who were already finding it difficult to meet the financial needs of their own families were not able to provide assistance for their teen sons' children, according to the fathers.

The types of relationships the fathers had with the young mothers of their children were also explored. These relationships fell into three basic categories: friendly and positive, romantic and loving, and negative and hostile. The categories that emerged in this study were similar to Hamer's (2001). However, not every relationship fit nicely into one category. What was significant was that the type of relationship the father had with the mother of his child seemed to influence his fathering behavior. Most of the fathers stated that their relationships with the mothers were generally friendly and positive. These relationships were not typically romantic and loving (although some fathers suspected the mothers wanted such), but rather casual and amicable both before and after the birth of their children. These relationships were characterized as positive because the fathers had amicable relationships with the mothers.

In these friendship situations, the fathers generally said they were encouraged to visit with their children as often as they wanted. Although the fathers used the term "friend" to describe the mothers in this category, the term seemed loosely defined and used since it also depicted relationships in which some of the fathers exploited the mothers, even after the births. For instance, a couple of fathers described how they pretended to have some feelings for the mothers in order to avoid having them seek future child support. A few discussed how they were "using" the mothers for sex. In addition, some had sexist orientations to their relationships and seemed to care little about the mothers' needs and concerns. Regardless of their motives, what was common about the relationships in this category was

Discussion and Conclusion

177

that they "got along," and that, by their own definitions, these mothers were "friends."

The second most reported form of relationship between the father and the mother of his child was described as romantic and loving. The fathers were usually already in a romantic, loving relationship before the pregnancy. These relationships tended to have a positive impact on their fathering behavior. Becoming fathers under these conditions, they reported, tended to enhance their relationships with the mothers, many of whom they planned to marry. Because of the close nature of this type of relationship, the fathers spent more time with their children and provided more economic support in general than did fathers who defined the relationship as friendship.

Finally, some fathers had negative, unfriendly relationships with the mothers. This was the least reported type, and these antagonistic relationships usually developed after the pregnancies. Thus, fatherhood status appeared to initiate these negative relationships. Fathers who categorized their relationships with the mothers in these terms were most likely independent fathers. They were more apt to blame the mothers for the pregnancies and the decisions to bear the children. Not surprisingly, these relationships created negative conditions for paternal behaviors. These young fathers provided less economic and nurturing/emotional support for their children than did other fathers with more positive relationships with the mothers.

The friends of the adolescent fathers were not influential on the teen fathers' conceptualizations of fatherhood or on their paternal behaviors. This finding was interesting considering that when fathers discussed their activities, interests, and hobbies, they usually mentioned activities they did with their friends. However, they did not turn to their friends for advice or assistance regarding fatherhood problems or concerns. Furthermore, their behaviors as fathers, such as the time spent with their children, were not influenced by their friends. In fact, most fathers reported that they spent about as much time with their friends after becoming fathers as they did before (although there were a few of exceptions). Likewise, their fatherhood status did little to impact their friendships; the teens stated that very little had changed in their relationships with their peers.

What their peers were most influential in impacting, however, was the fathers' sexual behavior before becoming fathers. Although most fathers reported that having sex with many young women was not

178 VOICES OF AFRICAN-AMERICAN TEEN FATHERS

personally important to them, it was, however, important in meeting the approval of their friends, supporting some of the assertions made in Anderson's (1989, 1990) study. The more young women with whom they had sex, the greater the perceived status among their peers. It is not clear whether this actually affected their becoming fathers, because most adolescent fathers reported that although they knew many young women with children, they knew few male adolescents with children. Only a few said they had a friend who was also a teen father. This supports the literature somewhat in that more than half of all teen mothers are impregnated by older men (Lindberg et al. 1997; Kansas Department of Health and Environment 2002).

The youngest fathers in the study experienced elevation in status among their peers because of their fatherhood. According to them, their peers admired and "respected" their new status. This finding may support some of the literature (Dash 1989; Anderson 1989, 1990) which suggests that adolescent parenthood is seen as a symbol of adulthood status among African-American youth.

Next, the challenges and concerns African-American fathers had as parents were examined. Some of these were at the individual level and were youth related. For instance, one of the greatest challenges for most of the fathers was making the transition to fatherhood. Many had trouble identifying with the fatherhood role because of their adolescence. Sometimes their youth was used as a crutch or explanation for their inabilities or reluctance to provide economic or nurturing support for their children. Some explained that they did not know how to be parents and were too young to act as one.

Another concern was related to their relationships with the mothers of their children. Negative relationships with the mothers presented problems in their abilities and/or willingness to do fathering. They did not separate the relationship with the mothers from their children. Therefore, if they did not like the mothers or had a bad relationship with her, they were not likely to attempt to spend very much time with their children (because they did not want to be around the mothers), and they were not likely to attempt to provide any economic support. The fathers felt less obligated to provide financial support if they did not have a positive relationship with the young mothers. Thus, negative relationships presented a challenge, in their views, to enacting fatherhood roles.

Some of the fathers feared that the mothers would eventually implement legally enforced child support. This was a concern that was expressed by many. Although nearly all of them planned to provide economic support as adults, they did not want to be pressured or required to provide this support. As "men" they wanted to do this on their own volition. Although providing support was perceived as a responsibility, both how much support they provided and how they provided it were perceived as a choice. Thus, they resented the idea that they may be stripped of this decision. Interestingly, the fathers mentioned that most of the mothers did not threaten to demand formal child support; the mothers' main requests centered on wanting the fathers to spend more time with their children and/or with them.

Another concern discussed was "losing freedom." The fathers defined this loss as loss of "free time" (e.g., feeling as if they were not able to spend enough time with their friends, or believing that they might not be able to do activities because of time spent with their children), loss of or limitations in choices of careers and schools (e.g., feeling pressured to find a job or join the military as opposed to going to college), and loss of mental or emotional freedom because of the pressures and responsibilities of being a parent. What was key in these findings, however, was that their "loss of freedom" appeared to be simply a concern. Very few of the young fathers adjusted their lives to accommodate their conceptualizations of fatherhood.

Other challenges and concerns pertained to the fathers' poverty or low socioeconomic status. For instance, many talked about how they had trouble making economic provisions for their children. Their reasons for this difficulty were based on reality—they had no money to give. Lack of monetary resources was related to not wanting to work "undesirable" jobs they perceived as demeaning (e.g., "flipping burgers") and/or that paid minimum wages, not having much time to work because they were still in school, not having reliable transportation or access to transportation, and not having parents who were in economic positions to help them financially provide for their children. Generally, the teens felt that they were not able to adequately perform their fatherhood roles because of their limited socioeconomic resources.

Other structural and culturally related challenges included the poor, segregated neighborhoods in which they lived. The young men discussed how prevalent drug exposure existed in their communities

180   VOICES OF AFRICAN-AMERICAN TEEN FATHERS

and schools and how their neighborhoods were infected with drug trade, violence, poor housing conditions, and unemployment and underemployment. They were concerned about these conditions and their children being raised in them. Many fathers also experienced or observed racism daily. These challenges will be further discussed in the next section.

Finally, the last research question dealt with how African-American teen fathers experience and construct their sense of masculinity. This issue was explored because of the significance it has for the enactment of manhood and fatherhood. Masculinity was intricately associated with the teens' definitions of fatherhood (e.g., traditional notion of provider/breadwinner), their positions and behaviors in relationships (e.g., dominance and self-focused behaviors in male-female relationships), and in their interactions with others (e.g., "tough guy" behavior among peers). How African-American young fathers express masculinity is important in understanding how they perceive and perform as men and as fathers. Social ecology and gender theory best explains how masculinity, social structure, and interaction intersect in the lives of African-American teen fathers.

THEORETICAL RELEVANCE OF FINDINGS

Social ecology and gender theory provide useful perspectives in trying to understand the subjective meanings African-American teens have of their fatherhood experiences. These theoretical paradigms are important explanatory tools for my observations. Social ecology theory suggests that certain events are best analyzed by considering the social-structural context in which they occur, their social meanings, and the cultural context in which they exist (Bronfenbrenner 1979). The significance of culture and structure is as important in understanding teen pregnancy and parenthood as are individual factors. The ecological framework was used in this study to understand African-American teen fathers' family lives, their obligations, and their decisions in terms of their social, cultural, and structural environments. Bronfenbrenner (1979) provided a theoretical framework for understanding the role each of these elements played in their everyday lives as fathers.

Bronfenbrenner (1979) theorized that these multiple environments are best conceptualized as four spheres: micro-, meso-, exo-, and macro-systems. In the current study, the microsystem included the

Discussion and Conclusion 181

dyadic relationship between the teen father and his child. Furthermore, other microsystems were discussed as well such as the dyadic relationship between the father and the mother of his child, the relationship between the teen father and his adult father, as well as others.

Bronfenbrenner (1979) talked about the mesosystem in terms of the relationships between microsystems and other settings. In this study, mesosystems would include the father-child relationship and how it associated with other microsystems, such as the teen's relationship with the mother of his child, as well refer to how the teen's relationship with his child was influenced by the relationship (or lack thereof) with his adult father, etc.

The exosystem included the broader institutions discussed in this study, mainly the economic and political institutions, and how they affected teen fathers and influenced their daily lives as fathers. Greater focus was placed on the economic realm, as seen in the teens' discussions and their references to poverty, residential segregation, and lack of resources, and how these factors impacted their fatherhood experiences.

Finally, such factors as values, laws, and customs, which make up the macrosystem, were addressed to explain how these factors may have encouraged or discouraged certain family formations (e.g., prevalence of female-headed household among African Americans), shaped the teens' conceptualizations of fatherhood (e.g., provider, nurturer, etc.), and influenced the teens' fathering behaviors. These concepts will be further addressed in the following paragraphs.

Where do the young men in the current study observe the practice of socially approved fatherhood, and is this important in order to enact it? According to Billson (1996), one of the factors that encourages the decision to accept a new identity is having models to demonstrate appropriate behavior for a particular identity. Thus, if teen fathers are to act appropriately in traditional masculine roles of fathers (providers), or even in other roles (e.g., involved nurturers), then they must see such behavior modeled by others. One young man in the current study mentioned how great his mother was but that the one thing she could not do for him was "teach me how to be a man." There seems to be some credence in what Billson (1996) stated if this young man's statement is also applied to fatherhood.

Most of the fathers conceptualized their roles of fatherhood around traditional definitions (provider). However, the question still remains of where they learn the ideals if they are not directly taught them or if they are not prevalently exposed to such practiced behaviors. Young men in American society are simply socialized to accept this ideal through a number of conduits: media (especially television), school, family members, social policies, law, peers, etc. (Myers 1998). The fathers in this study could not articulate where their conceptualizations actually originated, but they did know that their ideals were "right" and were expected of them. Some of these expectations were impressed upon them by their mothers—"she told me that I needed to be a man now." Regardless, their fatherhood ideals were deeply ingrained.

The prevalence of female-headed households and absent fathers can be understood in light of a number of macrostructural factors: limited economic resources, high rates of unemployment and underemployment, high imprisonment rates, poor access to health care, institutionalized racism, etc. These factors create a limited pool of "marriageable" African American men, and thus father-absent homes (Wilson 1987; Allen and Connor 1997). Evidence of this is seen in the prevalence of African-American teen fathers who live in homes without these adult men but who are expected to enact fathering behaviors in which their own adult fathers found it impossible or challenging to do.

Furthermore, the teen fathers in the current study are cognizant of the grave circumstances of their lives: high crime rates; high incidence of incarceration of other young male African Americans; intense exposure to drugs; homicides that had taken their male friends' and family members' lives; the neglect, pain, and anger they and many others have felt from their fathers not being involved (or being minimally involved) in their lives; and the disproportionate rates of unemployment and underemployment of other African-American men they knew (even among those who were college educated). These fathers are less likely to live as long as their white counterparts, and are not likely to outlive their female partners or wives (Staples 1985; Franklin 1989). The young fathers in this study felt the stigma of their race, and many dealt with racism on a daily basis. Several knew of others who felt helpless about their economic situations and felt hopeless about their futures. The environments in which they live are likely to promote feelings of hopelessness, according to the literature (Staples 1985; Wilson 1987; Myers 1998). So how do they deal with

Discussion and Conclusion 183

such alienation and hopelessness? How do they cope with trying to maintain their sense of masculinity in the face of such obstacles?

Some of the fathers were cogent enough to understand the link between these negative macrostructural factors and their culture. For example, one of them described these intersecting factors as their "neighborhood mentality." The "mentality" referred to a climate or culture produced by poor socioeconomic conditions, neighborhood segregation, and racism. This culture included a commonly accepted sense of hopelessness about the future and a tolerance of the circumstances in which they lived, according to the fathers. In turn, the people, the residents, re-created and reproduced the very poor, hopeless circumstances in which they lived. This is similar to what Lewis (1966) wrote in "The Culture of Poverty" many years ago. For instance, according to some of the fathers in the study, the people around them were complacent about their poor socioeconomic conditions and bleak futures, feeling they could do little to prevent or to change them. Their neighbors and communities, according to the fathers, accepted the perceived "pathologies" (e.g., crime, rampant drug use, teen pregnancy, father-absent homes, etc.) of their culture as "a way of life." If the perceptions of the fathers were correct, then this study supports the literature pointing to racial segregation and discrimination as the key factors associated with unemployment, underemployment, high crime rates, and feelings of alienation and hopelessness among poor, urban African Americans (Wilson 1987; Sampson and Wilson 1995; Massey and Denton 1993). Still, African-American teen fathers are expected (and this expectation is internalized) to become providers and nurturers in the face of these obstacles and what they perceive as bleak futures for themselves.

In the context of these conditions, these fathers (similar to most men in American society) perform masculinity and what it is to "be a man" by pursuing competitiveness, aggression, and dominance (Thompson 1989). However, when men of color are restricted in how and where they can pursue these traits (whether this is perceived or real), how, then, do they enact them, or do they enact them at all? They express their masculinity in untraditional or in socially disapproved manners (Staples 1985; Coates 1987; Franklin 1989; Thompson 1989). For instance, although men in this society are taught that they should become providers (meaning breadwinners), many socioeconomically poor African-American men are forced to modify this

184   VOICES OF AFRICAN-AMERICAN TEEN FATHERS

meaning or to adapt this concept to their environments. For instance, the concept of *provider* to the fathers in this study was synonymous with "helping the mothers out" or providing *some* assistance, but not being sole providers or significant contributors. The teens knew many African-American men who were unemployed, underemployed, lacked college education, and were not able to provide adequately for their children. Likewise, the fathers in this study were particularly concerned about not being able to adequately provide when they become adults, although they hoped they could do so. Knowing the role of traditional provider might be out of reach, they adopted a different social meaning of "provider"—they "helped out" or provided some monetary assistance toward the care of their children. The majority of teens adopted a traditional notion of fatherhood as provider, but they modified this meaning (partially or totally) because of their inabilities, or concerns about ability, to enact them.

This modified, adapted version of provider may have been further encouraged by their observations that their mothers and other women around them were the providers. Because of this (and the uninvolved parenting from the men around them, including their own noncustodial fathers), they may have developed a different notion or variation of the concept of provider. Namely, their role as fathers and as providers was expected to be more supplemental in nature. Their mothers enacted the traditional provider role as breadwinner in their families (perhaps this is why they expected the same of the mothers of their children). Nonetheless, their mothers acted as providers out of necessity and because of the circumstances brought on by the structural factors previously discussed. Nonetheless, the teen fathers are expected (and have internalized this expectation) to enact a role that has been culturally modified for them (although out of necessity), and a role that has been significantly shifted to members of the opposite sex in their culture.

Although the young fathers were taught to be ambitious and aggressive, they were also taught that they could not express such aggression in the workplace or in the pursuit of a vocation or career. Several had mentioned ideal jobs and careers (e.g., lawyer, engineer, professional athlete) they would have liked to have pursued, but throughout the course of the interviews they indicated beliefs that their lives were destined to low-paying jobs with little potential for career advancement or financial fulfillment. Institutionalized and individual racism played a role in why they thought they could not fulfill these dreams, or become "real men" in the workforce. For example, one father discussed how despite his efforts to advance in his current job he felt that racism continued to thwart his advancement. He believed that his experience was typical of African-American men in general. Many fathers adapted to their real and/or perceived limitations and adopted different methods of expressing male aggression. One of these adaptations involved expressing masculinity through efforts of "gaining respect."

The question is how African-American men obtain and experience respect, which is perceived as an important quality of their manhood, when they are not able to express their masculinity in traditional ways. Many young men in this study obtained respect via their peers and relationships with their female partners. Anderson (1990) observed that African-American youth gained "respect," admiration from peers, and a sense of manhood by being street tough, becoming drug dealers, carrying weapons, and having an abundance of money. As previously written, negotiating respect (which may involve violent behavior) is a cultural adaptation to the lack of gainful employment, poverty, lack of hope for the future, stigma of race, and the lack of faith in the legal system (Myers 1998; Anderson 1999). The young fathers in this study discussed many instances in which appearing tough among their peers and "getting respect" were very important. In fact, obtaining this respect almost cost the life of one of the fathers in the study. Anderson (1999) wrote that the "code" (street rules and protocol) and the negotiation of respect that is at its core are adaptations of masculinity in response to being poor, oppressed, and minority. Fighting and proving they were tough among their peers were commonly mentioned in the interviews in this study.

With their female partners, the young fathers in the current study emphasized their central importance as a man, in essence creating and reproducing the very nature of gender (West and Zimmerman 1987). Treatment of women as second class, for instance, was obvious with some of the young fathers interviewed, as well as were double standards regarding sex. Despite the cultural barriers they experienced, they had no problems "doing gender." Franklin (1989) described how African-American men, because of the barriers and limitations they experienced in trying to enact "productive" aspects of masculinity, express masculinity through sexual aggression, violence, and sexism. Although the fathers in the present study did not discuss sexual aggression or violence in their relationships, sexism definitely existed, and many had subjugating views about women and their roles in relationships.

For instance, in the negotiation of condom use they displayed traditional performances of gender. The findings suggested that the choice to use condoms was perceived as the man's prerogative. The fathers possessed more influence and control of contraceptive use, which supported prior research that found that women were less likely to be assertive with condom usage if the partner resisted (Detzer et al. 1995; Wingwood and DiClemente 1998). Thus, the expression of masculinity, or male dominance, in male-female interaction was apparent in the negotiation of condom use. Power, control, and male entitlement were at the core of their refusal to use them.

It should be stressed that social constructionist gender theory does not ignore individual agency. Regardless of the structural and cultural context, the fathers in this study were still responsible to some extent for their behaviors as parents and for their behaviors in relationships. That many differences existed among the fathers in all respects and that exceptions existed to all of the major findings of this study are an indication that the teen fathers made personal choices and enacted certain behaviors independent of their environments and community culture. Youth in itself also influences paternal behaviors regardless of cultural and structural factors.

In conclusion, masculinity was not a lost issue upon African-American teen fathers but was modified and expressed in ways that were potentially a detriment to their children, to their relationships with the mothers of their children, and to themselves. One of the principal ways in which they constructed their sense of masculinity and as men was through pursuing respect. This "respect" was obtained sometimes dangerously (e.g., fights, gang membership, association with drugs and weapons), sometimes sexually (impressing friends with the number of women with whom they have had sex), and sometimes by their dominance in male-female relationships (e.g., as demonstrated with condom use), even at the expense of life-altering consequences (unwanted pregnancy). The point is that African-American teen fathers have internalized and accepted the American standards of masculinity and fatherhood; however, various factors prevent the expressions of these behaviors. As a result, culture, social structure, and masculinity intersect in the lives of these fathers to produce parenting behaviors that fall in aberration to the standards of what is traditionally expected of fathers. The conceptualization and practice of fatherhood is redefined to be consistent with the oppression, alienation, and challenges they experience.

In the next and final chapter, Dr. Rhonda Lewis, PhD, MPH, will talk about where we should go from here in terms of serving and meeting the needs of young African-American fathers.

Chapter 10

Where Do We Go from Here?
Designing a Plan of Action

Rhonda Lewis

Several implications for action exist related to understanding the social construction of African-American adolescent fatherhood. The author identified three categories (provider, involved nurturer, and independent father) in which African-American adolescent fathers conceptualize their role as fathers, how the conceptualization impacts their roles as fathers, and their relationship with significant others and how this influences their roles as fathers. The *provider* is defined as a father that provides financial assistance for his child. The *involved nurturer* is defined by participants as being emotionally involved, physically present, and nurturing to his child. The *independent father* is defined as not particularly prepared to take on the fatherhood role and is detached from the role of father. In addition, the independent father blames the adolescent female for not taking responsibility for birth control.

The purpose of this chapter is to outline specific recommendations that could be used to design effective programs to help African-American adolescent fathers fulfill their fatherhood role. A number of the adolescent fathers reported that they were not ready for the responsibility of being a father but that they did want to provide financially for their children.

Rhonda Lewis, PhD, MPH, is Associate Professor of Psychology, Wichita State University.

Voices of African-American Teen Fathers
© 2006 by The Haworth Press, Inc. All rights reserved.
doi:10.1300/5477_11

THEORETICAL FRAMEWORKS

Four theoretical frameworks will be used to recommend prevention and intervention programs for African-American adolescent fathers and African-American males who may be at risk for early fatherhood:

1. The stages of change model (transtheorectical model) (Prochaska et al. 1992)
2. An Afrocentric perspective (Nobles 1998)
3. Brofrenbrenner's social ecology theory (Brofenbrenner 1979)
4. Bandura's social modeling theory (Ribes-Inesta and Bandura 1976)

Each model has implications for effective African-American adolescent fatherhood prevention (primary and secondary) programming (Mrazek and Haggerty 1994). A number of issues emerged from the study: (1) many of the adolescent fathers did not use a condom with their partners, (2) their conceptualization of fatherhood did not always translate into the actions of the role they described (with the exception of the independent father), and (3) in only a few cases did the adolescent fathers have an example of what a father should be to his children.

RECOMMENDATION #1:
DEVELOP AN ASSESSMENT TOOL

After examining the cultural context in which African-American adolescent fathers found themselves, the first recommendation would be to develop an assessment tool based on these results and develop questions using the stages of change model to document their condom use. Second, the assessment tool could document risk and protective factors (Hawkins and Catalano 1992) and cultural factors that might lend themselves to developing primary prevention programs for African-American male adolescents. Third, the assessment tool could identify the fatherhood characteristics of program participants and use that information to develop intervention programs to help African-American adolescent fathers fulfill their roles as fathers.

RECOMMENDATION #2: USE THE STAGES OF CHANGE MODEL TO ADDRESS CONDOM USE

From the assessment tool adolescent male condom use could be examined. For example, a number of adolescent fathers reported that they did not use a condom and that their female sexual partners did not require them to wear a condom. The stages of change model might be applied to help adolescent males increase their condom use if they are sexually active. The stages of change model (Prochaska et al. 1992) has the following five stages in which people find themselves in terms of behavior change:

1. The first stage is the *precontemplative stage* in which the person has not even considered using a condom.
2. The second stage is the *contemplative stage* in which the person thinks about using a condom but has not actually used a condom.
3. The third stage is the *preparation stage* in which the person has actually purchased condoms but has not used the condoms.
4. The fourth stage is the *action stage* in which the person actually begins using condoms during sexual intercourse.
5. The fifth stage is the *maintenance stage* in which the person uses condoms consistently and correctly every time he has sexual intercourse.

By applying the stages of change model, researchers or program planners could determine where African-American males are in terms of condom use and teach them effective ways of negotiating and communicating with their partners about condoms as well as dismissing the myths and embarrassment of purchasing condoms. Which stage the adolescents find themselves in would determine which intervention they would receive. In addition, a primary prevention program could be designed with African-American adolescents who have not fathered a child because of such an assessment, which may help prevent adolescent fathers who may be at risk from fathering a child. Also, from a secondary prevention perspective, adolescent fathers would be encouraged to avoid a second pregnancy.

RECOMMENDATION #3: IDENTIFY THE RISK, PROTECTIVE, AND CULTURAL FACTORS ASSOCIATED WITH EARLY ADOLESCENCE

The adolescent pregnancy prevention literature is particularly clear on the risks associated with adolescent pregnancy, including unsupervised free time, lack of condom use, and poor school grades (Card 1999; Gest et al. 1999; Holden et al. 1993; Lammers et al. 2000). Many of these studies have been conducted with adolescent females. Robbins and colleagues (1985) conducted a longitudinal study with both males and females to determine the antecedents of becoming a teen parent. They determined that school performance was a consistent predictor of adolescent pregnancy for both males and females. The study was conducted in the 1980s, thus more up-to-date research is needed to examine various risk and protective factors associated with adolescent pregnancy for both males and females.

It is important to document what the risk, protective, and cultural factors are for African-American adolescent males and develop comprehensive prevention programs that target this population. For example, incorporating a cultural component approach would be extremely beneficial. Nobles and Goddard (1999) defined culture as "the vast structure of behaviors, ideas, attitudes, values, habits, beliefs, customs, language, rituals, ceremonies, and practices peculiar to a particular group of people, and that it provides them with (1) a general design for living and (2) patterns for interpreting reality" (p. 285). In addition to examining the identified risk and protective factors, an intervention program might include an Afrocentric approach that would "reaffirm the right of African people to (1) exist as a people, (2) contribute to the forward flowing process of human civilization and culture, and (3) to share with as well as shape the world in response to our energy and spirit" (p. 288). An Afrocentric approach would put the existence of the African-American adolescent fathers into a broader context of life. For instance, Nobles and Goddard (1999) state that the Afrocentric approach refers "to the life experiences, history and traditions of African people as the center of one's analyses" (p. 286). The Afrocentric approach would allow researchers to explore the cultural context of African-American adolescent fathers and relate that approach to them fulfilling their roles as fathers in the way that African tradition has been demonstrated in past generations.

RECOMMENDATION #4: USE THE THREE IDENTIFIED CATEGORIES OF FATHERS TO DEVELOP AN EFFECTIVE INTERVENTION

The characteristics of the three identified father categories could be used to design an intervention to help African-American adolescent fathers fulfill their roles as fathers. A number of fathers had conceptualizations about what they wanted to be as fathers, but only the independent fathers' attitudes were consistent with their behavior. Many of the fathers that identified with the provider role were not able to fulfill that role because they were still in school and had to rely on their parents (mostly single mothers) to buy necessary items for their children. Although they identified with the provider role, they were not always able to fulfill that role they way they would like. Therefore, a tailored intervention focusing on job creation and developing job skills would be needed for this group of fathers.

The involved nurturers reported similar ideas of being involved with their children as being there and providing emotional support for their children. Perhaps parenting classes for both the adolescent female and male would be helpful in teaching young parents about what to expect in their new roles and what emotional support and being there truly means to an infant.

The independent father was not committed to his new role as father; therefore, an intervention is needed to help the fathers progress out of denial into accepting their responsibility for raising their children. Interventions might include coping with stress and parenting classes on adjusting to and fulfilling their new role.

Taken together, the assessment tool would be able to identify the characteristics of the particular fatherhood categories that emerge as well as additional fatherhood roles that at-risk African-American males might describe, and it could offer researchers a way to develop interventions designed for the various fatherhood categories. What follows is a discussion of how the Bronfenbrenner's (1979) social ecology model might be used to develop an intervention for African-American adolescent fathers at all levels of development.

Bronfenbrenner's (1979) model outlines four levels (individual, family, community, and societal/policy levels) whereby researchers can intervene to improve the quality of life in communities. Prevention programs could be designed that are constructed based upon the strongest father category that emerges.

First, researchers could develop assessment tools to identify African-American males who are at risk for becoming teen fathers and develop the appropriate intervention. For example, a majority of the teen fathers held beliefs that fathers are providers, and with this information prevention programs and interventions could be designed to address this conceptualization of fatherhood with realistic expectations about what fathers should be. As noted by the participant comments, although a majority of the teen fathers identified with the provider conceptualization of fatherhood, many of them were not fulfilling that role nor did they have males in their own lives that performed that function. Using Bronfenbrenner's (1979) social ecology theory, researchers could develop interventions that address individual factors, family factors, community factors, and societal-level factors.

Table 10.1 provides a description of what might be implemented for each father category at the individual, family, community, and societal level. For instance, if a researcher were to design an intervention program for an adolescent male that identified himself as a provider, the intervention might include at the individual level a program that would be designed to assist him with homework or job interviewing skills so that he could get a part-time job if he wanted one. In addition, an intervention might include learning how to cope with stress and how to use condoms correctly and consistently each time he has sexual intercourse. At the family level, the program might offer support groups for family members and money management classes for families so that each of the families can provide financial support to the adolescent father and the child. At the community level, businesses might generate coupons that the young father could earn to purchase needed items (blankets, furniture) that social services may not be able to provide. Instead of giving him a handout, the young father could do community service and earn points to purchase items for his child, or take classes on how to operate a small business. At the societal/policy level, businesses would be encouraged to hire African-American male adolescents, particularly African-American males who are fathers. Thus, by applying Bronfenbrenner's (1979) ecological model, the entire community can help teen fathers earn money for their children and fulfill their roles.

Where Do We Go from Here? Designing a Plan of Action

TABLE 10.1. Interventions by father category at the individual, family, community, and societal level.

Category	Individual level	Family level	Community level	Societal/ policy level
Provider	Ways to provide for children monetarily and nonmonetarily Communication skills Coping with stress Condom negotiation skills Parenting classes	Support groups for family members and mother of their child Communication skills between grandparents and teens	Positive father role models Change social norms around early fatherhood	Job training and job creation for adolescent males (particularly fathers) Educational attainment
Involved nurturer	Ways to interact with children at each stage of development Condom negotiation skills Parenting classes	Positive interaction with maternal grandparents	Positive father role models Change social norms	Job training and job creation for adolescent males Establishment of joint custody guidelines for unmarried parents
Independent father	Coping with stress and being a teen father Balancing their new role Positive play with children Condom negotiation skills Goal setting Parenting classes	Positive interactions with mother of the child	Positive father role models Change social norms	Job training and job creation Educational attainment

Last, in applying Bandura's (Ribes-Inesta and Bandura 1976) social modeling theory, these adolescent fathers reported not having many examples of fathers fulfilling any of the described roles. Embedded in gaining access to positive fatherhood models, an intervention should include specific instructions on how to translate the positive examples into action. Ribes-Inesta and Bandura (1976) offer four conditions necessary or effective modeling to occur: attention, retention, motor reproduction, and motivation. These conditions would be included within the comprehensive intervention for African-American adolescent fathers. First, *attention,* the person must first pay attention to the model. It is important for positive fatherhood models to be recruited and presented and for the adolescent father to pay attention to the model. Second, *retention,* the adolescent father must rehearse the behavior that was observed in order to act upon the behavior observed. Therefore, the intervention sessions would be developed so that adolescent fathers would practice being a provider and being an involved nurturer, for example. Third, *motor reproduction,* the father must produce the ability to replicate the behavior that has been modeled. For example, practicing interviewing skills, role-playing, changing a baby's diaper, or reading to an infant may be the behaviors that need to be replicated before behavior change would occur. Fourth, *motivation,* the final condition, the fathers must want to implement what was observed. Therefore, the adolescent father that pays attention, remembers the observed behavior, replicates the behavior, and applies the behavior will likely be successful in modeling fatherhood behaviors and fulfilling the role he has conceptualized. By including a modeling component, the fathers would get a chance to put their conceptualization of what fathers are into action.

LIMITATIONS

A number of limitations are noted with this approach. First, it might be difficult to fund such a project since most of the teenage pregnancy literature focuses on the female. Motivation from funders to focus on this issue of adolescent male fatherhood may be hard to find. Second, many of the fathers of adolescent mothers' children are adults, thus the sample from which to select adolescent male fathers might be small. Third, given the potential complexity of implementing such a program, involvement would be required from a number of partners, such as businesses, churches, and schools. It may be hard to find enough interest in the community to address this issue given that the community has so many other issues, such as youth violence, poverty, school finance, and unem-

Where Do We Go from Here? Designing a Plan of Action   *197*

ployment to address. Fourth, adolescent fathers might not be willing to participate in such a program if made available, and it would be difficult to motivate independent fathers who are not involved in their children's lives to participate.

In conclusion, the positive development of children is the critical aim of implementing such an intervention that would support African-American adolescent fathers. The hope is that the child would benefit from his or her father's involvement. It is important for researchers to discover and identify how African-American adolescent fathers construct their fatherhood roles, but an even more important step is to design a plan of action so that African-American adolescent fathers can fulfill their roles.

Appendix A

Interview Guide

PERSONAL DEMOGRAPHIC INFORMATION

1. How old are you?
2. What is your current marital status (married, single, divorced)?
3. How many years of school have you completed?
4. Are you in school now?
   If so, what year or grade?
5. Are you currently employed?
   If yes, how long have you been employed?
   Is this job part-time or full-time?
6. How many children do you have?
   What is/are the age(s)?
   Sex?
7. How old were you when you first became a father?
8. How many children live with you?
9. How many people live in your household (including yourself)?
10. How many people living in your home are under eighteen years old (including yourself if this applies)?
11. What is the highest level of education your mother has completed? Your father?
12. How much income do you think comes into your household per month?
13. Is anyone in your household receiving public assistance or welfare?

IDENTITY QUESTIONS

1. Will you please tell me a little about yourself?
2. How would you describe yourself?
3. What things are important to you?

Voices of African-American Teen Fathers
© 2006 by The Haworth Press, Inc. All rights reserved.
doi:10.1300/5477_12

200   *VOICES OF AFRICAN-AMERICAN TEEN FATHERS*

SOCIOECONOMIC CIRCUMSTANCES AND PERCEIVED FUTURE OUTLOOK

1. In your opinion, what would be your ideal job or career?
2. What type of job or career do you think you will have five years from now?
   Ten?
3. From what you have seen or experienced, are jobs available to most people around you?
   If so, what types?
   If not, why do you think this is the case?
4. Is higher education (such as college or university education) hard to attain for most people you see?
   Why or why not?
5. How do you feel about your neighborhood?
6. Is your neighborhood or community meeting your needs as a father, and if so, how?
   If not, why do you think it's not?
7. Is your neighborhood or community a good place to raise children?
   Why or why not?

TRANSITION TO FATHERHOOD

1. How did you feel and react when you found out that the mother of your child was pregnant?
2. How did the mother of your child react when she found out she was pregnant?
3. How did your family and your child's mother's family react to the pregnancy?
4. Has anything in your life changed since you have had a child, and if so how?
   If not, why do you think this has been the case?
5. What has been the biggest adjustment you have had to make since the birth of your child?
6. What things have been helpful or have made it easier for you to be a father, if anything at all?
7. What challenges do you face as a father?
   What hardships or trials have you experienced?
8. What has been the greatest thing about being a father?

Appendix A: Interview Guide 201

DEFINITION OF FATHERHOOD

1. How important is being a father to you? How responsible do you feel you should be at this point?
2. How do you define fatherhood/What does being a father mean to you?
3. What makes someone a good father? A good mother?
4. What can you tell me about your relationship with your own father?
5. Has your relationship with your own father (or the nonexistence thereof) shaped your own views about how you feel about fatherhood?
6. What things in your life, or people in your life, have (in your opinion) shaped how you feel about being a father?

SEXUAL EXPERIENCE AND BACKGROUND

1. How old were you when you first had sex?
2. How many sexual partners have you had to date?
3. How old is your baby's mother?
4. Did you and the mother of your child plan for the pregnancy to occur?
5. Was she using birth control? Were you using a condom?
6. What types of birth control methods have you and your female partner used?
7. Which birth control method works best for you?
8. Did you use protection the last time you had sex? If not, why?
9. Were you in love with the baby's mother when she got pregnant?
10. Are you in an intimate relationship with the baby's mother now?

FATHERHOOD INVOLVEMENT
AND PARENTAL SUPPORT

1. Describe your child (or children) to me.
2. How often do you see your child?
3. Do you have visitation rights?
   Are you pleased with them?
   Why or why not?
4. Where do you normally visit with your child?
5. Do you feel comfortable around your child?
6. Describe the way in which you and the baby communicate.
7. What activities do you do with your child?
8. Are you able to contribute to the support of your child?
   If so, could you please describe in what way(s) you do so, and how often?

VOICES OF AFRICAN-AMERICAN TEEN FATHERS

9. What is it like providing for your child?
10. Are there things that you really enjoy doing and things that you really don't like doing?
11. Who do you go to if you need help or advice?
    What else, if anything, do you find useful?
12. What sort of relationship do you want with your child as he or she gets older?
13. Does your paid employment have an impact on the way you father?

RELATIONSHIP WITH MOTHER OF CHILD

1. Does the mother of your child help or get in the way of your relationship with your child?
   What about your child's maternal grandparents (the parents of the child's mother)?
2. Is the mother of your child, in your opinion, satisfied with how much time you spend with your child?
3. Is the mother of the child, in your opinion, satisfied with what you have been able to provide for the child?
   Are you satisfied?
4. Is your child's mother receiving public assistance or welfare?
   If so, is it adequate or helpful in your opinion?
5. What is your current opinion about women and relationships?

PEER RELATIONSHIPS

1. Do you have any friends, and if so, could you please describe your friendship(s)?
2. How did your friends react when they found out you were going to be a father?
3. Are any of your friends teen fathers?
4. What are your friends' views about women—about being in relationships?
   About children?
   About sex in general?
5. Has your relationship with your friends changed since you have become a father?
   If so how?

Appendix A: Interview Guide 203

RELATIONSHIP WITH FAMILY OF ORIGIN

1. Describe your interactions/relationships with your family.
2. How often does your family (mother, father, sisters, brothers, etc.) interact with your child?
3. How do you think your own family of origin (the family in which you were raised) impacts your experience as a father?

OTHER QUESTIONS

1. What things, if any, do you feel that your community could provide that would make parenting easier for young adults?
   That your state or government could provide, if anything?
2. Are there any issues or questions I didn't cover that you would like to discuss?

Appendix B

Brief Biographies of Participants (Listed by Age)

Pseudonym	Bio

David

Fourteen years old
Has a four-month-old biracial son, Damon
Mother of his child is fifteen years old and white
Reported having had three sexual partners, including mother of child
Lives with his father, mother, and older sister
In ninth grade
Wants to be an English, social studies, or history teacher, in addition to being a writer

Malik

Fourteen years old
Has a six-month-old daughter, Jamillah
Mother of child is sixteen years old
Reported having had four sexual partners, including mother of child
Lives with mother and two sisters
In eighth grade
Wants to be a lawyer

Randy

Fourteen years old
Eight-month-old daughter, Brandi
Mother of child is fifteen years old
Reported having had six sexual partners, including mother of child
Lives with mother, grandmother, brother, and sister
In eighth grade

Voices of African-American Teen Fathers
© 2006 by The Haworth Press, Inc. All rights reserved.
doi:10.1300/5477_13

206 *VOICES OF AFRICAN-AMERICAN TEEN FATHERS*

Wants to be drafted into professional basketball right after high school

Jarrod
Fifteen years old
Has a three-month-old son, Demaris
Mother of child is seventeen years old
Reported having had two sexual partners, including mother of child
Lives with father and sister
In tenth grade
Wants to be a police officer

Jeremy
Fifteen years old
Has an eleven-month-old daughter, Jasmine
Mother of child is seventeen years old
Reported having had two sexual partners, including mother of child
Lives with his mother and older sister
In tenth grade
Not sure about plans after high school, but may go to college

Michael
Fifteen years old
Has two children: eleven-month-old son, Mike (whose mother is nineteen years old) and a two-month-old daughter, Crystal (whose mother is fifteen years old)
No information obtained on sexual history
Lives with mother and two older brothers
Was going into tenth grade the next month
Wants to be a professional basketball player

Tyreese
Fifteen years old
Has a one-year-old son, Aaron
Mother of child is sixteen years old
Reported having had seven sexual partners, including mother of child
Lives with his mother and stepfather, but has two older brothers (one is a preacher, and the other was recently incarcerated) and an older sister not living in their household
In ninth grade
Wants to be a professional athlete, but he is not sure about his own career or educational plans

Appendix B: Brief Biographies of Participants 207

Calvin

Sixteen years old
Has an eight-month-old daughter, Denae
Mother of child is eighteen years old
Reported having had four sexual partners, including mother of child
Lives with his mother, two sisters, and one brother
In tenth grade
Wants to be a mechanic

Clayton

Sixteen years old
Has an eight-month-old daughter, Kierra
Mother of child is fifteen years old
Reported having had six sexual partners, including mother of child
Resides with his mother, three sisters, a brother, and two nieces, with one sister currently pregnant
In ninth grade
Not sure about future career, but would like to own his own business

Eric

Sixteen years old
Has a four-month-old biracial son, Daniel
Mother of child is sixteen years old and white
No information obtained on sexual history
Lives with his mother and grandmother; no siblings
In tenth grade
Believes he will play professional football

Mark

Sixteen years old
Has a four-month-old son, Marquise
Mother of child is seventeen years old
Reported having had seven sexual partners, including mother of child
Lives with his mother and one of his two older brothers
In tenth grade
Wants to play football in college, then wants to play professional football

Bailey

Sixteen years old
Has a six-month-old son, Mykie
Mother of child is fifteen years old

208   VOICES OF AFRICAN-AMERICAN TEEN FATHERS

Reported having had five sexual partners, including mother of child
Lives with his mother; his older brother is in the army
In tenth grade
Will be starting a part-time job in a warehouse
Not sure about career or educational plans

Tevin   Sixteen years old
               Has a six-month-old daughter, Tracie
               Mother of child is nineteen years old
               Reported having had five sexual partners, including mother of child
               Lives with his mother, aunt, older male cousin, and three brothers
               In eleventh grade
               Wants to be a music producer, rapper

Alinius   Seventeen years old
               Has a three-month-old daughter, Starr
               Mother of child is sixteen years old
               Reported having had six or seven sexual partners, including mother of child
               Lives with his mother and two younger brothers
               In eleventh grade
               Wants to be a physician; plans to go to college and work part-time; not sure what his major in college will be

Carl   Seventeen years old
               Has a four-month-old daughter, Robin
               Mother of child is seventeen years old
               Reported having had two sexual partners, including mother of child
               Lives with his mother
               In twelfth grade and in an international baccalaureate program
               Plans to go to college and major in pre-law

Craig   Seventeen years old
               Has a two-year-old daughter, Joy
               Mother of daughter is sixteen years old
               Reported having had three sexual partners, including mother of child

Appendix B: Brief Biographies of Participants 209

Lives with his mother and sister
Works part-time at a factory at night
In eleventh grade at an alternative high school that is located in a mall
Plans to go into the air force

Darrius
Seventeen years old
Has a two-year-old son, Alex
Mother of child seventeen years old
Reported having had more than fifteen sexual partners, including mother of child
Lives with his grandmother, has no siblings, but several half and stepsiblings who reside with his mother in another state and with his father who lives in still another state
In twelfth grade
Not sure about career or educational plans after high school, but considering the music industry as a rapper

James
Seventeen years old
Has a seven-month-old son, Kenis
Mother of child is eighteen years old
Reported having had eight sexual partners, including mother of child
Lives with mother, mother's boyfriend, and two younger sisters
In eleventh grade
Wants to be a professional basketball player

Paul
Seventeen years old
Has an eleven-month-old daughter, Brianna
Mother of child is seventeen years old
Reported having had four sexual partners, including mother of child
Lives with his mother and grandmother
In twelfth grade
Does not plan to go to college, but unsure about what he will do when he graduates from school

Russell
Seventeen years old
Has a one-year-old son, Rus
Mother of child is seventeen years old
Reported having had seven sexual partners, including mother of child
Lives with mother and two brothers

VOICES OF AFRICAN-AMERICAN TEEN FATHERS

In eleventh grade
Plans to go to college but unsure about major

Steve   Seventeen years old
Has an eleven-month-old daughter, Shanelle
Mother of daughter is seventeen years old
The mother of his child has been his only sex partner
Lives with father, mother, sister (but also has another sister)
Going into the twelfth grade
Works part-time at a dry cleaners
After high school, plans to get a job at one of the local aircraft companies

Bill   Eighteen years old
Has a fifteen-month-old son, Justin
Mother of child is eighteen years old and white
Reported having had three sexual partners, including mother of child
Lives with mother and two sisters
Works part-time at a fast-food restaurant
In twelfth grade
Plans to go to college; might major in computer engineering

Brandon   Eighteen years old
Has a one-and-a-half-year-old son, Keeshawn
Mother of child is seventeen years old
Reported having had four sexual partners, including mother of child
Lives with his mother and older sister
Is in the twelfth grade
Plans to attend a community college after high school; not sure about major

Byron   Eighteen years old
Has an eleven-month-old biracial daughter, Asia
Mother of child is seventeen years old and white
Reported having had two sexual partners, including mother of child
Lives with his mother and sister
In twelfth grade
Works at a hardware/lumber store
Plans to go into the military after high school

Appendix B: Brief Biographies of Participants 211

Edward

Eighteen years old
Has a two-year-old son, Edward Jr.
Mother of child is seventeen years old
Reported having had six sexual partners, including mother of
child
Lives with mother and father; has no siblings
Has graduated from high school
Not employed; not in school
Wanted to be a professional basketball player, but not sure
about career plans—stated that he will probably get a job

Roman

Eighteen years old
Has a three-year-old son, Jamal
Mother of child is nineteen years old
No information on past sexual history obtained
Lives sometimes with mother, but mostly with his friends/ gang
members and considers himself financially independent
of his mother
Has no siblings
Not in school—dropped out; not employed
Has been in a gang for four years
No career or educational plans; believes he will end up incar-
cerated or in prison within next five years

Dwayne

Nineteen years old
Has two children: two-year-old daughter, Adrianne (whose
mother is nineteen years old) and an eight-month-old son,
Ricky (whose mother is eighteen years old).
Reported having had four sexual partners, including mothers
of children
Resides on college campus, stays at home on the weekends
Attends college, majoring in psychology
Works in the military reserve

Jermaine

Nineteen years old
Has two children: seven-month-old son, Nicholas (whose
mother is twenty-one years old), and a two-year-old son,
Cornell (whose mother is eighteen years old)
Reported having had ten or eleven sexual partners, including
mothers of children
Lives with his father, stepmother, biological sister, three
stepsisters, and two stepbrothers

212 VOICES OF AFRICAN-AMERICAN TEEN FATHERS

Graduated from high school
Used to work as an assistant manager at a restaurant until he got into legal trouble

Keith
Nineteen years old
Has a thirteen-month-old son, Todd
Mother of child is seventeen years old
Reported having had six sexual partners, including mother of child
Lives with his mother and two younger sisters; has also lived with his grandmother
In twelfth grade
Had no career or educational plans at time of interview

William
Nineteen years old
Has a nine-month-old daughter, Audrey
Mother of child is eighteen years old
Reported having had seven sexual partners, including mother of child
Lives alone, independently of his family
Graduated from high school
Works in customer service for a telemarketing company

References

Alan Guttmacher Institute. 1999a. *Facts in Brief: Teenage Reproductive Health in the United States.* New York: Author.

Alan Guttmacher Institute. 1999b. *Teenage Pregnancy: Overall Trends and State-by-State Information.* New York: Author.

Allen, W.D., and Connor M. 1997. "An African American Perspective on Generative Fathering." *Generative Fathering: Beyond Deficit Perspectives* (pp. 52-70). Edited by A.J. Hawkins and D.C. Dollahite. Thousand Oaks, CA: Sage Publications.

Allen, W.D. and W.J. Doherty. 1998. "Being There: The Perception of Fatherhood among a Group of African-American Adolescent Fathers." In *Resiliency in African-American Families* (pp. 207-244). Edited by H.I. McCubbin and E.A. Thompson. Thousand Oaks, CA: Sage Publications.

Andersen, M.L. 1993. "Studying Across Difference: Race, Class and Gender in Qualitative Research." In *Race and Ethnicity in Research Methods* (pp. 39-52). Edited by J.H. Stanfield II and R.M. Dennis. Newbury Park, CA: Sage Publications.

Anderson, E. 1989. "Sex Codes and Family Life among Poor Inner-City Youths." *Annals of the American Academy of Political and Social Science* 501:59-78.

Anderson, E. 1990. *Streetwise: Race, Class, and Change in an Urban Community.* Chicago, IL: The University of Chicago Press.

Anderson, E. 1999. *Code of the Street: Decency, Violence, and the Moral Life of the Inner City.* New York: W.W. Norton & Company.

Aronson, R.E., T.L. Whitehead, and W.L. Baber, 2003. "Challenges to Masculine Transformation among Urban Low-Income African Males." *American Journal of Public Health* 93(5):732-741.

Battle, S.F. and J.L.R. Battle. 1987. "Adolescent Sexuality: Cultural and Legal Implications." In *The Black Adolescent Parent* (pp. 125-136). Edited by J.H. Stanfield II and R.M. Dennis. Newbury Park, CA: Sage Publications.

Bengtson, V.L. and K.R. Allen. 1993. "The Life Course Perspective Applied to Families Over Time." In *Sourcebook of Family Theories and Methods: A Contextual Approach* (pp. 482-483). Edited by P.G. Boss, W.J. Doherty, R. LaRossa, W.R. Schumm, and S.K. Steinmetz. New York: Plenum Press.

Billingsley, A. 1992. *Climbing Jacob's Ladder: The Enduring Legacy of African-American Families.* New York: Simon & Schuster.

Billson, J.M. 1996. *Pathways to Manhood: Young Black Males Struggle for Identity.* New Brunswick, NJ: Transaction Publishers.

Voices of African-American Teen Fathers
© 2006 by The Haworth Press, Inc. All rights reserved.
doi:10.1300/5477_14

214   *VOICES OF AFRICAN-AMERICAN TEEN FATHERS*

Blankenhorn, D. 1995. *Fatherless America: Confronting Our Most Urgent Social Problem.* New York: Basic Books.

Bronfenbrenner, U. 1979. *The Ecology of Human Development: Experiments by Nature and Design.* Cambridge, MA: Harvard University Press.

Bryman, A. and R.G. Burgess. 1994a. "Developments in Qualitative Data Analysis: An Introduction." In *Analyzing Qualitative Data* (pp. 1-17). Edited by A. Bryman and R. G. Burgess. New York: Routledge.

Bryman, A. and R.G. Burgess. 1994b. "Reflections on Qualitative data analysis." In *Analyzing Qualitative Data* (pp. 216-226). Edited by A. Bryman and R.G. Burgess. New York: Routledge.

Bubolz, M.M. and M.S. Sontag. 1993. "Human Ecology." In *Sourcebook of Family Theories and Methods: A Contextual Approach* (pp. 419-448). Edited by P.G. Boss, W.J. Doherty, R. LaRossa, W.R. Schumm, and S.K. Steinmetz. New York: Plenum Press.

Cannon, L.W., E. Higginbotham, and M.L.A. Leung. 1988. "Race and Class Bias in Qualitative Research." *Gender and Society* 2(4):449-462.

Card, J. 1999. "Teen Pregnancy Prevention: Do Any Programs Work?" *Annual Review of Public Health* 20:257-285.

Castiglia, P.T. 1990. "Adolescent Fathers." *Journal of Pediatric Health Care* 4:311-313.

Centers for Disease Control and Prevention. 2004. "Youth Risk Behavior Surveillance—United States, 2003." *Morbidity and Mortality Weekly Report* 53(SS-2): 1-96.

Centers for Disease Control and Prevention. 2005. "QuickStats: Infant Mortality Rates by Selected Racial/Ethnic Population—United States, 2002." *MMWR Weekly* 54(05):126.

Chadwick, B. and T.B. Heaton. 1998. *Statistical Handbook on the American Family.* Phoenix, AZ: Oryx Press.

Chafetz, J.S. 1999. "The Varieties of Gender Theory in Sociology." In *Handbook of the Sociology of Gender* (pp. 3-23). New York: Kluwer Academic/Plenum Publishers.

Christmon, K. 1990. "Parental Responsibility of African-American Unwed Adolescent Fathers." *Adolescence* 25:645-653.

Coates, D.L. 1987. "Gender Differences in the Structure and Support Characteristics of Black Adolescents' Social Networks." *Sex Roles* 17:667-687.

Collins, P. 1994. "The Meaning of Motherhood in Black Culture" In *The Black Family: Essays and Studies* (pp. 165-173). Edited by in R. Staples. Belmont, CA: Wadsworth Publishing Company, Inc.

Connell, R.W. 1987. *Gender and Power: Society, the Person and Sexual Politics.* Stanford, CA: Stanford University Press.

Connell, R.W., N. Radican, and P. Martin. 1989. "The Changing Faces of Masculinity: The Problem of Change." In *Men's Lives* (pp. 578-585). Edited by M.S. Kimmel and M.A. Messner. New York: Macmillan Publishing Company.

References 215

Dallas, C.M. and S.P.C. Chen. 1998. "Experiences of African American Adolescent Fathers." *Western Journal of Nursing Research* 20:210-222.

Dallas, C., T. Wilson, and V. Salgado. 2000. "Gender Differences in Teen Parents' Perceptions of Parental Responsibilities." *Public Health Nursing* 17(6):423-433.

Danziger, S. K. and N. Radin. 1990. "Absent Does Not Equal Uninvolved: Predictors of Fathering in Teen Mother Families." *Journal of Marriage and the Family* 42:636-642.

Dash, L. 1989. *When Children Want Children: The Urban Crisis of Teenage Childbearing*. New York: William Morrow and Company, Inc.

Dawsey, D. 1996. *Living to Tell About It: Young Black Men in America Speak Their Peace*. New York: Anchor Books Doubleday.

Denzin, N.K. 1994. "The Art and Politics of Interpretation." In *Handbook of Qualitative Research* (pp. 500-515). Edited by N.K. Denzin and Y.S. Lincoln. Thousand Oaks, CA: Sage Publications.

Detzer, M.J., S.J. Wendt, L.J. Solomon, E. Dorsch, B.M. Geller, J. Friedman, H. Hauser, B.S. Flynn, and A.L. Dorwaldt. 1995. "Barriers to Condom Use among Women Attending Planned Parenthood Clinics." *Women & Health* 23(1): 91-102.

Dey, I. 1993. *Qualitative Data Analysis: A User-Friendly Guide for Social Scientists*. New York: Routledge.

DiClemente, R.J., M. Durbin, D. Siegel, F. Krasnovsky, N. Lazarus, and T. Comacho. 1992. "Determinants of Condom Use Among Junior High School Students in a Minority, Inner City School District." *Pediatrics* 89:197-202.

Dixon, J.C., and Rosenbaum, M.S. 2004. "Nice to Know you? Testing Contact, Cultural, and Group Threat Theories of Anti-Black and Anti-Hispanic Stereotypes." *Social Science Quarterly* 85(2):257-280.

Edin, K. and L. Lein. 1997. *Making Ends Meet: How Single Mothers Survive Welfare and Low-Wage Work*. New York: Russell Sage Foundation.

Fagot, B.I., K.C. Pears, D.M. Capaldi, L. Crosby, and C.S. Leve. 1998. "Becoming an Adolescent Father: Precursors and Parenting." *Developmental Psychology* 34(6):1209-1219.

Franklin, C. 1984. *The Changing Definition of Masculinity*. New York: Plenum.

Franklin, C. 1989. "Black Male-Black Female Conflict: Individually Caused and Culturally Nurtured." In *Men's Lives* (pp. 365-373). Edited by M.S. Kimmel and M.A. Messner. New York: Macmillan Publishing Company.

Franklin, D.L. 1987. "Black Adolescent Pregnancy." In *The Black Adolescent Parent* (pp. 15-39). Edited by S.F. Battle. Binghamton, NY: The Haworth Press.

Furstenberg, F.F. 1976. *Unplanned Parenthood: The Social Consequences of Teenage Childbearing*. New York: Free Press.

Furstenberg, F.F. 1985. "Adolescent Pregnancy: Contributing Factors, Consequences, Treatment, and Plausible Solutions." *Adolescence* 20:281-289.

Furstenberg, F. F., J. Brooks-Gunn, and S. P. Morgan. 1987. *Adolescent Mothers in Later Life*. New York: Cambridge University Press.

216 VOICES OF AFRICAN-AMERICAN TEEN FATHERS

Gasden, V. and R.R. Smith. 1995. "African American Males and Fatherhood: Issues in Research and Practice." *Journal of Negro Education* 63:634-648.

Gasden, V.L., S.E.F. Wortham, and H.M. Turner III. 2003. "Situated Identities of Young, African American Fathers in Low-Income Urban Settings." *Family Court Review* 41(3):381-399.

Gerson, K. 1997. "The Social Construction of Fatherhood." In *Contemporary Parenting: Challenges and Issues* (pp. 119-153). Edited by T. Arendell. Thousand Oaks, CA: Sage Publications.

Gest, S., J. Mahoney, and R. Cairns. 1999. "A Developmental Approach to Prevention Research: Configural Antecedents of Early Parenthood." *American Journal of Community Psychology* 27:543-565.

Gilgun, J.F. 1999. "Methodological Pluralism and Qualitative Family Research." In *Handbook of Marriage and the Family* (pp. 219-261). Edited by M.B. Sussman, S.K. Steinmetz, and G.W. Peterson. New York: Plenum Press.

Groening, M. 1989. "The Road to Manhood." *Men's Lives* (pp. 126-127). Edited by M.S. Kimmel and M.A. Messner. New York: Macmillan Publishing Company.

Grunbaum, J.A., L. Kann, S. Kinchen, J. Ross, J. Hawkins, R. Lowry, W.A. Harris, T. McManus, D. Chyen, and J. Collins. 2004. "Youth Risk Behavior Surveillance—United States, 2003." *Morbidity and Mortality Weekly Report* 53(SS-2):1-98.

Hajnal, Z.L. 1995. "The Nature of Concentrated Urban Poverty in Canada and the United States." *Canadian Journal of Sociology* 20:497-528.

Hamer, J. 2001. *What It Means to be Daddy: Fatherhood for Black Men Living Away from their Children*. New York: Columbia University Press.

Harris, J.L. 1998. "Urban African American Adolescent parents: Their Perceptions of Sex, Love, Intimacy, Pregnancy and Parenting." *Adolescence* 33:833-844.

Haveman, R.H., B. Wolfe, and E. Peterson. 1997. "Children of Early Childbearers as Young Adults." In *Kids Having Kids: Economic Costs and Social Consequences of Teen Pregnancy* (pp. 257-284). Edited by R.A. Maynard Washington, DC: The Urban Institute Press.

Hawkins, D. and R. Catalano. 1992. *Communities that Care*. San Francisco: Josey-Bass.

Hendricks, L.E., C.S. Howard, and P.P. Caesar. 1981. "Black Unwed Adolescent Fathers: A Comparative Study of Their Problems and Help-Seeking Behavior." *Journal of the National Medical Association* 73:863-868.

Hendricks, L.E. and T. Montgomery. 1983. "A Limited Population of Unmarried Adolescent Fathers: A Preliminary Report of their Views on Fatherhood and their Relationship with the Mothers of their Children." *Adolescence* 69:201-210.

Hendricks, L.E. and A.M. Solomon. 1987. "Reaching Black Male Adolescent Parents through Nontraditional Techniques." *Child and Youth Services* 9:111-124.

Henshaw, S.K. 1996. *U.S. Teenage Pregnancy Statistics*. New York: Alan Guttmacher Institute.

Henslin, J.M. 1993. *Sociology: A Down-To-Earth Approach.* Boston, MA: Allyn and Bacon.

Hill, R.B. 1990. "Economic Forces, Structural Discrimination and Black Family Instability." In *Black Families* (pp. 87-105). Edited by H.C. Cheatham and J.B. Stewart. New Brunswick, NJ: Transaction Publishers.

Holden, G., P. Nelson, J. Velasquez, and K. Ritchie. 1993. "Cognitive, psychosocial and reported sexual behavior differences between pregnant and nonpregnant adolescents." *Adolescence* 28:557-572.

Holstein, J.A. and J.F. Gubrium. 1995. *The Active Interview.* Thousand Oaks, CA: Sage Publications.

Huang, C.J. and J.G. Anderson. 1991. "Anomie and Deviancy: Reassessing Racial and Social Status Differences." Paper presented at the annual meeting of the American Sociological Association, August 1991, Cincinnati, Ohio.

Hughes, C. 1994. "From Field Notes to Dissertation: Analyzing the Stepfamily." In *Analyzing Qualitative Data* (pp. 35-46). Edited by A. Bryman and R.G. Burgess. New York: Routledge.

Institute of Medicine. 1994. *Reducing Risks for Mental Disorders: Frontiers for Preventive Intervention Research.* Edited by P.J. Mrazek and R.J. Haggerty. Washington, DC: National Academy Press.

Jaccard, J., P.J. Dittus, and V.V. Gordon. 2000. "Parent-Teen Communication About Premarital Sex: Factors Associated with the Extent of Communication." *Journal of Adolescent Research* 15(2):187-208.

Johnson, E.S., A. Levine, and F.C. Doolittle. 1999. *Fathers' Fair Share: Helping Poor Men Manage Child Support and Fatherhood.* New York: Russell Sage Foundation.

Joshi, N., and S. Battle. 1990. "Adolescent Fathers: An Approach for Intervention." *Journal of Health and Policy* 1:17-33.

Kalmuss, D., A. Davidson, A. Cohall, D. Laraque, and C. Cassell. 2003. Preventing Sexual Risk Behaviors and Pregnancy among Teenagers: Linking Research and Programs. *Perspectives on Sexual and Reproductive Health* 35(2):87-93.

Kansas Department of Health and Environment (KDHE). 1998. *Annual Summary of Vital Statistics 1988-1994.* Topeka, KS. Available online at: http://www.kdhe.state.ks.us.

Kansas Department of Health and Environment (KDHE). 2002. *Annual Summary of Vital Statistics 2002.* Topeka Kansas. Available online at: http://www.kdhe.state.ks.us/hci/as02/as2002.html.

Kaplan, E.B. 1997. *Not Our Kind of Girl: Unraveling the Myths of Black Teenage Motherhood.* Berkeley: University of California Press.

Kimball, C. 2004. "Teen Fathers: An Introduction." *The Prevention Researcher* 11(4):3-5.

Kimmel, M.S. 2000. *The Gendered Society.* New York: Oxford University Press.

Kimmel, M.S. and M.A. Messner. 1989. "Introduction." In *Men's Lives* (pp. 1-13). Edited by M.S. Kimmel and M.A. Messner. New York: Macmillan Publishing Company.

218   VOICES OF AFRICAN-AMERICAN TEEN FATHERS

Kinder, D.R. and T. Mendelberg. 1995. "Cracks in American Apartheid: The Political Impact of Prejudice among Desegregated Whites." *The Journal of Politics* 57(2):402-424.

Lammers, C., M. Ireland, M. Resnick, and R. Blum, R. 2000. "Influences on Adolescents' Decision to Postpone Onset of Sexual Intercourse: A Survival Analysis of Virginity among Youths Aged 13-18 Years." *Journal of Adolescent Health* 26:42-48.

Lerman, R. 1993a. "A National Profile of Young Unwed Fathers." In *Young Unwed Fathers: Changing Roles and Emerging Policies* (pp. 27-51). Edited by R. Lerman and T. Ooms. Philadelphia, PA: Temple University Press.

Lerman, R. 1993b. "Unwed Fathers: Who They Are." *The American Enterprise* 4:32-34.

Lewis, O. 1966. "The Culture of Poverty." *Scientific American* 115:19-25.

Lindberg, L., F.L. Sonenstein, L. Ku, and G. Martinez. 1997. "Age Differences between Minors who Give Birth and Their Adult Partners." *Family Planning Perspectives* 29(2):61-66.

Luker, K. 1996. *Dubious Conceptions: The Politics of Teenage Pregnancy*. Cambridge, MA: Harvard University Press.

Marsiglio, W. 1987. "Adolescent Fathers in the U.S.: Their Initial Living Arrangements, Marital Experience and Educational Outcomes." *Family Planning Perspective* 19:240-251.

Martin, J.A., B.E. Hamilton, P.D. Sutton, S.J. Ventura, F. Menacker, and M.L. Munson. 2003. Births: Final Data for 2003. *National Vital Statistics Reports* 54(2):57-58.

Massey, D.S. and N.A. Denton. 1993. *American Apartheid: Segregation and the Underclass*. Cambridge, MA: Harvard University Press.

McAdoo, J.L. 1990. "Understanding African-American Teen Fathers." In *Understanding Troubled and Troubling Youth* (pp. 229-245). Edited by Peter E. Leone. Newbury Park, CA: Sage Publications.

McCall, N. 1994. *Makes Me Wanna Holler*. New York: Vintage Books.

Messner, M.A. 1997. *Politics of Masculinities: Men in Movements*. Thousand Oaks, CA: Sage Publications.

Miller, D.B. 1997. "Adolescent Fathers: What We Know and What We Need to Know." *Child and Adolescent Social Work Journal* 14: 55-69.

Myers, L.W. 1998. *Black Male Socialization: Revisited in the Minds of the Respondents*. Stamford, CT: JAI Press, Inc.

Nobles, W. 1998. "To Be African or Not to Be: The Question of Identity or Authenticity—Some Preliminary Thoughts." In *African American Identify Development* (pp. 187-192). Edited by R.L. Jones. Hampton, VA: Cobb and Henry Publishers.

Nobles, W. and L. Goddard. 1999. "An African-Centered Model of Prevention for African American Youth at High Risk." In *African American Children, Youth*

References 219

and Parenting (pp. 115-129). Edited by R.L. Jones. Hampton, VA: Cobb and Henry Publishers.

Okely, J. 1994. "Thinking through Fieldwork." In *Analyzing Qualitative Data* (pp. 13-34). Edited by A. Bryman and R.G. Burgess. New York: Routledge.

Patton, M. 1990. *Qualitative Evaluation and Research Methods*. Newbury Park, CA: Sage Publications.

Philliber, S., L. Brooks, L.P. Lehrer, M. Oakley, and S. Waggoner. 2003. "Outcomes of Teen Parenting Programs in New Mexico." *Adolescence* 38(151):535-554.

Pirog-Good, M.A. 1995. "The Family Background and Attitudes of Teen Fathers." *Youth and Society* 26:351-376.

Popenoe, D. 1996. *Life Without Father*. New York: Free Press.

Prochaska, J., C. DiClemente, and J. Norcross. 1992. "In Search of How People Change: Applications to the Addictive Behaviors." *American Psychologist* 47: 1102-1114.

Rein, L.M., K.R. Ginsberg, D.F. Schwartz, J.A. Pinto-Martin, H. Zhao, A.P. Morgan, and G.B. Slap 1997. "Teen Father Participation in Child Rearing: Family Perspectives." *Journal of Adolescent Health* 21(4):244-252.

Reinharz, S. 1992. *Feminist Methods in Social Research*. New York: Oxford Press.

Ribes-Inesta, E. and A. Bandura. 1976. *Analysis of Delinquency and Aggression*. Hillside, NJ: L. Erlbaum Associates.

Robbins, C., H. Kaplan, and S. Martin. 1985. "Antecedents of Pregnancy among Unmarried Adolescents." *Journal of Marriage and the Family* 47:567-583.

Roberts, D. 1998. "The Absent Black Father." In *Lost Fathers: The Politics of Fatherlessness in America* (pp. 145-161). Edited by C.R. Daniels. New York: St. Martin's Press.

Robinson, B.E. 1988. "Teenage Pregnancy from the Father's Perspective." *American Journal of Orthopsychiatry* 58:46-51.

Rhodes, E.B. 2000. "Fatherhood Matters." *The American Prospect* 11(9):48-52.

Sampson, R.J. and W.J. Wilson. 1995. "Toward a Theory of Race, Crime, and Urban Inequality." In *Crime and Inequality* (pp. 37-54). Edited by J.H. and R.D. Peterson. Stanford, CA: Stanford University Press.

Seward, R.R. 1991. "Determinants of Family Culture: Effects on Fatherhood." In *Fatherhood and Families in Cultural Context* (pp. 218-236). New York: Springer Publishing Company.

Sidel, R. 1996. *Keeping Women and Children Last: America's War on the Poor*. New York: Penguin Books.

Stack, C. 1997. *All Our Kin*. New York: Basic Books.

Staples, R. 1985. "Changes in Black Family Structure: The Conflict Between Family Ideology and Structural Conditions." *Journal of Marriage and the Family* November: 1005-1013.

Stokols, D. 1996. "Translating Social Ecological Theory into Guidelines for Community Health Promotion." *American Journal of Health Promotion* 10(4):282-298.

220 VOICES OF AFRICAN-AMERICAN TEEN FATHERS

Strauss, A. and J. Corbin. 1990. *Basics of Qualitative Research: Grounded Theory Procedures and Techniques.* Newbury Park, CA: Sage Publications.

Sullivan, M.L. 1989. "Absent Fathers in the Inner City." *Annals of the American Academy of Political and Social Science* 501:48-58.

Taylor, R.A. 1997. "Who's Parenting? Trends and Patterns." In *Contemporary Parenting: Challenges and Issues* (pp. 69-91). Edited by T. Arendell. Thousand Oaks, CA: Sage Publications.

Thompson, C. 1989. "A New Vision of Masculinity." In *Men's Lives* (pp. 586-591). Edited by M.S. Kimmel and M.A. Messner. New York: Macmillan Publishing Company.

Thornberry, T.P., C.A. Smith, and G.J. Howard. 1997. "Risk Factors for Teenage Fatherhood." *Journal of Marriage and the Family* 59:505-522.

U.S. Census Bureau. 2000. http://factfinder.census.gov.

Ventura, S.J. 1994. "Recent Trends in Teenage Childbearing in the United States" *Statistical Bulletin* 74(4):10-7.

Ventura, S.J., S.C. Curtin, T.J. Matthews. 2000. Variations in Teenage Birth Rates, 1991-1998: National and State Trends. *National Vital Statistics Reports* 48(6): 14pp.

Ventura, S., T.J. Matthews, and B.E. Hamilton. 2001. Births to Teenagers in the United States, 1940-2000. *Vital Health Statistics Reports* 49(10):24.

Warner, S. and K.M. Feltey. 1999. "From Victim to Survivor: Recovered Memories and Identity Transformation." In *Trauma & Memory* (pp. 161-172). Edited by L.M. Williams and V.L. Banyard. Thousand Oaks, CA: Sage Publications.

Weinman, M.L., P.B. Smith, and R.S. Buzi. 2002. "Young Fathers: An Analysis of Risk Behaviors and Service Needs." *Child and Adolescent Social Work Journal* 19(6):437-453.

West, C. and D. Zimmerman. 1987. "Doing Gender. *Gender & Society* 1:125-151.

White, J.L. and J.H. Cones. 1999. *Black Man Emerging: Facing the Past and Seizing a Future in America.* New York: Routledge.

Wichita/Sedgwick County Weed & Seed Steering Committee. 2002. Weed & Seed Report. Wichita, KS. Unpublished.

Wichita-Sedgwick County Department of Community Health, University of Kansas School of Medicine/Department of Preventive Medicine, Wichita State University. Community Health Assessment Project (CHAP). Wichita, KS: University of Kansas School of Medicine; 1997.

Williams, D.R. 1998. "African-American Health: The Role of the Social Environment." *Journal of Urban Health* 75(2):300-320.

Williams-McCoy, J.E. and F.B. Tayler. 1985. "Selected Psychosocial Characteristics of Black Unwed Adolescent Fathers." *Journal of Adolescent Health Care* 6:12-16.

Wilson, W.J. 1987. *The Truly Disadvantaged: The Inner City, the Underclass, and Public Policy.* Chicago, IL: The University of Chicago Press.

References   221

Wilson, W.J. 1996. *When Work Disappears: The World of the New Urban Poor.* New York: Vintage Books.

Wingwood, G.M. and R.J. DiClemente. 1998. "Partner Influences and Gender-Related Factors Associated with Noncondom Use among Young African American Women." *American Journal of Community Psychology* 26(1):29-51.

Wolcott, H.F. 1990. *Writing up Qualitative Research.* Newbury Park, CA: Sage Publications.

Xie, H., R.B. Cairns, and B.D. Cairns. 2001. "Predicting Teen Motherhood and Teen Fatherhood: Individual Characteristics and Peer Affiliations." *Social Development* 10(4):488-511.

Zucchino, D. 1997. *Myth of the Welfare Queen.* New York: Scribner.

Index

Abandonment by fathers, 26, 101, 106, 115. *See also* Absence of fathers
Abortion
  teen fathers, this study, 61, 69-74, 87, 171-172
  young men, 18, 19, 172
  young women, 15
Absence of fathers. *See also* Abandonment
  and culture, 18, 183
  impact on teen fathers, 20, 98, 175
  and "moral decline," 12, 22
  result of socioeconomic consequences, 34, 35, 182
Adolescent. *See also* Teen fathers; Teen mothers
  birth control pill use, 1, 62, 65, 67, 134
  condom use, 1, 13
  contraceptives, 13, 14, 18, 19, 171, 186
  culture, 31, 40
  pregnancy, 1-2, 5-10, 12-15
  sexual behaviors, 1, 13, 14, 18
Adoption, 69-74, 172
Affirmative action, 33
African Americans. *See also* Teen fathers
  census, 34
  childbearing, 7
  culture, 14, 37, 39, 40
  discrimination toward, 32, 183
  education, 31, 32, 33
  employment, 20, 23, 24, 28, 32-35, 38

African Americans *(continued)*
  familial experiences, 20, 24, 26, 31, 33-35, 128-129
  male-female relationships, 36, 62
  marriage rates, 24, 33-35, 182
  mortality rates, 33, 46
  poverty, 31-35, 36, 39, 73, 179, 181, 183, 185
  stereotypes, 32, 40, 62
  stigma, 14, 17, 20, 39, 182, 185
  unemployment, 31-35, 40, 46
  violence, 30, 32, 40, 161, 164-165, 180, 186, 196
  in Wichita, KS, 46
African-centered, 192. *See also* Afrocentric perspective
Afrocentric perspective, 190. *See also* African-centered
Aid to Families with Dependent Children (AFDC), 23, 34. *See also* Public assistance; Temporary Assistance for Needy Families (TANF); Welfare benefits
Asian Americans, 7, 46, 167

Breadwinners
  assuming role, 41, 115
  defined, 77, 78, 116, 172, 183
  and masculinity, 37, 39, 180
  mothers' enactment of, 184

Caregivers, 87-89
Child care, 148

Voices of African-American Teen Fathers
© 2006 by The Haworth Press, Inc. All rights reserved.
doi:10.1300/5477_15

224   VOICES OF AFRICAN-AMERICAN TEEN FATHERS

Child custody, 106, 107
Child support
  adult fathers, 23
  concern about, 123, 125, 130-132,
    136, 139, 154-156, 179
  desire to pay, 124
  and masculinity, 124-125
  provision by teen fathers, 80, 122
  provision by teen fathers' parents,
    112, 128
  and relationship with children's
    mothers, 124, 125, 129, 176
Church, 47, 48, 56, 59, 165, 196. See
    also Religion
Civil rights, 33
Code of the streets, 39, 185
Communication between parents, 61,
    64-66, 71, 171, 172
Crime. See also Criminal activities
  African-American community, 31,
    145, 182, 183
  and masculinity, 36
  and young mothers, 12
Criminal activities, 1, 31, 40, 57. See
    also Crime
Cultural influence
  community, 40, 161, 183
  defined, 192
  disadvantaged, 18, 37
  experience of teen fathers, 31, 158,
    184
  masculinity, 37, 40
  poverty, 14, 15, 39, 183
  procreation, 18, 174, 180
  youths, 40, 41
Culture of fatherlessness, 22
Culture of poverty theory, 14, 183

Deadbeat dads, 23
Deindustrialization, 31, 35
Discipline, 175
Divorce, 103, 105, 115
Drugs
  among African Americans, 31, 34

Drugs (continued)
  in communities, 20, 33, 39, 179-180,
    182 183
  and masculinity, 40, 186
  nonmarried mothers, 12
  teen fathers, 80, 81, 106, 122, 135,
    137, 140, 158, 161-164, 173
  youths, 30, 31, 39

Education
  and African Americans, 31, 32, 33
  and teen fathers, 25, 28, 30, 33, 44,
    45, 52, 149, 150, 168, 184
  and teen mothers, 1, 8, 9, 15, 196
Environment
  adaptation to, 184
  associated factors, 46
  communities, 15
  ecological framework, 29, 180
  influences of, 14, 15, 33, 97, 161,
    182, 186
Exchange theory, 24-25, 80
Exosystem, 29, 181

Family. See also African Americans,
    familial experiences
  extended families, 26, 72-73, 172
  female-headed households, 12, 23,
    26, 33, 34, 40, 98, 175, 181,
    182
  matriarchal structure, 12, 96, 109
  nuclear, 33, 35
  single adult fathers, 11
  single mother, 2, 11, 12, 26, 33, 34,
    40, 98, 175, 181, 182
  single parent, 7, 12, 96
  as socialization agent, 25-26, 174
Father-centered programs, 23, 35, 47,
    189, 190-196
Fathers, adults. See also Teen fathers
  barriers to fatherhood, 34, 37
  as breadwinners, 37, 39, 41, 183
  deadbeat, 23

Index

Fathers, adults *(continued)*
  economic provider, 24, 34, 37, 38, 40
  father-child involvement, 2, 18, 23-24
  initiatives for, 23
  role of, 2, 37
  single parent, 11
  socioeconomic factors, 24, 35, 183-184
  teen pregnancy, 2, 10, 16
Feminine roles, 36-37, 108, 112, 115

Gender
  condom negotiation, 186
  constructing fatherhood, 104
  differentiations in parenting roles, 88, 89, 104, 148
  "doing gender," 64, 185
  male socialization, 101
  masculinity, 166
Gender theory, 21, 28, 36-41, 180-187
General social survey, 32
Grandparents
  assistance provided by, 80, 81, 89, 135
  impact on teen fathers' parenting, 67, 95, 131
  treatment toward grandchildren, 124, 131

Hispanics, 7, 19, 32, 46
Housing segregation, 32, 181, 183
Human ecology theory, 21. *See also* Social ecology theory

Identity theory, 21
Imprisonment, 163, 182. *See also* Prison
Income. *See also* Socioeconomic status
  African-American men, 35, 38, 78
  African-American women, 24
  gap between blacks and whites, 32

Income *(continued)*
  impact on marriage and family, 33, 35
  teen fathers, 3, 7, 45, 46, 77, 83, 127, 145, 156, 173
  teen mothers, 8, 10, 18
Infant mortality rate, 33, 46
Interactionist view, 18

Macrosystem, 29, 181
Masculinity
  adoption, 73
  "being strong" (macho), 102-103, 166, 183
  breadwinner, 34, 37, 39, 180
  child support payment, 124
  condom use, 186
  fatherhood, 34,, 36-41, 77, 96, 180, 186
  "gaining respect," 185
  gender theory, 36-41
  goals of this study, 30
  impact of racism on, 168-170
  "saving face," 101
  sexual aggression, 185-186
  status symbol ("being a real man"), 140, 173
Media, 40, 182
Mesosystem, 29, 181
Microsystem, 29, 180, 181
Military service
  aspirations of, 66, 83, 127, 151, 179
  current occupation, 102
Minimum wage, 158
Modeled behavior. *See also* Role model; Social modeling theory
  conditions necessary for, 195-196
  family impact, 174
  and identity, 38, 104, 181
  inappropriate forms, 104
  masculinity, 103-104
  mothers' behavior, 116
  positive, 195
Moynihan report, 12

226 VOICES OF AFRICAN-AMERICAN TEEN FATHERS

Neighborhoods
culture, 19, 30, 162
differences in, 18-19
disadvantages, 180
poverty, 31, 145, 161
segregated, 32, 179, 181, 183
this study, 46

Postindustrialization, 24
Poverty. *See also* Income;
    Socioeconomic status
    African-American families, 15,
        31-32, 34, 35, 36, 39, 73
    culture of, 14, 15, 183
    female-headed households, 34
    teen fathers, 98, 113, 114, 145, 179,
        181, 183, 185, 196
    teen mothers, 1, 5, 7-9, 10, 12, 15,
        23
Prevention strategies, 190-193
Prison, 8, 91, 163, 166, 182, 208
Public assistance. *See also* Aid to
    Dependent Families with
    Children (ADFC); Temporary
    Assistance to Needy Families
    (TANF); Welfare benefits
    among African Americans, 31
    and fathers, 34-35
    legal issues, 132
    stereotypes, 32
    teen fathers' experience with, 28, 98
    young mothers, 11, 131, 135

Racial discrimination, 32, 167, 170, 183
Racism
    adapting to, 39, 73-74, 113
    challenges to youths, 38, 143, 145
    employment, 20, 31, 32, 38,
        184-185
    teen fathers' experiences with,
        167-170, 180, 182
Religion, 19, 56, 73, 172. *See also*
    Church

Research methods for study
    analysis of data, 58-60
    background, 46
    consent form, 51-52
    interview questions, 48-49
    interviewing process, 47, 50-51,
        53-56
    recruitment strategies, 47, 51-53
    reliability, validity, and
        generalizability, 57
    sample (subjects), 43-46, 56-57
    transcription, 57
Role conflict, 94
Role model, 103. *See also* Modeled
        behavior; Social model theory
Role strain, 79, 82, 157, 173
Role theory, 21, 81

Sexism, 20, 62, 176, 186
Social constructionist theory, 30, 186
Social ecology theory
    African-American teen fathers,
        30-35
    cultural impact, 18
    masculinity, 180
    prevention, 190, 194
Social modeling theory, 190, 194. *See*
        also Modeled behavior; Role
        model
Social network, 41
Social services, 194
Social support, 95
Socialization
    adult fathers' impact on, 116
    adult mothers' impact on, 26
    family as primary agent, 25, 96
    fatherhood responsibility, 24
    and masculinity, 101
    media's impact, 40
    peer influence, 27-28
Socioeconomic status
    fathers, 24, 25, 34
    impact on family, 33

Socioeconomic status *(continued)*
  teen fathers, 18, 43, 45, 112, 170, 179
  teen mothers, 9
Stages of change model, 191
Stereotypes, 11, 32, 62
Strain theory, 120
Symbolic interactionism, 21

Teen fatherhood. *See also* Teen fathers
  challenges, 28, 104, 109, 113, 114,
    131, 145-170
  cultural influences, 15, 18, 19, 20,
    158, 161-162, 174, 180, 183,
    184, 186, 192
  paternal behavior
    as disciplinarians, 175
    independent (absent), 22, 89, 91,
      92-96, 11, 123, 133, 135, 140,
      148, 154, 164, 169, 173, 177,
      190, 194
    general involvement, 20, 22-25,
      75-96, 172, 189, 193
    as nurturers, 78, 85-92, 107, 111,
      115, 126, 129, 141, 157, 160,
      173
    as providers (economic), 41,
      76-84, 89, 90, 106, 111, 155,
      156-159, 160, 173, 193, 194
  perceptions of
    independent (absent), 75, 85,
      92-96, 130, 172, 173, 189
    nurturer, 75, 78, 84, 85-92, 96,
      129, 173, 189
    provider (economic), 59, 75,
      76-84, 85, 99, 112, 114, 116,
      154, 172-173, 180, 184, 189
  role expectations, 20-22
  socioeconomic challenges to,
    156-159
  as status symbol, 15, 18, 19, 139-141
Teen fathers. *See also* Teen fatherhood
  associated risk factors, 2, 20
  attitudes toward marriage, 22
  attitudes toward parental status, 22,
    28, 145, 146-148, 178

Teen fathers *(continued)*
  attitudes toward pregnancy, 16, 19,
    22, 17, 22
  babysitting, as fathers, 87, 88, 90
  as breadwinners, 77, 78, 115, 116,
    172, 180, 184
  child support, 80, 112, 122-125,
    128-135, 139, 143, 153,
    154-157
  concept of family, 128-129
  condom use, 61-67, 95-96, 79, 95,
    96, 134,171,186, 190-191, 194
  contraceptive use, 19, 61-67, 171,
    186, 191
  discrimination, 167-170
  education, 18, 28, 168
  employment, 23-24, 28, 82-83, 115,
    156, 167, 180, 185, 196
  freedom, 28, 148-152
  good, defined, 76, 81, 85, 90, 91, 93,
    96, 106, 116, 143
  mothers' expectations of, 21
  mothers' perception of, 23
  paternity, identification of, 17
  perception of "good mothers," 113,
    115, 130, 134, 135
  preparedness for, 146-148
  prevalence of, 2, 16-18
  recruitment as research subjects, 23,
    43, 47
  relationship with children's mothers,
    26-27, 117-136, 153-156,
    176-177
  relationship with own father, 26,
    97-108, 175
  relationship with own mother,
    108-116, 175-176, 178-179
  relationship with peers, 27-28,
    137-143, 177-178
  sexual behaviors, 19, 61, 66, 62, 63,
    64, 79, 118-122, 130, 138,
    140, 146, 176-178, 184-186,
    191, 194
  socioeconomic status or factors, 18,
    19, 22, 24-25, 28

228 *VOICES OF AFRICAN-AMERICAN TEEN FATHERS*

Teen fathers *(continued)*
  statistics, 16-18
  support systems for, 24-25, 28
Teen mothers
  associated factors, 10-15
  childbearing statistics, 6-7
  consequences of, 7-9
  marriage, 5, 8, 9, 12, 14, 19
  pregnancy statistics, 1, 5-6
  sociopolitical issues, 10-12
Temporary Assistance to Needy
      Families (TANF), 11, 23, 34.
      See also Aid to Families with
      Dependent Children (AFDC);
      Public assistance; Welfare
Transportation
  employment, 158-159, 179
  involvement with children, 123,
      159-160, 174
  poverty, 145
  provision to children, 158
Transtheoretical model, 191

Unemployment, 31-35, 40, 46. *See also*
      African Americans,
      employment

Violence
  concerns about by teen fathers, 143,
      161
  culture, 40
  masculinity, 185-186
  neighborhoods, 23, 164, 165, 180
  single mothers, against, 11
  stereotypes, 32, 40
  youths, 30, 196

Welfare benefits. *See also* Aid for
      Dependent Families with
      Children (AFDC); Public
      assistance; Temporary
      Assistance for Needy Families
      (TANF)
  adolescent parents, 1, 135
  burden to system, 11, 162
  and fathers, 24
  stereotype, 11
Whites
  adolescent parents, 2, 7
  contraceptive use, 18
  family composition, 34
  socioeconomic factors, 31, 32